The Political History of Contemporary India

The Political History of Contemporary India

P. S. Choudhary

KUNAL BOOKS
New Delhi-110002 , India

KUNAL BOOKS
4596/1A, First Floor,
11, Daryaganj, New Delhi-110002
Phones: 9811043697, 011-30125412
E-mail: *Kunalbooks@gmail.com*

The Political History of Contemporary India

First Published 2010

ISBN - 978-81-910085-7-9

Published in India by Prem Singh Bisht for Kunal Books, and printed at **Deepak Offset Press**, Delhi.

PREFACE

The chronological history of India dates back to about 34,000 years ago, when the first traces of human existence on the Indian subcontinent were found. Since then, it has hosted some of the greatest civilizations that have significantly shaped up human history. A chronological history of India spans the modern day geographical landscapes of countries like India, Pakistan, Bangladesh, Sri Lanka, Nepal and Bhutan. The Indus Valley Civilization began in 3300 BC, and flourished around 2600 BC, after which, the Aryans, a semi-nomadic tribe, is believed to have migrated from central Asia or Northern Iran.

The people of India have had a continuous civilization since 2500 B.C., when the inhabitants of the Indus River valley developed an urban culture based on commerce and sustained by agricultural trade. This civilization declined around 1500 B.C., probably due to ecological changes. During the second millennium B.C., pastoral, Aryan-speaking tribes migrated from the northwest into the subcontinent. As they settled in the middle Ganges River valley, they adapted to antecedent cultures.

The political map of ancient and medieval India was made up of myriad kingdoms with fluctuating boundaries. In the 4th and 5th centuries A.D., northern India was unified under the Gupta Dynasty. During this period, known as India's Golden Age, Hindu culture and political administration reached new heights.

Politics of India take place in a framework of a federal parliamentary multi-party representative democratic republic modeled after the British Westminster System. The Prime

Minister of India is the head of government, while the President of India is the formal head of state and holds substantial reserve powers, placing him or her in approximately the same position as the British monarch. Executive power is exercised by the government. Federal legislative power is vested in both the government and the two chambers of the Parliament of India. The judiciary is independent of the executive and the legislature.

According to its constitution, India is a "sovereign socialist secular democratic republic." India is the largest state by population with a democratically-elected government. Like the United States, India has a federal form of government, however, the central government in India has greater power in relation to its states, and its central government is patterned after the British parliamentary system. Regarding the former, "the Centre", the national government, can and has dismissed state governments if no majority party or coalition is able to form a government or under specific Constitutional clauses, and can impose direct federal rule known as President's rule. Locally, the Panchayati Raj system has several administrative functions.

At the federal level, India is the most populous democracy in the world. While many neighboring countries witness frequent coups, Indian democracy has been suspended only once Nevertheless, Indian politics is often described as chaotic. More than a fifth of parliament members face criminal charges.The transformations in Indian society, economy and polity have gathered speed since the early 1990s, and are particularly manifest in the national and regional elections since 1997. This is an opportune moment to consider the growing body of data that attempts to make sense of these changes and to understand their likely significance as India becomes increasingly important as an economic and political force.

Contents

1

Political Development in India

Among the people who lived in the north of India four thousand years ago, the most advanced were the Dravidians. The Dravidians, in fact, were more civilized than the Aryans who later fought and defeated them. The suggestion has been made that the ancestors of these same Dravidians might have been the people who developed the civilization of the Indus Valley at an earlier age. So far, this is no more than speculation; if it can be proved, it will bridge the thousand year gap in Indian history following Mohenjo-Daro. The Aryan conquest of the more highly civilized Dravidians would then be comparable to the German conquest of Rome in the 5th century A.D.

At any rate, we know that about four thousand years ago a people calling themselves Aryas, or noblemen, entered India through Afghanistan. They were of the same stock as the Persians and spoke a language similar to Persian, Greek, Latin, Teutonic, and Slavonik. The Aryans came in successive waves, some as migrants bringing their whole families with them. The Dravidians and the aboriginal tribes fought tenaciously for a long time, but gradually some of them were absorbed by the Aryans and the rest retired to central and southern India.

During the next fifteen hundred years the Aryans developed a remarkable civilization in the north and the Dravidians prospered in the south. Cultural intercourse between the two was slow because of the dense jungles and the Vindhya Mountains in the center of India. With the passage of time, however, there was a fusion of the two cultures, out of which grew the religion known as Hinduism. Sanskrit, the language of the Aryans, became the medium of religious expression throughout the land, much as Latin was in Europe in the middle Ages. The Dravidians, however, retained their language, and developed a great literature of their own.

The Aryans spread toward the east, skirting the desert region below Punjab. Their migrations usually followed one of the great rivers of India, which could be utilized for irrigation. Territorial expansion forced the Aryan tribes to band together into larger units for protection against sudden attacks by the aborigines. Some of these units later became kingdoms, others formed republics. It is interesting to observe that around 600 B.C. there were fifteen republics in northern and eastern India.

A good deal of warfare was carried on between the various kingdoms and republics, individually or in combination with others. In the fourth century B.C., however, there arose an illustrious general named Chandragupta Maurya, who brought the whole of northern India under his rule. The brightest period of the Maurya Empire was during the reign of Chandragupta's grandson, Asoka, who became famous for his zeal in propagating the Buddhist faith and his earnest solicitude for the welfare of the people.

After Asoka, the Maurya Empire began to decline, and soon various factions fell to fighting for supremacy. It was not until the fourth century A.D. that northern India was again united, this time by the Gupta emperors, who reigned for over two hundred years. Toward the latter part of the seventh century A.D., northern India was again split up into a number of independent states. From the eleventh century A.D. onward, a series of Arab, Turkish and Afghan invasions finally resulted in the establishment of the Moghul (or Mongol) Empire in India.

Southern India, until the coming of the Moghuls, had followed its own course, undisturbed by the happenings beyond the Vindhya Mountains in the north. Great empires rose and fell there, as they did in the north. But the sixteenth century saw the establishment of Moghul power under Akbar the Great over practically the entire length and breadth of India. Disruption set in with the reign of Akbar's great-grandson, Aurangzeb; and in the chaotic period following his death in 1707 many groups bid for power, but by this time a different set of newcomers had arrived-the Portuguese, Dutch, French, and British.

This almost continual internal warfare was not peculiarly Indian. Countries all over the world were torn by periodic waves of warfare. These struggles, in fact, were not always confined to any one country, but were often continent-wide in scope. Internal warfare went on constantly not only in countries of tremendous size, such as China, but also in smaller countries, such as Great Britain. Permanent peace was not established in Britain until the English Revolution of the 17th century.

Internal warfare itself had very little to do with the Indians' late entrance into modern civilization, just as internal peace established by the British is not necessarily hastening it. The causes lie elsewhere. We will understand them better after we learn something about the social, economic and cultural development of the Indians prior to the coming of the Europeans. Since we do not yet know what kind of society the MohenjoDaro people had, our knowledge of Indian society begins with the Aryan conquest of India. The Aryan tribes settled down in the Indus valley in small communities or villages.

A group of villages comprising a tribe had a chief at its head, who was elevated to that position due perhaps to seniority in the tribe or to military prowess. The chief had an advisory body-the Samiti, or popular assembly of the tribe. In the early days, land was held in common by the tribe. Individuals owned movable things, such as ploughs, cattle, horses, gold, ornaments, household furniture and utensils, and weapons. The priests received gifts on all religious occasions, but they were gifts of personal property-land could not be given away, sold or bartered.

Primarily a pastoral people when they first entered India, the Aryans gradually turned to agriculture. State governments took care of irrigation and organized standing armies, for which they received a share of the produce of the land. With the increase in population and the development of a standing army, the masses of the people were able to devote themselves entirely to civilian occupations. Land being plentiful, the excess population cleared the forests and established villages of their own, patterned after the parent village.

Increased demand for handicraft products resulted in specialization of work. The woodworker, being carpenter, joiner and wheelwright in one, made carts and chariots. The metal worker, using the wing of a bird in place of bellows to fan the flames of the furnace which smelted ore, made copper, bronze or iron kettles and other domestic utensils. Caravans plied regularly overland through Baluchistan between India and the Near East, carrying Indian muslin, silks, brocades, gold, silver, copper and bronze ware.

The Dravidians in the south carried on an extensive seagoing trade with Egypt, Western Asia, Greece and Rome, exporting ivory, pepper, rice, ginger, cinnamon, spices, precious stones, coral, pearls, textiles, silk, tortoise shell, teakwood, and even peacocks and monkeys. By the fourth century B.C. trade was flourishing; the republics had disappeared; chiefs had crowned themselves kings and succession had become hereditary. The basis of Indian society, which continued almost unchanged up to the 18th century, was firmly established.

The unit of Indian society became the village, as it was in the rest of the world, including Europe in the pre-industrial period. The vast majority of the population lived in selfsufficient, autonomous villages. The peasants did not live in individual farmhouses surrounded by their fields. Each village was a cluster of cottages, enclosed by a stockade or wall with gates for the purpose of defense. On the outskirts of the village lay the arable land; beyond it were the pasture, and the woodlands separating one village from another.

The bulk of the populations were tillers of the soil. The arable land was divided among the farming families, according to their size, but the pasturage and the woodlands were always held in common by the villagers. Scattered over an expanding territory, and facing the problem of slow means of communication, the communities tended to become economically and socially self-sufficient.

Each village had its potter, who turned out on his wheel the simple utensils needed by the peasants; the carpenter who built and repaired the ploughs; the blacksmith who made axes and other necessary tools; the fisherman, the butcher and the scavenger; the priest and the teacher (although often the priest was also the teacher); the clerk who attended to legal documents and wrote out correspondence between people of different villages; the town herdsman who looked after the cattle and returned them at night to their various owners; and the ever-present astrologer, who advised as to the days, and even hours, auspicious for planting and harvesting, the celebration of marriages and other festive occasions.

The professional men were not paid by individuals according to the work done; they were supported by the community as a whole. As the number of professionals increased, they tended to establish villages of their own. Thus we find records of villages peopled entirely by members of a particular craft: carpenters, blacksmiths, coppersmiths, goldsmiths, potters, jewelers, etc.-catering to the needs of several neighboring villages.

The political structure of the village communities was organized on a functional basis. In the early days, when the villages were smaller, the inhabitants assembled in a nearby grove to discuss public affairs. The final decision had to be either unanimous, or, if they failed to reach unanimity, the matter was settled by a committee of referees. Later, a more elaborate structure was built up. The people of each village annually elected a council of five, known to this day as the Panchayat (Panch means five). This council elected one of its number as its President.

The Panchayats met regularly in an assembly hall-a raised platform open on all sides, with a roof supported by pillars. In very small villages the shade of a tall tree sufficed as an assembly hall. The Panchayat's functions were to dispense local justice, to supervise irrigation, to build fences and snares and appoint watchmen for protection of the crops from pests, to keep in repair the village wells, tanks, roads and drainage system, to see that craftsmen and other professionals were provided for, to extend hospitality to travelers passing through the village and furnish them with guides, and to collect taxes on behalf of the government.

Most of the work in the villages was done cooperatively. The villagers, under the supervision of the Panchayat, built and repaired roads, sunken wells and tanks, and made fences and snares. Women considered it a civic honor to contribute their share to municipal activities, both manually and politically. In activities that involved group action by several villages, as, for example, in time of drought, the presidents of the several Panchayats met and worked out plans for common action.

There were two seasons of harvest. The farmers grew a great variety of foodstuffs, such as wheat, beans, corn, maize, barley, sesamum, and rice. Fruits were also bountiful, of which the mango was-as it still is-the most popular. While the men tilled the soil, the women spun and wove on charkas (spinning wheels) and on handlooms. The villagers made their own clothing, much as the peasants of Europe did in the middle Ages.

Although there was some money in circulation, very little was used in the villages. When anyone needed something he did not himself produce or make, he exchanged part of his own product for that of another. To facilitate such transactions there were market towns for every ten villages-as there were in medieval Europe-where people gathered periodically to barter goods. Production in villages was strictly for consumption, and surplus products were bartered for useful and necessary things rather than to make a profit.

Each village paid a single tax collectively to the central government. It was a tax not in money, but in kind, and amounted to anywhere from one-twelfth to one-sixth of the total raw produce of the land. A portion of the total produce was also set aside by the village for emergencies such as droughts and famines. In contrast to the simple, placid, and even monotonous life of the village, city life was dynamic and colorful. The cities were well-planned rectangles, divided into four wards. There were four gates in the wall surrounding each city for defensive purposes.

Houses were built either of wood, or brick and stone, depending upon the material nearest at hand. Streets were provided with water courses carrying drainage from the houses to the moats outside the city. Severe penalties were inflicted for misuse of the drainage system. Thousands of vessels filled with water were placed at regular intervals in the streets, for fire prevention. At the entrances and exits to the cities were taverns for passersby and guest houses for travelers, maintained by the municipality. Municipalities also maintained "spinning houses" where women who were without families or any means of subsistence could work for a living.

The growth of trade resulted in the development of customs similar to those in Europe in the Middle Ages. Specialized workers banded into craft guilds to protect their economic interests. Not only that, but each craft and profession tended to localize itself into certain sections of cities, much as they still do in cities like Benares, where one finds jewelers' streets, goldsmiths' streets, weavers' streets, and streets where only musicians, dancers and other entertainers live. When the members of a craft became too numerous, they founded a village of their own in the suburbs.

The list of arts and crafts practiced in those days was a long one. There were workers in gold, silver, copper, brass, bronze, and tin; shipbuilders, carriage makers, builders of furniture and houses; weavers, leather workers, potters, and confectioners; barbers, masseurs, beauticians and garland-makers; jewelry, ivory, glass and porcelain workers; architects, sculptors, masons, musicians, dancers and actors; and seamen, pilots, and guides of caravans.

Each of these had its own craft guild, and their laws were similar to those of the craft guilds of Europe: At the head of each guild were a president, a treasurer and a supervisor, elected by the members of the craft. The president's function was to enforce the laws of the guild; the treasurer saw to it that members who were for one reason or another incapacitated, and families of deceased members, were financially taken care of; and the supervisor inspected the work of the craftsmen to ensure a high standard of quality. In large centers of commerce the various craft guilds also elected a supreme leader, whose function was to arbitrate inter-craft disputes.

As in Europe, to learn any one of the arts and crafts, boys and girls were apprenticed to master craftsmen at an early age. The apprentices lived in the homes of their teachers, and assisted in all work around the house while learning their trade. Traveling in those days was slow and tedious, and full of danger.

Merchants in their travels were often attacked by bandits or aboriginal tribes. Thus the merchants, too, banded together and formed guilds, and even engaged mercenary soldiers for their protection. The leaders of the merchants' guilds also represented them at the courts of the kings.

In contrast to the villages where barter was used, flourishing trade developed a monetary economy in the cities and gold became the medium of exchange in commercial transactions. Since merchants could not carry large amounts of gold on their persons, banking and credit systems came into existence. With increased profits and expanding commerce, the money lender made his appearance. He was to play a significant and vicious role in the life of the Indians for many centuries, even to the present day.

The municipal government of the cities was in many ways similar to that of the villages. The four wards elected their own councils, which looked after local affairs. The merchants paid one-fiftieth of their income as tax to the government, and the artisans contributed a day's work each month. A duty of one-twentieth was levied on indigenous merchandise coming into a city, and foreign imports paid a duty of one-tenth. As elsewhere, the actual amount of taxes paid varied considerably under different rulers and at different periods.

So far we have described what might be called local selfgovernment in the villages and cities. In contrast to the simplicity of local village and city administrations, the central government of the states was highly complicated and elaborately systematized. For efficient handling of all state activities, government officers were divided into district officials and city officials. District officials were in charge of irrigation, land measurement and collection of land revenue, agriculture, forestry, timber works, metal foundries and mines, maintenance of highways and planting of milestones at every mile.

City officials comprised six boards of five members each, whose functions included supervision of manufactories, public buildings and taverns; care of the sick and burial of the dead; extension of hospitality to strangers and supplying them with guides when they left the city; registration of births and deaths; inspection of weights and measures; keeping accurate records of new and secondhand merchandise sold in the cities; collection of a sales tax of ten per cent; and the upkeep of public works, harbors and temples.

Warfare had progressed far beyond tribal skirmishes. The department of war was divided into the Admiralty, Transport and Commissariat, the Infantry, the Cavalry, the Chariots and the Elephants, with a committee of five heading each division. Curious how the idea of the panchayat - the council of five-is carried into all branches of the government. The state supplied the soldiers with weapons and horses, and compensated the families of soldiers who died during their employment.

This was the economic and political structure of India until the Moghul invasion in the sixteenth century. The political and economic structure was scarcely affected by the Moghul conquest. The changes which occurred were those of personnel rather than of the system. Hindu kings, after they accepted the suzerainty of the Moghul emperor, were allowed to remain rulers of their territories, on payment of an annual tribute. Many Hindu revenue collectors were replaced by Moghuls.

The villagers continued to pay their tax in produce as before, and to administer their local affairs through the traditional panchayat. City administration remained the same, although the amount of taxes fluctuated from time to time. The Moghuls-who were Moslems-soon, became an integral part of Indian life, as had the Aryans and Dravidians. Intermarriage between all three was not uncommon. Moghul emperors had Hindu ministers and even appointed Hindus as generals of their armies; and Hindu kings employed qualified Moslems in posts of authority.

There was no discrimination on the basis of conqueror and conquered, nor on differences in religion. The most significant point is that both during the peaceful period under Moghul rule and the period of internal strife which followed later on, the masses of the people lived harmoniously irrespective of their religious differences. The vast majority of Indians continued to live in small villages, following their traditional and hereditary vocations. Hindu children at the age of five and Moslem children at the age of 4 years, 4 months, and 4 days, went to school to study reading, writing and arithmetic-the former under the village priest, and the latter under the local mullah, or Moslem divine.

They were also taught a little history and geography by rote, in the form of verses made up of historical incidents and names of peoples, countries, oceans and rivers. Education was rudimentary in the villages; few villagers attended the universities. Crafts were handed down from parents to children and apprentices, so there were no special schools to teach them. Village life in India, as elsewhere, followed a monotonous pattern, relieved by occasional festivities. The three principal stages in the life of a human being were celebrated by both Hindus and Moslems. Whether a family affair or a religious occasion, the whole village or several villages together participated.

The birth of a child was celebrated with appropriate ceremonies and the distribution of gifts to relatives and neighbors. In the seventh year Moslem children were circumcised, which was an occasion of great rejoicing and entertainment according to the means of the family. Hindu boys belonging to the three higher castes-Brahmans, Kshattriyas and Vaisyas - went through the ceremony of the sacred thread in their ninth year. This ceremony introduced the boy to the rights and duties of a man.

During the ceremony the boy learned the basic religious hymns and donned the sacred thread. This consisted of three strands of cotton, each strand formed by three or nine threads, and the cotton must have been gathered from the plant by the hand of a Brahman and carded and spun by persons of the same caste. The sacred thread was hung from the left shoulder and fell on the right hip. Marriage was less a personal than a family affair. While the children were quite young, parents looked for suitable marriage partners for them.

Hindu children had to marry within their caste. It was often impossible, in a small village, to find a suitable match for a boy or girl, so parents consulted marriage brokers, who traveled from village to village carrying a list of prospects. As was customary among agricultural people the world over, Indian children were betrothed early, and marriages were consummated at an age lower than that of today. Since the Indians have been strongly condemned for the practice of comparatively early marriage, it may be mentioned in passing that parallels can be found even in England in medieval times.

"It was not unusual for parents," writes L. F. Salzmann, "to arrange marriages for their children while they were still infants; even the actual marriage ceremony was sometimes performed when the bride and bridegroom were so young that they had to be carried to the church and could not repeat all the words of the service." The age of marriage rose higher with the industrialization of Europe. The Indian emperor Akbar, in the middle of the sixteenth century, fixed the minimum age of marriage at 16 years for boys and 14 years for girls.

The wedding of a boy or girl was the most important occasion in family life, since it contained in miniature customs and traditions that had accrued since early tribal days. Among Hindus marriage ties were formed not only between families of the same caste, but of the same family traditions and even of the same homeland from which the original tribe migrated. It was also an occasion of festivity for the entire village, or, in the case of cities, of the entire ward.

After a suitable match had been arranged and the auspicious day and hour for the ceremony fixed by the astrologer, invitations were sent out to all the relatives of both parties through courier, itinerant barber, traveling craftsman or special messenger. The marriage ceremony took place in the home of the bride. The cottage was decorated with garlands of flowers and festoons of mango leaves. The neighbors decorated their cottages, too.

On the day of the wedding the bridegroom, dressed in new clothes and wearing garlands of flowers, arrived at the bride's home. He was attended by a large party of friends and relatives, and, if finances permitted, a band of musicians. The entire village joined the bride's family in welcoming the guests. It was customary for the host to feed the bridegroom's party, and, if they came from a considerable distance, to lodge them overnight. The neighbors brought gifts of food, which was served on long plantain leaves. They also supplied quarters for the guests. There was much music and singing of wedding songs by the entire assembly.

The marriage ceremony was performed by the village priest in the case of Hindus, and the Moslem divine in the case of Moslems. Customarily the bridegroom stayed overnight with his new relatives. Upon his arrival home, his family was obliged to give an equally elaborate affair for the friends and relatives of the bride. After the wedding, the wife became a member of her husband's family. Funerals were also attended by much elaborate ceremony. Among the Hindus the practice of cremation had long superseded interment of the deceased, but the Moslems buried their dead.

At the edge of the village, if possible by the bank of a river, the Hindus burned the bodies of the dead. In a different location, also on the outskirts of the village, was the burial place of the

Moslems. Besides these three occasions, the Hindus had many religious holidays and the Moslems in course of time developed some of their own. Although these religious days were scattered throughout the year, the majority of the people, being peasants, celebrated those which coincided with their period of leisure after the harvesting of the crops.

The two most popular festivals among the Hindus were Holi and Diwali. Holi was in honor of the most popular incarnation of God in Hindu mythology-the Lord Krishna, god of love and wisdom. It was a spring festival similar to the Easter festival of the Greeks. During Holi all the villagers put on garlands of flowers, lit huge bonfires, danced and sang love songs, and scattered red powder and squirted colored water at one another, symbolic of Krishna's escapades with the milkmaids of Mathura.

Diwali, or the Festival of Lights, somewhat comparable to Hallowe'en or All Saints Day, was celebrated in the autumn to give a cheerful welcome to the spirits of the sainted dead who were permitted to visit their earthly homes and familiar surroundings once a year. To guide them on the right paths, the villagers arranged a series of earthenware lamps on their verandahs, window sills and doorsteps. The village at night looked as though lit up by hundreds of glowworms.

Apart from their strictly religious ceremonies, the Moslems had their seasonal festivals as well-the Nau-roz in the spring and the Shab Barat in the autumn. Nau-roz was celebrated in large gardens and riverside parks with music and flowers. During Shab Barat the Moslems used fireworks and illuminated their homes and Mosques. The villagers often gathered at dusk at the panchayat hall for community singing and dancing. The musical accompaniment was supplied by bamboo flutes and drums. Groups of strolling players-somewhat similar to the European Comedia del Arte-toured the villages and regaled the people with plays based on mythology and the epic poems.

These players carried with them a synopsis of the stories, and improvised their dialogue and songs, incorporating many allusions to local history and humorous anecdotes about local characters. The plays invariably contained a generous amount of singing and dancing. The audience sat in a circle, leaving an open space in the center for the players. Four singers sat in four corners of the open space, transforming it into a stage. The players and the musicians in their colorful costumes sat at one side. When the cue came for an actor to make his appearance, he would rise from the sidelines and enter upon the imaginary stage.

As in modern musical comedies, the moments of intense emotion were always given over to songs. For instance, when a boy told a girl, "I love you," and the girl said, "How much?" the four singers in the corners of the stage rose and sang in chorus, describing how much the boy loved the girl. If the occasion called for it, the actors in the center of the stage danced; otherwise, they simply sat out the song, and resumed where they left off when the song was over.

The monologist and the debating team were other types of traveling entertainers. The monologist used no costumes or make-up. Sitting crosslegged, he told stories from history or mythology, partly in prose and partly in song, using only his arms and facial expression for dramatic emphasis. The debating team consisted of two men with their musical accompanists. The performance was unrehearsed. One debater would improvise a riddle in song; the other debater had to sing his reply. It called for nimble wits and versatility as a ballader.

Sometimes the village audience would suggest a subject of debate; one of the traveling team would take the affirmative and the other the negative. Each one had to illustrate his point by telling in song an appropriate story from mythology or history. The style was somewhat similar to that of the Calypso singers of Trinidad. There were also traveling acrobats, jugglers and musicians. Puppet shows were given at fairs in market towns, and performances by trained bears and tigers.

Outdoor sports such as wrestling, swimming, archery, sword play, fencing with sticks, and many other indigenous games, were enjoyed by the Indian people. In those days every householder kept arms for protection from bandits and wild animals, and was a proficient hunter. Field hockey was also a popular sport. Wealthy city folk indulged in fencing, polo, horseracing and dog-racing. For indoor pastime they played card games, chess and backgammon, and gambled with dice.

2

The Political Awakening of India

Egypt is a simple problem; India is a complex one. Egypt is a limited inhabited area with a small population generally homogeneous in race, language, religion, and historical development. India is a vast continental area inhabited by one fifth of mankind, diverse in race and language, variegated in religion and historical experience. India, like Egypt, is a land with an ancient history, with a people recently awakened to national consciousness and to the realization of the significance of western ideas.

Like Egypt, too, India seeks freedom from the rule of the British, to whom it is chiefly indebted for initiation into western ways. In common with the valley of the Nile, the valleys of the Indus and the Ganges rank among the great source reservoirs of the world's civilization. Furthermore, India, as well as Egypt, had experienced centuries of alien rule before the coming of the British. From the monuments and other remains, scholars have been able to unravel the history of Egypt with comparative accuracy and definiteness for more than three millenniums prior to the Christian era.

The memorials of ancient India are no less extensive and interesting but the historical investigator is able to glean from them few definite facts for the establishment of even the outline of the country's early annals. The curtain rises in the sixth century before Christ and reveals a settled society which postulates centuries of development. In that century occurred two epochal events: the great religious revolution inaugurated in the Ganges valley by Buddha and the appearance of the Persian armies on the northwest frontier, establishing the first clearly historical contact between India and the West.

Two centuries later Alexander the Great, who had already brought Egypt and other lands under his sway, appeared with his all-conquering Macedonian phalanx in the valley of the Indus. For at least two hundred years Greek influences continued to stream, or at least to trickle, into India; Greek visitors to India recorded their observations; regular commercial intercourse between India and the West was established. This cultural and commercial contact between India and the West, though perhaps never extensive, continued unbroken until the rise of Mohammedanism at the beginning of the seventh century of our era.

Buddhism reached its climax in India in the third century before Christ under the empire of Asoka, the most extended and enlightened rule ever developed in India prior to the seventeenth century. The decline of Buddhism and the revival of Hinduism had already progressed far when the first Mohammedan contacts with India were established at the beginning of the eighth century. It was not until the beginning of the eleventh century that any part of India was brought under Mohammedan sway, and not till two hundred years later was a distinctively Mohammedan Indian state established in the land with its capital at Delhi.

The founder of this state, a Mohammedan and oriental contemporary and compeer of Richard the Lion-Hearted, has left as his splendid memorial the highest minaret in the world, the Kutab Minar, which still overlooks the plain of Delhi and preserves his name. By this time Mohammedan faith and rule had been spread across northern India from the mouths of the Indus to the delta of the Ganges. This Mohammedan empire was not preserved intact, for there were soon almost as many Moslem kingdoms in India as there had been Hindu states for centuries out of mind.

It was, therefore, a welter of petty states ruled by Moslem shahs and Hindu rajas that made up the India of 1498. In that memorable year there landed on the southwestern coast of India a Portuguese expedition under the command of Vasco da Gama, whose coming was to bring India into far closer relations with Europe than had ever before subsisted. The extension of Mohammedan power in India had been accompanied by a renewal of trade intercourse with the West. It was about 1293 that India was visited by Marco Polo on his way from the court of Kublai Khan back to Venice. His description is the first account of India by a Christian from Western Europe.

In the two centuries between Marco Polo and Vasco da Gama various Europeans, both traders and Catholic friars, had visited India and recorded their observations and experiences. The West was getting acquainted with India and placing a steadily increasing value on its trade. Vasco da Gama opened an allsea route, which at that date was both quicker and cheaper than any other between western Europe and southern Asia.

The consequent monopoly of the rapidly expanding trade with the East was enjoyed by Portugal until the close of the sixteenth century, when the folly of Philip II, who had added Portugal to his Spanish dominions, provoked the Dutch and English into successful competition for that rich prize. In general, the Dutch directed their activities to Malaysia and the English to India. English relations with India became the monopoly of the English East India Company chartered by Queen Elizabeth in 1600, which retained its privileges in whole until 1773, and in part till 1858.

In the seventeenth century three centers were established-Madras, 1639; Bombay, 1664; Calcutta, 1689-from which English power in India was to develop in the eighteenth century. The English came to trade; they remained to rule. Synchronously with the growth of European interests in India, there had grown up a vast Mohammedan empire, which for a time seemed likely to succeed in subduing the whole peninsula to its sway.

This empire of the Great Mughals, founded at Delhi by Babar in 1526, reached its zenith under Akbar, 1556-1605, the contemporary of Queen Elizabeth, and under Aurangzib, 1658-1707, the contemporary of Louis XIV. Under these monarchs more of India was embraced within a single empire than at any time prior to British rule, except under Asoka two thousand years earlier. It was the break-up of the Mughal Empire after the death of Aurangzib, and the ensuing struggle between Mohammedan and Hindu that opened the way for the establishment of a new alien rule in India.

In the eighteenth century four powers-two Asiatic, the Persians under Nadir Shah and the Afghans under Ahmad Shah, and two European, the French led by Dupleix and the English led by Clive-struggled for the mastery of India. By 1763 three had failed; the English alone survived, and their territorial possessions in India amounted to less than a thousand square miles. The English had merely won a clear field; it remained to be determined whether they could establish political control over the numerous heterogeneous and conflicting states.

Beginning with Bengal in 1765, the British have added province to province and kingdom to kingdom, until, for the first time in history, a single power holds dominion over the whole land from Cape Comorin to the Himalayas, and all the borderlands as well are brought under its control. The British have converted India from a geographical expression into an empire, from a congeries of peoples into a nation.

Historians have been wont to speak of the unification of Italy and the unification of Germany as the two greatest and most characteristic political achievements of the nineteenth century, but have taken no thought of the more remarkable achievement of the unification of India. The annexation of Bengal made the English East India Company not merely a wealthy and powerful trading corporation but the ruler of an area and a population exceeding those of the British Islands. The first legislative effort to deal with this curious situation was Lord North's regulating act of 1773.

This measure provided for the exercise of jurisdiction jointly by the English government and by the Company. The dual control, as this arrangement was called, subsisted, with some modifications, until 1858. The English government was represented in India by a governorgeneral and council; Indian interests were represented in the English government by a special minister, the president of the board of control. The Company was deprived of its trade monopoly in 1813 and of all its trade privileges in 1833.

It was not until after the Mutiny that the anomalous continuance of the Company as a ruling power was terminated on November 1, 1858, when the British Crown assumed full control of the government of India. The president of the board of control became secretary of state for India, and the governor-general became viceroy. The essential element in the change was the establishment of the complete and direct supremacy of parliament over India, with the consequent definite location of responsibility. An informed judgment on Indian affairs, if not a representation of the interests of India, was assured to the government in London by the substitution for the old board of control, of a council of India to advise and assist the secretary for India.

On this council a majority had to have seen service in India, and in practice nearly every appointee complied with that requirement. In India the viceroy, like the governor-general previously, was to be advised and assisted by a council of four in executive and administrative matters. Under an act of 1853 this number was enlarged to twelve by the addition of other nominated members for purposes of legislation. In provincial administration, likewise, the existing status was continued with slight modifications.

The governors of Madras and Bombay were to be appointed by the Crown and assisted by councils; the other governors were appointed by the viceroy and acted without councils. The government was entirely in the hands of the British and no native was admitted to one of the higher offices or to the councils. Natives were employed only in the subordinate ranks of the administration. Hitherto there had been little consideration of British aims with reference to India and there was no formally avowed policy. The English position in India had been that of an exploiter. The dividends had been territory, cash, and mutiny.

The act of 1858 passed by parliament did not alter the case. The Queen's proclamation, however, in addition to proclaiming amnesty and religious toleration, included the sentence: "And it is Our further will that, so far as may be, Our subjects, of whatever race or creed, be freely and impartially admitted to offices in Our service, the duties of which they may be qualified by their education, ability, and integrity duly to discharge." Whatever this meant specifically, its general significance clearly indicated a new and more sympathetic attitude toward the government and people of India.

The Indian councils act of 1861 supplemented and modified the act of 1858 and provided the system under which Indian legislation was framed until 1892. The constitution of the governor-general's council was modified for executive purposes, and for legislative purposes it was to be supplemented by from six to twelve nominated members, of whom at least half must be nonofficials and might include natives, as actually became the practice. Legislative councils were revived in Madras and Bombay and authorized for Bengal, where one was established in 1862; and the governor-general might introduce them into other provinces as he did into the Northwest Provinces in 1886 and into the Punjab in 1897.

The governor-general's council might legislate for all India, and provincial councils for the provinces concerned. In both cases the executive had control of the matters introduced and a veto on the enactments. These bodies were really committees to frame laws, not legislative bodies empowered to consider the general welfare and take measures freely with reference to that end. Native members were not introduced to represent the natives but to acquaint the British with native opinion and conditions. The secretary of state in presenting this measure to parliament explicitly disavowed the idea of a representative legislative body in India as absolutely impracticable.

Municipal institutions, or, perhaps better, some forms of community organization, seem to have been a very ancient development among the peoples of the so-called Aryan race. Consequently, such institutions have long subsisted in India, but their operations have naturally been of a primitive and limited sort. In creating municipal organizations in India the British government does not seem to have built upon these foundations, but, rather, to have introduced schemes of its own invention. As early as 1850 an act permitted the establishment of municipal committees or councils in the Northwest Provinces, the Punjab, and Bombay; in 1856 there was an act for Bengal, and in 1865 for Madras.

These measures allowed some nonofficial membership, permitted in principle rather than in practice choice by election, and sought to stimulate local interest and taxation with reference to a limited number of subjects. Lord Mayo, who became viceroy in 1869, faced a difficult financial situation which he sought to remedy in part by transferring certain matters, with the accompanying financial burdens, to the control of local jurisdictions which should exercise the function of levying the necessarily increased taxes involved.

Only the arrangement for Madras was enacted under his administration in 1871, but under his successor similar acts were framed for the other provinces. These measures emphasized the nonofficial membership, definitely introduced the practice of election in a limited way, and considerably extended the scope of jurisdiction to include, among other local matters, education. The plan was a financial expedient and was generally the subject of native protest because of the increased taxation. It did, however, involve a beginning in self-government and election, and it helped to educate some of the people of India to show interest and activity in public concerns. The municipal population potentially affected by the scheme was only one tenth of the total in the provinces concerned, and there remained a minority of these communities in which the councils were not introduced.

Under the second Gladstone ministry, 1880-1885, Lord Ripon and later Lord Dufferin were appointed viceroys of India and signalized their administrations by further measures for the development of the system of local councils. By new acts for each of the provinces in which the system of municipal councils had been authorized the size of the councils was increased; the proportion of official members was limited to one third; greater freedom of election was extended and encouraged; the choice of the chairman by election was permitted; the field of municipal legislation was enlarged; but certain reservations for executive control were included as both negative and positive safeguards.

These measures, with some revision, have since continued in force, and have worked with a reasonable degree of satisfaction, in some cases excellently, but in some cases unfortunately. The number of such municipalities in 1906 was 749, involving a population in excess of 16,000,000, or approximately seven per cent of the total for British India. These do not include the three great commercial centers, Calcutta, Bombay, and Madras, with their large foreign populations, which are administered under special acts of more liberal character.

The novel feature of Lord Ripon's reforms provided for the creation of somewhat similar boards in rural local jurisdictions and the districts throughout British India except Burma. This innovation called forth no little debate and, in the nature of things, has worked rather less satisfactorily than has the system of municipal councils. In 1913 there were 198 district boards with 5,032 members, of whom 2,364 were elected, while the local boards numbered 536 with a membership of 8,005, of whom 3,711 were elected.

At the same date the number of municipalities was 712, consisting of 9,718 members, of whom 5,005 were elected. It will be seen, then, that there was a total of nearly 25,000 members of these various sorts of councils, of which number over 11,000 were elected; by far the larger proportion of the members were natives. These figures are significant for the evidence they give of the extension of the practice of self-government, thus fulfilling Lord Ripon's declaration that his plan was "chiefly desirable as an instrument of political and popular education."

The creation of the municipal and local councils was, however, part of a plan of administrative decentralization to relieve the paid officials from various duties and some responsibility and to lessen the financial burdens of the central and provincial governments, especially in matters which were of local interest but which involved increasing expenditure. The British officials were, in many cases, more anxious to secure information from competent natives which would assist them in administration than to afford the natives free debate and full responsibility in the matters concerned.

British opinion, both at home and in India, revealed serious doubt of the wisdom of the measures, and even strong disapproval of them. Indian opinion was little friendlier because of the increased taxation and because of the restrictions upon the independence and responsibility of the councils. By failing to attend sessions and by unreadiness to participate in a spirit of independence coupled with cooperation, the native members often failed to get from the new institutions the full benefits which were available or to convince the British officials that the system was sufficiently worth while to justify more hearty efforts for its success.

Notwithstanding the difficulties, the indifference, and the opposition, the latest reports available, those for 1920, show that the system is expanding; that native participation and elections are both on the increase; and, perhaps more interesting still, that in a considerable number of cases women may vote, and in some cases are eligible for the council. While Lord Ripon's reforms of 1883 and 1884 established district and local rural councils with Indian members and with elective privileges, in the United Kingdom itself it was not until 1888 that the local-government act established elective county councils, and not until 1894 that the elective parish councils were created.

It may also be noted that while the reform acts of 1832, 1867, and 1884 made successive extensions of the franchise, it was not till 1918 that a considerable portion of the male population of the United Kingdom received the right to vote, at the same time that the parliamentary franchise was extended to women. These facts need to be taken into consideration in passing judgment on the British policy in India. Returning, then, to the subject of the major councils, we find that there was a growing demand for the revision of the act of 1861.

This was accomplished by the Indian councils act of 1892. The measure provided for the increase of the number of nonofficial, and hence of native, members in the legislative council of the governor-general and in the provincial councils; the election of such members was permitted by a clumsily worded and indirect provision; and the privileges of debating the budget and of interpellation were accorded. While in 1861 there had been deliberate avowal of the purpose not to create "a petty parliament," this measure involved more important steps in that direction, but the intimation that it anticipated the introduction of the representative system was promptly denied and reasons were adduced why the idea was impractical for India.

The act of 1892 was destined to remain in force only half as long as its predecessor before demand for still more liberal privileges made its revision necessary. It was criticized because the Mohammedans, the landowners, and the commercial classes, did not receive adequate representation, whereas thirty-six per cent of the nonofficial members of the councils belonged to the legal profession, this percentage being much larger in the elective portion of the membership.

Whatever faults there may have been, the act of 1892 was a step in advance which led logically to further steps affected by the Indian councils act of 1909. Before considering that measure, it will be desirable to go back and take into account other developments which were contributory to this result. In India there was the demand for participation not merely in the legislative but also in the administrative work of government. In the subordinate posts numerous natives had long been employed, but there was a natural resentment that all, or nearly all, the higher posts were reserved for Englishmen.

After fruitless minor efforts at adjustment and after investigation and report by a special commission, several reforms were introduced in or about 1892, that is at about the date of the Indian councils act just discussed. These changes included the definite division into the Indian civil service, the provincial service, and the subordinate service. The two latter were almost wholly reserved for natives, and the terms of competition for appointment in the first were modified so as to give Indian candidates a reasonable chance.

In addition there are certain small special services. Such as forests, engineering, and public works, for which practically all the appointees are necessarily British. The situation in the three principal services in 1904 was that, of 1,370 posts paying above £1800, 1,263 were held by Europeans, 15 by Eurasians, and 92 by natives; while of 26,908 posts paying under £800, Europeans held only 5,205, while Eurasians held 5,420, and natives 16,383. Though these figures do not show a marked change in favor of the natives, they do indicate that the trend was clearly in that direction.

The training of natives in the practical tasks and responsibilities of administration must necessarily be accounted one of the important items in preparation for selfgovernment. While some recognition of the importance of education had been given by the British in India at earlier dates, the system really rests upon two fundamental documents, a minute drafted by Lord Macaulay in 1835 and the despatch of Sir Charles Wood in 1854 with the accompanying orders.

These documents laid down the principle of education in English and placed the emphasis almost exclusively upon higher education. Since then there has been extensive development of secondary and collegiate schools and the numbers who have received training in them have been ample -indeed, in excess of the opportunities for corresponding employment. Serious criticisms have been made against the system at almost every point, but in two particulars which must be noted. In the first place, few of the institutions aside from those under mission control give attention to supplementing literary instruction with any form of character training.

The other important objection is to the failure to provide scientific, technical, and vocational training which would fit the beneficiaries for employment and service in varied fields and make them participants in the development of the nation's economic life. In contrast to the disproportionate attention to the development of higher education has been the neglect or, at best, unsystematic and slight consideration and support accorded to elementary education. Illiteracy in India is appalling, and as late as 1907 less than two per cent of the population was in attendance upon any form of elementary schools, most of which were of very inferior character.

The government felt that it was inexpedient, if not impossible, to increase taxation to provide the necessary means for an adequate educational system, and did not see its way to secure the funds by retrenchment of expenditures for other matters. Furthermore, it must be remembered that the three great measures regulating education in Great Britain itself bear such recent dates as 1870, 1902, and 1918.

To no small degree is the growth of unrest in India directly traceable to the faults of the educational system. The former and actual students of the high schools and colleges have furnished the most numerous and aggressive element in the several forms of agitation and outbursts of discontent. The great gulf between the highly educated few and the ignorant masses is a calamity of incalculable proportions and significance.

While the problem of education has been handled considerably better in India than in Egypt, the success of the British in dealing with questions of assessment and taxation in Egypt has not been duplicated in India. The permanent settlement of the revenue, that is, the establishment of a permanent assessment, effected in Bengal in 1793 under the administration of Lord Cornwallis, has won praises from the most bitter critics of the British, but the reason is that the permanence of the assessment has made impossible any readjustment upward so as to increase the revenue to meet changes in values and in needs.

The settlements or assessments of the land revenue in other parts of India have been vigorously attacked because they are for fixed periods and do permit changes in the assessment. Such changes have been made and rates increased from time to time. These have led to complaints both of injustice in fixing the rates and of overtaxation. Successive administrations have steadily endeavored to mitigate the causes of complaint wherever the justice of the methods employed was questioned.

Under the rule both of the Company and later of the Crown there have been English civil servants in India who have displayed remarkable ability to enter into the life of the country and to labor sympathetically for the welfare of the people. British and Indians alike unite in honoring the memory of men like Sir Thomas Munro and James Thomason. Several governors-general and viceroys, likewise, have exhibited a keen interest in measures for the welfare of the Indian peoples and sought to carry out reforms of benevolent character and of deep significance.

The name of Lord William Bentinck will always be honorably remembered for the suppression of *sati*, or widow-burning, and of *thagi*, an evil which permeated the life of the country and has given us the word thug. That he was able successfully to brave the deep-seated prejudices of the people in these matters is reasonable evidence that reforms of even more far-reaching importance might have been worked out by others laboring with equal courage, devotion, and sympathy. A later viceroy whose name is remembered with similar respect was the Marquess of Ripon, whose reforms in the matter of local councils have already been considered.

Just as in Egypt, the British in India have been accused of neglecting the development of sanitation, and even more of failure to take adequate measures against the chronic evil of India, famines. These criticisms do not mean that the British have not done a vast amount of work to remedy evils and to provide against plague and famine, but that they have not accomplished the desired ends. Anyone who has read Mr. Kipling stories *William the Conqueror and The Tomb of His Ancestors* has vivid pictures in mind of the splendid work done.

Even so it is an obvious excuse for criticism that after more than a century of British rule, there should be possible such frightful ravages as have resulted from both plague and famine in the past quarter century, not to mention the disgustingly unsanitary conditions which are still tolerated even in the largest and most Europeanized cities. No doubt ignorance and superstition, religion and caste have been obstacles to radical measures, but one may question whether all these would not have yielded to firm but sympathetic pressure had such measures as those of Lord William Bentinck been followed up consistently through the three generations since he left India.

Accusations made by vehement nationalists like Lajpat Rai, or by somewhat more moderate writers such as Romesh Chunder Dutt, that England has preferred revenue from India to reform for India are certainly exaggerated. Even though one dismisses as by-gones, which these Indians do not, the rapacity and greed under the Company in the eighteenth century on which Burke poured forth the vials of his indignation, or conditions far less objectionable during the later Company days in the early nineteenth century, there remains to be considered the situation under the government of the Crown.

Great Britain has taken no governmental tribute from the people of India, but it has charged to the Indian exchequer expenses which the Indians allege are imperial, not Indian, and, in some cases, the British have considered the point sufficiently well taken to cause them to transfer certain items. The chief accusation, however, is what the Indian economists and agitators describe as the economic drain, which they attribute to the suppression of native industry, the manipulation of trade, and interest charges on railroad bonds and other capital investments.

The charge cuts deeper, however, for it goes beyond the mere economic drain to allege either serious errors in policy, such as preferring railway construction to canal and irrigation works, or deliberate sacrifice of Indian welfare to English economic advantage, as in yielding to the protests of the Lancashire cotton spinners against certain tariff duties. It would seem that there is too much smoke to preclude the existence of some fire.

The correspondence of the directors of the East India Company with their officials and agents in India affords plentiful evidence of their loyal devotion to dividends, and their opposition to measures either of imperial or of reform character which might appear in any way to endanger the size of the annual net income. None the less the agents of the Company did carry forward almost unremittingly a policy of conquest and of territorial absorption within India, which reached its climax in the extensive annexations effected by the great Marquess of Dalhousie, who was governor-general from 1848 to 1856.

Dalhousie was a devout, indomitable Scotchman who was intensely convinced that he was engaged in a great humanitarian undertaking-a conviction which an impartial reader will be inclined to share-but his too masterly policy overreached itself. The great Mutiny of 1857 was the result. Since then Great Britain has abandoned the policy of annexations within India and has been content to allow the native princes to govern, under its supervision, the considerable portions of the country which had not already been incorporated into British India.

Since the Mutiny, British policy with reference to India has been in the control of the secretary of state for India, a member of the British cabinet, responsible to parliament. His vision of India has been obtained from the point of view of the United Kingdom and of imperial interests. Down to the Anglo-Russian agreement in 1907 British imperial policy was dominated by fear of Russia, sedulously cultivated by returned civilians and military men from India As a consequence of this situation, the British in India turned their activities from annexations within India to a policy of annexations along the frontiers and of building up buffer states under British influence for protection against the Russian bear's "irresistible advance into India." Imperialism in India had given place to imperialism in Asia.

As the old policy attained its climax under Lord Dalhousie, so this new policy finally overreached itself in the too masterly activities of Lord Curzon of Kedleston as viceroy from 1899 to 1905. He carried out annexations on the northwest frontier which he organized into the Northwest Frontier Province, and he sent the Younghusband mission to Tibet in 1904 and Sir Louis Dane to Afghanistan in 1905. These measures include the latest annexations of territory to the Indian Empire and the latest extensions of the British sphere of influence in territories adjacent to India.

The horrid contrast of this splendid and expensive imperialism with the misery of plague and famine in the land could not fail to produce a reaction. It is a tribute to the development of the Indian peoples under British rule in the intervening half century that instead of Mutiny there was Unrest. The half century had been marked by the development of the councils, national, provincial, and local; by great material development in the construction of railways, telegraphs, canals, and irrigation works; by famine relief and measures against disease; by improved financial arrangements; by civil service reforms; and by the spread of education-all which have been discussed; and by many minor measures of amelioration.

What had been the reaction of all these on the Indian mind? What, moreover, is the character of Indian mentality? It has been the fashion, as exemplified by Mr. Kipling, to consider the Indian mentality and western thinking as incommensurate. The Indians, not merely the Hindus, but also the Mohammedans, emphasize their spiritual-mindedness as contrasted with the material-mindedness of the occidentals. The Hindu has been exalted for his ability for abstruse and lofty thought.

While there is perhaps some truth in all these notions, yet much is certainly to be found in the intellectual life of India to-day which is comparable with the mysticism and scholastic philosophy of the European Middle Ages, rather than with the present-day traits of western peoples. Generalizations, always dangerous, are nowhere so likely to lead to false conclusions as in India. Its diversities of conditions really forbid generalization.

Over against the abysmal ignorance of the vast masses there stand experimental scientists with broad philosophic vision like Sir J. C. Bose, and liberal-minded, well-balanced statesmen like Lord Sinha. The leadership of large sections of Indian opinion and action to-day has, however, been assumed by men of a different stamp. These belong to the higher castes, many of them Brahmins, who have received western education in the schools and colleges.

That education has unfortunately been of the sort that passes examinations but not of the kind that trains the mind to grapple with problems and face situations involving hard facts. It has taught the student to memorize many facts, whether he understands and accepts them or not, in order to satisfy the examiner. It has, on the other hand, given him the ability to read, outside the curriculum, books of advanced, if not incendiary thought. This reading, without the check of the careful analysis and searching criticism of the classroom, results in uncontrolled thinking, loose reasoning, and often irrational, even dangerous, conclusions.

In talking with men of this class one is frequently surprised at their adolescent evasion of facts, inability or unwillingness to reason logically, and imaginative zeal to arrive at conclusions in realities as well as in ideas regardless of intervening obstacles. The British problem is to find the needed supply of wise and sympathetic mentors for this group of men, mostly young, who are leading India they know not whither. They are as sheep without a shepherd. India needs good scout-masters skilled not in the craft of the forest or in jungle lore but in the lore and craft of politics, economics, sociology, and religion.

The British civil, educational, and other services have provided not a few such excellent scout-masters, and the mission schools and colleges have furnished more. The supply of these men is woefully inadequate and in recent years has been decreasing not only relatively but absolutely. The real problem of the future of India is to increase greatly the supply of such wise and tactful guides. Force has been the stern schoolmaster of India for centuries, and has failed; the warm heart and the sympathetic hand are yielding the desired results where they have a chance.

This, however, is getting ahead of the story, for we have been trying to collect and collate the data necessary for understanding the situation in India after Lord Curzon gave place to the Earl of Minto in 1905. Two items still remain for consideration, the attempts of the leaders of India to organize for the promotion of their aims and the external influences which may have been operating to stimulate their thought and action.

Since its organization in 1885 the Indian National Congress, an entirely unofficial and voluntary organization, chiefly but not exclusively Hindu, and largely Brahmin, has been the most widely recognized and influential spokesman of Indian opinion. The original platform of the congress did not present immoderate demands, but did contend for much more than the British authorities have yet been prepared to concede.

In the earlier years, and even as late as 1915, both the government and the congress recognized the desirability of maintaining some contacts. Several English people, including some prominent retired civil servants, have given their sympathy to the congress. Five times in the first thirty years, the presidency of the congress was held by Englishmen. Three times a Parsi, Mr. Dadabai Naoroji, was chosen to preside, and on three other occasions Mohammedans were selected for the presidency, which has at other times been held by Hindus.

The registered attendance during this period averaged 775 annually. It reached 440 the second year and did not fall so low again until 1909, while it reached the maximum in the Calcutta meeting of 1906 due to the efforts to protest against the partition of Bengal. Radicalism grew steadily in the congress until it reached a climax in the stormy session at Surat in 1907, after which followed a period of milder councils. During the first twenty years, then, the congress movement had been gaining steadily in momentum. Not unfriendly relations had subsisted between it and the government, but as the years passed without producing any particular impression upon the government, the more radical elements gained strength.

Meanwhile external events were wielding an increasing influence upon Indian thought. It was the unwritten law of the British, never honored in the breach, not to permit any military reverse to pass without being promptly avenged. The consequent occidental prestige for invincibility remained unshattered until the crushing and unretrieved defeat of the Italians by the Abyssinians at Adowa in 1896. The success of the Boers in South Africa in withstanding for three years the greatest military effort which the British Empire had ever yet put forth was expensive to British prestige in Indian eyes, and was not redeemed by the concession of responsible government to the two Boer states five years later, in 1906.

A more convincing blow to European prestige was the defeat of Russia by Japan, an Asiatic nation, smaller, less populous, and poorer than India, and, unlike India, but recently emerged from its medieval seclusion. Russia, furthermore, was that nation in awe of which Great Britain had held its breath and maneuvered its imperial policy for two generations. With such a convincing demonstration, why should India continue to cower before the British? India had been taught and believed that England must be tolerated to save India from the worse evil of Russian despotism.

Whatever remained of that danger was removed by the Anglo-Russian agreement of 1907, which followed upon British success in out-maneuvering Russia in Tibet and Afghanistan in 1904 and 1905. Freed from the Russian menace, there remained no foe against which India needed British protection; India was free to deal with Great Britain on the merits of the question. The situation was not unlike that which arose in North America after the French menace had been removed from England's continental colonies by the treaty of 1763.

Within the British Empire, India had not received equitable treatment. It was true that the British monarch now plumed himself with the splendid title of Emperor of India and that Edward VII had recently been proclaimed at a magnificent darbar at Delhi in 1903. In the imperial conferences, however, which had been held occasionally since the Queen's jubilee in 1887, India had been accorded no part. India was good for show but not for counsel.

In various ways India had contributed to the British success in South Africa, but the British government failed to assure Indian laborers and others in South Africa fair treatment after the war, and had left them to win their own battle as best they might. Then, too, Australia and Canada, other self-governing dominions, had contemptuously shown their unwillingness to accord the Indian equal treatment with the white citizens of the empire, but, rather, sought to exclude him as undesirable. Such denial of equitable treatment not only hurt the Indian pride, but it sapped the Indian confidence in British fair-mindedness and justice.

In India itself things had not been going well. The financial crisis which affected the United States and other countries in the nineties of the last century hit India even more severely. Before that crisis had passed came famines more widespread than any in the modern history of the country. In 1900 the famine area was three and one-half times greater than the United Kingdom, with a population two and one third times as great. At one time the numbers gathered in relief camps equaled the population of Greater London.

Then came the bubonic plague first appeared in India in 1896 and has become endemic. In 1904 it caused more than 1,000,000 deaths and in the last twenty years 10,000,000 deaths. Against this dark background, in lurid contrast stood out the bustling and expensive imperialism of Lord Curzon. Finally he, quite unwittingly, threw the lighted match into the tinder by proclaiming the partition of Bengal in 1905. The division of this province, which exceeded the area of the United Kingdom by twenty-five per cent and the population by seventy-five per cent, was an obvious administrative necessity and was arranged on lines which were apparently expedient politically since they recognized the predominantly Mohammedan population of the sections which were separated to form a new province.

This was denounced as British favoritism to the Mohammedans, since in the original province the Hindus had constituted the majority. The action was interpreted as a departure from the avowed British policy of not interfering in religious matters. In race and language there was no differentiation between the districts incorporated in the new province and the portions of Bengal left in the old province. It was easy to raise the cry that the British had cut in pieces "Mother Bengal," and that they had done so for their own evil purposes.

Agitation ran rife; acts of violence occurred; the Indian national congress assembled in Calcutta in 1906 with unrivaled attendance and joined in denunciation of the outrage; and the *swadeshi* boycott of English goods was initiated. Never was such pressure brought to bear on the British government to reverse one of its policies in India. When Lord Curzon's quarrel with Lord Kitchener resulted in the former's resignation in 1905, it was confidently hoped that the change of administration would be accompanied by a reversal of the act, especially as the Liberal party had recently come into power in England. Mr. John Morley, the new secretary of state for India, however, declared the matter a *chose jugie* and adhered strictly to that policy.

Mr. Morley, and the new viceroy, the Earl of Minto, undertook to divert attention by liberal reforms of the national and provincial legislative councils. Progress was slow, for the reforms which were first outlined in a minute by Lord Minto in 1906 were not embodied into law until the passage of the Indian councils act of 1909, though Mr. Morley had called to the council of India in 1907 two Indians, one a Hindu and one a Mohammedan, and in 1909 an Indian was for the first time admitted to the viceroy's executive council; he was a Hindu, Mr., later Lord, Sinha.

The new councils act included provisions for enlarging the provincial legislative councils and giving them nonofficial majorities; for enlarging the legislative council of the viceroy, but retaining an official majority with a veto over the provincial councils; for representation of the Mohammedan minority; for the election of a proportion of the members of both the viceregal and provincial councils, with an arrangement of electoral constituencies; for increased privileges of budget discussion and interpellation; for the right to introduce resolutions; and for the later extension of executive and legislative councils to other provinces.

Comparison with the act of 1892 shows that the increase of privileges was both liberal and genuine. The Indians were given much larger opportunities for acquiring experience in the handling of important public questions and for exercising very considerable influence upon government policy. The presence of the official majority in the viceroy's council was a definite but reasonable restriction upon complete native control and responsibility.

It was justifiable as an intermediate step and also because the councils were only in the slightest degree representative of the peoples of India; they merely represented certain interests. In other respects the measure was disappointing to the reformers in the congress party and open to reasonable criticism, but it was a long step forward and a genuine one. Experience of its actual working, on the whole, quite thoroughly justified the wisdom both of going so far, and of not going further. These Morley-Minto reforms were not brilliant or epoch-making achievements, but they proved to be good solid statesmanship, constructive and progressive.

In all fairness, they must be judged as an effort to establish not a permanent but a temporary system. The period of unrest which had started with the partition of Bengal was practically terminated by the reforms of 1909. The councils act of 1861 had remained in force thirty-one years; the councils act of 1892, seventeen years; the MorleyMinto reforms of 1909 were destined to only a decade of life before being superseded. The immediate result of the reforms was favorable. Lord Minto left India amid approving plaudits in 1910, and his successor, Lord Hardinge, was welcomed in a similar spirit.

The visit of King George V and Queen Mary for the proclamation of their accession at a great *darbar* at Delhi in 1911 was the first event of its kind and evoked great enthusiasm. The announcement on this occasion of the transfer of the capital from Calcutta to Delhi was perhaps a clever move, but the revision of the partition of Bengal which gratified Hindu sentiment was bound to give offense to the Mohammedans who had profited from the previous arrangement.

The Mohammedans of India had been much slower than the Hindus to avail themselves of the privileges of western education, but with the opening of the twentieth century this situation had begun to change. Furthermore, the Mohammedans had held aloof, as a rule, from the Indian national congress movement and had been inclined to find their interest in supporting British rule rather than in sympathizing with the Hindu reformers. Even when the All-India Moslem League was formed in 1905 this attitude persisted. Education and events in other parts of the Moslem world were already modifying their views, when the revision of the Bengal settlement gave added incentive to change, which was still further accentuated by other events outside India.

In 1904 the Anglo-French agreement confirmed the English position in Egypt and the French hold on Morocco; the Anglo-Russian agreement of 1907 practically brought Persia under the sway of the two contracting powers; Italy seized Tripoli and Rhodes in 1911; and the Balkan wars of 1912-13 stripped the Ottoman Empire of most of its European lands. The Christian powers were apparently banded in an unholy league for the destruction of the political power of Islam, which could only be interpreted as precursing the subversion of the faith as well.

The consequent growth of the Pan-Islamic movement did not fail to attract followers in India. The success of the Young Turk revolution of 1908 caused the more restless Moslem spirits in India to link up with its leaders and to draw inspiration from them. This tendency became pronounced at the time of the Balkan wars, when the Moslems of India bore their gifts to their sorely tried Ottoman brethren. The Indian Mohammedans were drifting rapidly into the same dubious position as the Hindus with reference to the British government.

Then came the World War. With surprising unanimity the Indian peoples, as well as the Indian princes, rallied to the support of the British Empire against the Germans. There seemed to be a sudden realization that, whatever its faults, British rule was preferable to German. The services of Indian troops on the western front in France in 1914-15 were of indispensable importance. Indian troops, often Mohammedans, did valiant service also in Mesopotamia, Palestine, and East Africa against Mohammedan coreligionists.

The viceroy's legislative council passed important war measures not dissimilar to those enacted in England itself, voted unanimously a gift from the Indian government of £100,000,000 for the imperial war expenses, and later approved a loan for an additional £100,000,000 which was promptly subscribed. Whether these acts were spontaneous and disinterested or not, India had clearly earned the right to have its affairs regarded by the British government in the future from "a new angle of vision," as Premier Asquith expressed it.

The first evidence of such a change came when a native prince of India and a former Hindu member of the Indian legislative council were seated with the representatives from the self-governing dominions in the first Imperial war conference. Recognition as a partner with the self-governing dominions in the empire suggested a larger measure of self-government for India. The first steps to this end were taken by Lord Hardinge before the close of his administration in 1916. His successor, Lord Chelmsford,. later in the same year submitted to the government in London his project for reforms, but there were destined to be long delays before the British ministry and parliament could find time free to devote to Indian constitutional questions.

The delay made the extremists in India increasingly impatient-a marked contrast to the patience of the Egyptian nationalists until after the armistice. The congress and the

Moslem league drew closer together with the growing power of the radical element in each. Both met at Lucknow in 1916 and adopted resolutions embodying radical and insistent demands for the largest measure of self-government and for other reforms. It was on this occasion that the theosophical Mrs. Besant began the exercise of her remarkable and inflammatory influence upon the congress movement. Thus began a second period of unrest which apparently reached its culmination in the arrest of Mr. Gandhi in 1922.

The year 1917 saw an adjustment of the long-standing grievance over the cotton duties, the appointment of the Sadler commission to inquire into educational questions in India and of the Holland committee to study the industrial situation, the termination of indenturing Indians to work in the Fiji and West Indian islands, and other reforms. Toward the end of the year Mr. Montagu, who had been Mr. Morley's under-secretary, became secretary of state, for India and arrived in India to confer upon the question of governmental reforms in accordance with an announcement that the policy would be not only "the increasing association of Indians in every branch of the administration, but also the greatest development of self-governing institutions with a view to the progressive realization of responsible government in India as an integral part of the British Empire."

Though the announcement was carefully safeguarded with cautionary restrictions it marked a long step in advance since Mr. Morley had accompanied his reforms with a vigorous denial that he contemplated the ultimate bestowal of parliamentary institutions upon India. Mr. Montagu completed his inquiries and conferences in India by signing in April, 1918, with Lord Chelmsford, the viceroy, a report which was presented to parliament in July. Long delays still ensued, which, indeed, contributed somewhat to the value of the result, before the measure was finally passed in December, 1919.

This government of India act of 1919 created a council of state of not more than sixty members, of whom not more than one third may be officials. This is an entirely new body and forms the upper house of the national legislature. The former legislative council has become the lower house, with the name of legislative assembly. It is composed of one hundred and forty-four members, of whom one hundred and three are elected and, of the remainder, only twenty-six may be officials. The term of the council of state is five years, and of the assembly, three years.

In cases of disagreement the two bodies may sit in joint session to determine their differences. The reserve power which had been invested in the national legislature prior to this act of 1919 had, with this creation of a native majority, to be transferred to the viceroy, who, in certain cases, is granted power to "certify" measures as vital to the peace, safety, and welfare of India. The viceroy's executive council, which now numbers eight, has charge of the various departments of administration. The reforms in the national government of India are paralleled on a somewhat more liberal scale by changes in the provincial government.

In the eight more important provinces (Burma has since been included) not only were there important changes made in the legislative councils and their powers and in the extension of the franchise, but a reform of vital significance was introduced in the character and powers of the provincial executive. These administrative powers are divided into two classes, one dealing with the "reserved" subjects, and other dealing with the "transferred" subjects. The "reserved" subjects are those which involve imperial interests, and remain in the charge of the governor-in-council. The "transferred" subjects, which deal with purely provincial matters, such as education, are under the charge of the governor assisted by ministers who are intended to be responsible to the legislative council of the province.

This novel constitutional scheme, which its inventors have called dyarchy, involves certain obvious limitations upon the freedom of action of the legislative chambers. This scheme was devised for the explicit purpose of transferring power and responsibility for certain matters of provincial, as contrasted with imperial, interest, to the people of India. It is confessedly an awkward arrangement, and its real justification is that it has been created to meet a peculiar necessity. It can scarcely be regarded as other than a temporary expedient, and as a step toward the gradual transfer of the direction of other departments of administration and legislation to native control, as rapidly as experience appears to justify such action.

It was recognized that these important changes in the government of British India would have an inevitable reaction upon the government of the numerous native states. Accordingly, provision was included for the establishment of a chamber of princes, in which the rulers of these states might meet for conference and action upon matters of general concern. Another important provision of the act recognized its provisional character, and required that once in ten years there should be a parliamentary commission of inquiry into the workings of the government, the progress of the people, and proposals for further changes in the form of government.

This provision, which is, to all intents and purposes, a scheme for the consideration of constitutional amendments, is of the highest importance, since it definitely commits the British government to a policy of progressive bestowal of self-government, and no longer leaves the question either to chance or to spasmodic adjustment. The act obviously falls short of conferring upon India full dominion status, as the most advanced leaders in India had desired, and even demanded, as the necessary minimum.

On the other hand, moderate opinion in India recognized the remarkable generosity of the new measure in the amount of self-government conferred, as contrasted with the measure of 1909. There was no longer any disavowal, by the statesmen of England, of the development of a genuine legislature, or of representative institutions, or even of a preliminary stage of responsible government. The measure did actually create a legislature based in large measure upon elections in accordance with the representative principle, and it contained also definite provision for the development of ministerial responsibility.

Naturally, British opinion, both in India and at home, was sharply divided upon the expediency of the measure. In both cases a large majority recognized the necessity, if not the wisdom, of the act, but in both groups there were numerous outspoken opponents who denounced the new governmental scheme as fraught with ruinous consequences. They declared that the people of India were not fitted for such responsibility, that the new legislatures and ministers could not be trusted to work with the best interests of the whole of the Indian people in mind, and especially did they denounce the surrender of British imperial interests.

Before the new acts were placed upon the statute book two events occurred which radically altered the situation in India. The first of these was the passage of the so-called Rowlatt acts. The other was the killing of nearly four hundred Indians and the wounding of about three times as many more by the orders of General Dyer at Jallianwala Bagh, at Amritsar, on April 13, 1919. With the close of the war it was felt that the lapse of the special powers conferred by the defense of India act, corresponding to the British defense of the realm act, would deprive the government of the necessary powers for the prevention or suppression of sedition.

To meet these situation two measures were framed by a committee under the presidency of Mr. Justice Rowlatt of the high court. In the legislative council, these proposals were denounced in the most vigorous terms by the native members, and the government was fully warned not merely of the inexpediency but of the danger of enacting these proposals. They were, however, passed by the votes of the official bloc in the council. In fact, the acts remained inoperative, and the only result of their passage was to inflame public opinion.

The measures were not unreasonable or harsh as compared with similar laws in western countries, but the government would have been wise not to have pressed the measures prior to the establishment of the new legislative chambers under the Montagu-Chelmsford act which was soon to become a law. Of the second matter, the unfortunate and ghastly affair at Amritsar, in the Punjab, it is sufficient to quote from the despatch of the British government: "The principle which has consistently governed the policy of His Majesty's Government in directing the methods to be employed where military action in support of civil authority is required, may be broadly stated as using the minimum force necessary.... It must regretfully, without possibility of doubt, be concluded that Brigadier-General Dyer's action at Jallianwala Bagh was in complete violation of this principle."

The only charitable view is that in ordering a body of soldiers to fire without warning upon a defenseless mob General Dyer lost his head. The British government was slow in appointing the socalled Hunter commission to investigate the affair, and it was more than a year after the tragedy before the commission's report appeared. These delays gave added weight to the fiery denunciations of the affair by the agitators throughout India.

Though the report unqualifiedly condemned General Dyer's action, and both the government of India and the British government at home disavowed the affair, General Dyer was let off with mere dismissal from the service, and other officers in the Punjab who were more or less implicated in this and other measures for the suppression of disturbances in that province not merely escaped without any penalty but like Sir Michael O'Dwyer, lieutenant-governor of the Punjab, were retired on pensions chargeable to the Indian revenues.

It was these two affairs which turned Mr. Gandhi into a thoroughgoing opponent of the British government, which he rightly claimed he had hitherto loyally supported, and made him the greatest leader that the people of India have produced. There is no more striking or interesting personality in the world today than this prophet, this holy man, who suddenly rose to the leadership of the people of India. He was a man of fifty, educated in the British schools in India, at London University, and at the Inner Temple, where he read for the bar.

The major part of his mature life had been spent in South Africa, where he had acquired renown as the champion of the rights of his fellow Indians. Mr. Gandhi's power rested primarily upon his personality. His saintly character, his ascetic life, and his lofty spiritual principles have won universal admiration, and it is little wonder that the highly religious and mystical natives of India have revered him as a holy man and have, in spite of his own behest, insisted upon calling him Mahatma Gandhi, that is, the prophet Gandhi. It would be difficult to find any western parallel for the intense devotion to a man which the people of India have given to Mahatma Gandhi.

Only in the Middle Ages of Europe may one find a counterpart to the mysticism, asceticism, and sanctity of Mr. Gandhi, but not even St. Francis of Assisi is an adequate parallel, nor does even the crusading zeal and enthusiasm aroused at the council of Clermont afford a comparison to the passionate devotion of the natives of India to their prophet.

In entering the field of political agitation in India, Mr. Gandhi was attempting a far more difficult role than he had practiced on the smaller stage of South Africa. Likewise, in attempting to preach for the three hundred millions of people of India ideals similar to those of a religious ascetic, he was attempting, as no other character in history has done, to carry his ideals to their logical conclusion in the sphere of government. Even Jesus of Nazareth had declared that his kingdom was not of this world, and had enjoined his followers to "render to Cζsar the things that are Cζsar's."

In proclaiming his doctrine of *swaraj*, Mr. Gandhi confused the idea of personal *swaraj*, or self-control, with national *swaraj*, or self-government. He insisted that the principles, which all religions teach, of the development of self-control as the way of righteousness and salvation, were equally applicable in the larger sphere of the regulation of masses of peoples in social and political affairs. One cannot but be astounded into admiration for the boldness and magnificence of his idealism, and one feels almost a sense of horror at applying cold reason to his great program. Even he himself seemed at times to waver in the face of the frightful evidence of the impracticability of his teachings.

The doctrine of *swaraj* in political matters was not original with Mr. Gandhi. It had long been the ideal of the educated classes in India. It was only in his lofty spiritual interpretation of the doctrine that he was an innovator. The other elements of his practical program were likewise borrowed, but also more or less spiritualized by his idealism. The idea of *swadeshi*, that is, home industries, had been one of the essential factors in the disturbances of 1906, but Mr. Gandhi declared not merely foreign goods, but all the material inventions, machines, and enterprises of the West, satanic, and bade his followers turn from them and return to the use of the distaff, the spinning wheel, the plow, and the flail, which had been the implements of Indian industry for thousands of years.

The western civilizations of Persia and Greece and Rome and the empires of the foreign conquerors from Alexander to the Great Mughals had all passed away, but India alone stood firm after four thousand years, with the same religion and culture, the same economic and social system. The salvation of India obviously lay in rigorously throwing aside the material evils of the moribund civilization of the West and in disφwning the British government, which his logic led him to denounce as satanic. He called upon the people to return to the eternal verities of the spiritual life of India embodied in the *Mahabharata* and the *Bhagavadgita*.

To emphasize this teaching, he not only enjoined but practiced the use of the old-fashioned spinning wheel, the *charka*, for the making of the rough home-spun cloth in which he clad himself, and which he exhorted his followers to make and wear. The third great ideal which he preached was that of brotherhood of the peoples of India. No one has ever struck so tremendous a blow at the system of caste as has Mr. Gandhi, both by precept and example. He has endeavored to persuade the Brahmin to overcome his scruples, and even to sit at table with "untouchables," that is, persons of the lower castes.

One cannot doubt that the future historians of India will record that one of the greatest forces in the molding of unity of the peoples of India has been the work of Mahatma Gandhi in his labor to unite them all, regardless of caste or race or creed, into one great brotherhood of Indian people. To the logic of this exalted ideal Mahatma Gandhi was not unfaithful. He recognized that in this great brotherhood not only must all the castes of Hinduism be merged but that Hindu and Mohammedan must be brought into affiliation.

This led to the adoption of the fourth, and in some respects the most serious, item in his program, the acceptance of the caliphate doctrine and agitation current among the Mohammedan leaders under the inspiration of the hot-headed Ali brothers. The caliphate movement owed its origin in the first place to the Pan-Islamic agitation and later to the movement led by the Young Turks, which resulted in the revolution of 1908 in the Ottoman Empire, but it received still greater stimulus from the steady breakdown by Christian European powers of the independence of Mohammedan states in the early years of the twentieth century.

The World War witnessed the further disintegration of Turkish power, and the abortive treaty of Sθvres confirmed the results by stripping the Ottoman Empire of still more provinces, leaving to it little more than a fragment of Asia Minor. The war had also witnessed an attempt to deprive the Ottoman sultan of the caliphate. The dissatisfaction of the Mohammedans of India over certain internal matters, and the alarm at the steady decline in the extent of independent Mohammedan states had, however, not resulted in any serious manifestations in India until the treaty of Sθvres.

The Mohammedans of India had first organized themselves for political purposes in 1905 in the All-India Moslem League, which was in general sympathetic to British rule and antagonistic to the congress movement. This original attitude had been slowly shifting until 1916, when the league took action in identical terms with the congress in demanding self-government for India.

The caliphate question had no proper relation to political questions in India, but the Ali brothers, who had long been in sympathetic relations with the Young Turks, seized upon the treaty of Sθvres as a convenient political weapon to arouse Mohammedan sentiment in India to the danger of Christian aggression against Islam, and to the special menace of British rule in India to the interests of that country in general and of its Mohammedans in particular. The acceptance by Mr. Gandhi of the caliphate issue was a perfectly natural political agreement to clinch the coöperation of Hindu and Mohammedan in the struggle for national self-government.

The immediate purpose of the noncoφperation program was to withdraw support from the British government in India, and particularly to refuse any participation in the inauguration of the Montagu-Chelmsford reforms. Mr. Gandhi and his followers believed that it was possible, by maintaining a policy of nonresistance, to render the reforms ineffective and the British administration helpless. He did not contemplate the use of violence, but consistently denounced it. None the less, sporadic outbreaks of violence continually occurred.

As a consequence, the moderate element among the Indian population decided to accept the measure, and to coφperate in inaugurating the new legislative assemblies. This was the first blow to the success of the Gandhi program. A second blow came from the Moplah affair in the western part of the Madras presidency. This was an attack by a fanatical group of Mohammedans upon their peaceful Hindu neighbors to convert them forcibly to Mohammedanism. The result was a grim scene of violence and bloodshed, which brought home to the Hindu population with great vividness that the much-heralded brotherhood of Hindu and Moslem might not result in an equal partnership, but in domination by the more vigorous and strenuous Mohammedans.

Meanwhile the Duke of Connaught, the last surviving son of Queen Victoria, came to India in 1921 as a personal representative of George V to inaugurate the new legislative assemblies, the assembly of the princes, and the more important provincial assemblies. In his various addresses he endeavored to allay the bitterness of race feeling, and to win for the new reforms a favorable trial. Later in the same year the government in London decided that the Prince of Wales should make an extensive tour of the Indian Empire.

In many respects the occasion seemed to be highly unpropitious. His arrival in Bombay was the signal for serious rioting, and at Madras, Calcutta, and Allahabad, the hartal, or boycott, and other forms of unfriendly demonstration were disagreeably successful. As time went on, however, sentiment began to change, and the reception accorded to the prince from city to city became less hostile and more friendly. His reception in the native states was not merely friendly but highly gratifying. The closing weeks of his visit were spent at Delhi and in the

Punjab, where he even visited Amritsar without any serious unpleasantness.

Meanwhile the successful introduction of the reform measures and operation of the new legislatures were counteracting the efforts of the agitators. Shortly after the inauguration of the new assemblies, Lord Chelmsford completed his term as viceroy, and was replaced by Lord Reading. Upon his arrival in India the new viceroy held extensive conferences with Mr. Gandhi and through him even communicated with the Ali brothers. Efforts to establish an understanding between the government and the various agitating elements went to the length of a proposal, at the close of 1921, for a round-table conference. It did not require much consideration, however, to show that such a proposal was inexpedient, if not entirely impracticable.

This was made particularly clear by the continued irresponsibility of the Ali brothers, who were finally arrested and given jail sentences. The Indian national congress in December, 1921, met at Ahmedabad, the home of Mr. Gandhi. The question of putting into full force the noncoφperation program was discussed with approval, but the determination of the time for action was left to Mr. Gandhi, who was practically intrusted with dictatorial powers by the congress.

As Mr. Gandhi confronted the immediate possibility of inaugurating his plan, he seems to have realized that the various acts of violence which have just been mentioned made it clear that noncoφperation might be proclaimed as a measure of passive resistance, but that, in spite of his first intentions, it would result in worse violence and more bloodshed. While he was in this frame of mind there occurred at Chauri Chaura in the United Provinces a mob attack which resulted in the burning of a police station with about twenty native policemen, early in February, 1922.

Mr. Gandhi promptly denounced the affair, and declared that he would fast for several days as his personal expiation for the outrage. His indecision and hesitation grew more obvious, though the extremists were doing their best to spur him to action. During this period, the question of Mr. Gandhi's arrest was a subject of general discussion. The natives declared that the British government did not dare touch him, and charged the authorities with injustice in their arrest of minor agents.

The decision of the matter was precipitated in a way that could scarcely have been anticipated. Mr. Montagu, the secretary of state for India, who had been responsible for the reform policy and who was considered as being too lenient in dealing with the Indian situation, had evidently been for some time the object of attack by his more conservative colleagues in the ministry. The publication by him of a despatch from Lord Reading dealing with the Mohammedan issue, without the customary consultation with the prime minister and his colleagues, led to his dismissal on March 9, 1922.

The following day Mr. Gandhi was placed under arrest, promptly tried, and sentenced to jail for six years without labor. The coincidence had a noteworthy effect upon Indian opinion, and since that time the government of India has followed a strong and consistent policy of enforcing law and order and has impressed upon the popular mind the genuineness of British power by sending bodies of troops on long marches through the country, simply as a matter of demonstration.

The new legislative councils have, under the circumstances, been working even more satisfactorily than might have been expected, and this fact has had a beneficial influence. It is, of course, easy to bring criticisms against them, either from the British or from the Indian point of view, with reference to lack of adequate representative basis, to personnel, to procedure in debate, to ability and readiness to assume responsibility along with privilege, and in other matters, but it must be remembered that things are in the experimental stage, and perfection cannot be expected at once, especially as it has not been attained in western lands.

The most serious problem, however, is that of financial deficits, which have appeared in each of the budgets handled by the assemblies. In face of the spirit of unwillingness to increase taxation the only recourse lies in economies. As a consequence the demand for a large decrease in the British army in the country, and even of the native portion of the army, has been greatly intensified. The saving in expense would be prompt and obvious, and it would be consonant with the desire for native self-rule, as opposed to British control. If looked at merely by themselves, the figures for the size of the army and for military expenditures are large, but if considered relatively with the population of the country, they are quite small.

The number of British troops in India is about one to 4,500 of the population, and the number of native troops about one to 1,800, or a total army of one to every 1,300 of the population. The annual cost is approximately one dollar per capita for the population. It will be seen, therefore, that the military establishment can hardly be regarded as excessive in size or cost. Its necessity has been shown constantly in the past four or five years by the serious troubles on the northwestern frontier, which have been almost continuous, as well as in the serious Afghan war of 1919.

A more reasoned and scientific undertaking to deal with the financial situation was the request for the creation of a commission of inquiry into expenditures. This commission, similar to the Geddes commission in England, is now at work under the presidency of Lord Inchcape, and may be expected to offer useful recommendations.

Since the arrest of Mr. Gandhi, the influence of the national congress has steadily declined. It is reported that the number of registered supporters is now only 25 per cent of what it was in 1921, and that the financial support has suffered a similar decline. Moreover, serious divisions have appeared in the congress party. One part, under the leadership of Mr. C. R. Das, who has recently been released from prison, advocates participation in the elections which will occur some months hence, in order to achieve their aims either by direct action in the councils or by pursuing a wrecking policy. This party, however, was defeated at the meeting of the national congress held at Gaya, in December, 1922, by the faction which proposed to adhere strictly to the extremist noncoφperation policy.

Though the outlook for the successful application of an added measure of self-government under the Montagu-Chelmsford reforms is hopeful, it is not certain. The problems are tremendous, the difficulties enormous; the bulk of the people is illiterate; the extension of education progresses slowly; the economic and financial questions offer serious perplexities. To overcome these obstacles India's greatest asset is the will to win in the establishment of self-government and to prove to the world its equality with the progressive nations of the West.

Having studied the program of the political movement in India down to the present moment, it is now desirable to survey the more important factors in the Indian situation, in order to understand the problems to be faced in the development of a system of self-government by the Indian peoples. In the first place, the Indian Empire comprises an area somewhat in excess of 1,800,000 square miles, that is, somewhat more than the area of the United States east of the Rocky Mountains.

About 700,000 square miles of this area are contained in native states, ruled by their own princes, with their own administration and laws in each case. Over these native states the British government exercises a certain benevolent supervision. In some of them the administration is highly progressive, and the conditions are better than in British India itself. This is apparently, however, the exception rather than the rule. Administration through native states, from the point of view of the British control, is a simple procedure, and has thus far afforded the imperial government a minimum of anxiety.

Partly owing to this circumstance and partly owing to other reasons some persons have recently seriously proposed the breaking up of British India into a suitable number of small states, and placing them under native rulers. It would seem to be apparent that such a suggestion is both reactionary and impracticable, and that it would also fail to prove a solution of the problem of self-government acceptable to the people of India. The population of the native states, by the census of 1921, was 71,936,736.

The remainder of the Indian Empire, customarily spoken of as British India, has an area of about 1,100,000 square miles, and its population in 1921 was 247,138,396. This territory is divided into fifteen provincial units, of which nine have a population varying from 7,500,000 to 46,000,000, and areas varying from 53,000 square miles to 230,000 square miles. The remaining provinces are much smaller in area and in population, and the separate existence of each is due to some peculiarity in geography, race, or history.

The nine principal provinces mentioned are Assam, Bengal, Bihar and Orissa, Bombay, Burma, Central Provinces and Berar, Madras, the Punjab, and the United Provinces. The history of the administration of these provinces has been already fully discussed. The major portion of the population of India belongs to the Indo-European or Aryan stock, but in southern India a large proportion of the population belongs to the Dravidian family. Besides these two main groups, ethnologists recognize at least five other distinct racial stocks among the peoples of India.

The diversity of languages is even greater. It is estimated that considerably more than one hundred different distinctive languages are spoken within the Indian Empire. Eleven languages are spoken by more than 10,000,000 persons each. Twelve others are spoken by more than 1,000,000 each, and ten others are spoken by more than 300,000 each, the last figure representing approximately the number to whom the English language is the native speech.

The peoples of India are indebted to the British and to their educational system for the gift of a common tongue in which to carry forward their nationalist propaganda. This somewhat humiliating fact has led to various suggestions of developing one of the more common native languages as the national speech. All suggestions to this end have hitherto met with such serious objection as to render any successful outcome unlikely, though Hindustani most nearly meets the requirements.

While, as has been seen, only about two thirds of India is directly under British rule, and more than one third remains under the control of a large number of petty native princes, yet British rule has given a definite unity to the Indian Empire, such as has never existed before. It has also established and maintained absolute peace throughout the country ever since the Mutiny of 1857 and, despite the sporadic outbreaks of violence during the recent period of unrest, has maintained throughout the empire the rule of law and order, and enforced a civilized system of administering justice.

These blessings were absolutely unknown to India prior to British rule. The existence of the vast number of petty states with the confusion of race and language and religion, involving innumerable and incessant wars, formerly prevented any possibility of the establishment of law and order. The prevalence of *dacoity* and *thagi*, in other words, of brigandage and organized pillage and murder, has been eliminated only as the result of the establishment of British sovereignty.

The principal religion in India is Hinduism, which numbers approximately 218,000,000 followers. Next in order come the Mohammedans, numbering nearly 70,000,000. Buddhism has become almost nonexistent in India proper; nearly all its 11,000,000 adherents within the empire are to be found in Burma. About an equal number practice some form of animistic religion. The Sikhs include about 3,000,000.

The number of Christians is at present about 5,500,000, an increase within the past decade of over 40 per cent. Indeed, Christianity is the only one of the religions in India which has made progress out of proportion to the increase in population. It may be observed that its converts have come in major part from the lower classes. About 500,000 of the Christians are so-called Syrians, that is, represent a form of Christianity introduced into India many centuries ago, traditionally, by the apostle, St. Thomas. The Roman Catholics number about 2,000,000 and the Anglicans somewhat over 500,000. Christians, Mohammedans, Buddhists, and Sikhs do not recognize caste.

Caste is an institution associated with Hinduism. The question of how far caste is a religious institution and how far it is social, economic, or political, is one upon which experts are not agreed. At any rate, religion is only one factor in the case, and, to a certain extent, a caste is a sort of profe-ssional, trade, or labor guild. The spread of modern ideas, especially the extension of rapid means of transporta-tion and communication, and the growing complications in the provision of food supplies, have had a powerful effect in breaking down certain of the religious formalities and restrictions associated with caste.

There have not been wanting, in recent years, advocates within Hinduism itself of the removal of many of these forms. Mr. Gandhi's attitude on the question of the "untouchables" is the most important illustration of the case. The aggressive activities of the Brahmins as leaders in the nationalist movement and in other respects during the past two decades have produced as a reaction the development of a vigorous non-Brahmin movement. This has acquired such headway in the Madras presidency that the elections of the present assemblies resulted in a non-Brahmin majority, and, consequently, in the selection of nonBrahmin ministers.

These circumstances have naturally tended to emphasize the economic, political, and social aspects of caste, as questions of debatable character. These facts, taken together with the consequent breakdown of the rigid restrictions of religious formalism, have led to an increased emphasis upon the purely religious or spiritual aspect; perhaps one should say of Hinduism rather than of caste. The existence of the large number of castes with the hitherto rigid separations cutting across the economic, social, and political structures has been a serious factor in the disintegrative character of Indian society in all its aspects.

The growth of an Indian nationalist movement, therefore, will, of necessity, involve the softening of caste distinctions in many respects. The peoples of India have not been dwellers in cities, but in small villages and hamlets. In 1881 there were no cities in India with 1,000,000 population, and but five with more than 200,000. The census of 1921 showed two cities with more than 1,000,000, and ten others in excess of 200,000. The number of cities of more than 50,000 increased during the forty years from sixty to seventy-five. The total urban population at the present time amounts to less than five per cent of the population.

The percentage of urban population in the United States by the census of 1920 was 51.4. Agriculture, then, is the occupation of the major portion of the population. The annual area under crops in British India approximates very closely one acre per capita. Of this area, about 20 per cent is supplied with irrigation. There exist large areas of cultivable lands which are not adequately utilized, while other areas, particularly in the Ganges valley, suffer badly from overcrowding.

It is a difficult problem to overcome the inertia of the natives sufficiently to secure their migration from the overcrowded districts to the regions where land is more readily available. There has, however, been considerable progress in the extension of the actually cultivated area, the increase amounting to not less than 20 per cent in the past twenty years. In addition to rice and wheat, the more important crops include cotton, jute, and tea. The development of irrigation has, of course, been undertaken by the government, and considerable success has been attained in securing the stabilization of crops in spite of fluctuations in the rainfall.

The amount of works for this purpose already constructed has been very large, and the process of extension is still going on. The British administration has also undertaken extensive work in the supervision and care of the forests. India has a considerably varied supply of minerals, but the size of the output remains comparatively small, including as its main items coal, petroleum, salt, gold, and manganese ore. The manufacturing industries of most importance are those of cotton and jute. The number of mills working these materials increased from 237 with 295,000 employees in 1903 to 359 with 546,000 workers in 1921.

While various efforts have been made to establish factories of the modern type under native management, they have not usually been attended with success, and most of the companies are under European management. One notable example of native management is that of the group of ironworking enterprises controlled by the Tata Sons Corporation, but even they have relied, to some extent at least, upon the services of Europeans. There is no doubt a large field for the development of manufacturing enterprises in India, and it will be an important step in advancement when the Indian people learn to invest their money instead of hoarding it.

It ought not to require a large amount of advice and assistance by western experts to give success to such undertakings. The failure to secure the investment of native capital has been particularly notable in the construction of irrigation works, of railways, telegraph lines, and highways. Money for these purposes has had to be borrowed chiefly in England, though there is no doubt adequate wealth was lying idle in India, which might have been enlisted for these purposes, and so have retained the interest payments within the country.

The development of the railway system, as well as of irrigation, has been one of the important safeguards against famine, though the two have not been similarly appreciated by the people. The total mileage of railways in operation in 1921 was slightly in excess of 37,000, largely state owned and partly state operated. They are, unfortunately, however, built upon three different gauges, which prevent interchange of equipment, and makes necessary frequent transfer both for passengers and for freight. There were in 1920 over 88,000 miles of telegraph lines, and the postal service is widely extended and efficient.

In the matter of external communication the British have resisted every suggestion of developing railway communication from India to outside countries. There can be little doubt that England will soon find it absolutely essential to reverse this policy, and to link up her railways from Burma to other parts of the Indo-China peninsula and to China itself, while, to the northwest, the time can scarcely be long delayed when connections will be established with the Russian Trans-Caspian line and, through Persia, with the Bagdad railway.

Practically all Indian foreign trade and intercourse is carried on by sea, as it has been ever since the arrival of the Portuguese. This trade is mainly handled through a few ports, Karachi, Bombay, Colombo in Ceylon, Madras, Calcutta, and Rangoon, and to a slight extent through some minor ports. The extension of the trade of India has been remarkable. The figures for 1921 represent a growth of forty-sevenfold over those for 1834, the first year after the abolition of the trading privileges of the East India Company. The absolute growth, however, has been vastly greater in the past sixty years, during which period the increase has been sixfold.

The total foreign trade of India in 1921 amounted to approximately $1,800,000,000. In the same year the United States with one third the population had a foreign trade three times that of India. For many years the amount of exports has considerably exceeded the imports of merchandise, but in 1921 the figures were sharply reversed. On the other hand, the imports of treasure, that is, of gold and silver, have regularly been enormously in excess of the exports. This may be taken as evidence to some extent of hoarding, but it is also explained in part by use for ornaments. The stock of jewelry worn on the person is the Indian woman's savings bank deposit. These figures do not seem to confirm the theory of economic drain of India by England, which has been referred to previously.

The total of imperial and provincial revenues of India has increased from less than £60,000,000 in 1892 to over £135,000,000 in 1920, a gain of about 128 per cent whereas 25 per cent of the expenditures in 1892 was payable in Great Britain, and in 1920 only 18 per cent was so payable. Though the absolute amount had grown from £15,000,000 to £27,000,000, the increase was not commensurate with the rise in prices. It would appear, therefore, that the government is endeavoring to lessen the causes for complaint with regard to these expenditures. In this connection it is pertinent to note that in the same period the railway mileage was increased from 17,000 to 37,000, the mileage of telegraph lines doubled, and vast outlays made for irrigation works which, incidentally, include at present more than 3,000 miles of navigable canals.

The funds for these capital expenditures have had to be obtained, in large part, from Great Britain, so that corresponding interest payments must flow from India to Great Britain. As in the case of Egypt, so with India, England has been charged with a failure to develop properly sanitation and education. That England has done a large amount in the way of sanitation and of public health measures cannot be denied, but anyone who has walked the streets of even Calcutta and Bombay cannot have helped being impressed that certain obvious measures for public health have not been taken.

The most distressing of these is the failure to segregate the lepers. One, of course, recognizes that the enforcement of sanitary measures affords peculiar difficulty because of the embarrassments created by the existence of caste. The teachings of most of the religions of India, especially of Mohammedanism and only to a less degree of Hinduism, inculcate temperance, with special reference to the use of intoxicating drinks. Consequently, another charge brought against the English has been the spread of the drink traffic.

This was one of the points on which Mr. Gandhi laid considerable stress. It fitted into his program both with reference to exaltation of traditional native principles and of boycotting the English government, because the manufacture and sale of drinks are carried on under government licenses and pay considerable revenue to the government. This created a sort of native anti-saloon movement which was promptly seized upon by a well-known American prohibition campaigner, popularly known as "Pussyfoot" Johnson, who pursued his activities in India for some months.

The development of public education in India has already been discussed. The recent report of the Sadler commission will undoubtedly remove some of the worst evils, and is already clearly resulting in some marked improvements. The most essential is the emphasis which is being placed upon the development of residential colleges. The superiority in this respect of the church colleges has been convincing, and it is anticipated that emulation of their example will yield improved results in the institutions under the control of other faiths or under public management. More notable improvements are being introduced in secondary education, which has, until recently, received inadequate consideration.

The serious criticism with regard to both these fields is that attention has been too largely devoted to literature, rather than to professional, technical, or vocational education, which would prepare the graduates for definite careers of usefulness. Recently, however, there has been a distinct change for the better in this direction. One of the most essential types of special schools is that for the training of teachers, and particular attention is being given at present to the development of normal schools as an indispensable preliminary to the extension of primary education.

The growth of primary education under provincial supervision in recent years has been rapid. The number of primary schools for males grew from 114,000 with 4,400,000 pupils in 1913 to 133,500 with 4,950,000 in 1920, while the number of primary schools for females in the same period grew from 13,700 with 830,000 pupils to 21,700 with 1,175,000 pupils. The total number of educational institutions has increased from 148,500 in 1902 to 202,900 in 1920. While the number of male students increased during this period from 4,083,000 to 6,829,000, the number of female pupils grew from 446,000 to 1,377,000.

This evidence of the rapid extension of female education is one of the most significant factors in the case, for in India, as in Egypt, the breakdown of the social barriers which have kept women in seclusion and ignorance must be regarded as prerequisite to the development of society to anything corresponding substantially to western standards. In the development of primary education and of the education of women, the influence and actual contribution of Christian missions have been of the greatest importance.

Western influences are, of course, responsible for the development of journalism in India. There are not only a considerable number of newspapers in English and other European languages for the benefit of western residents, but there are also numerous periodicals published in each one of the more widely used native languages. Some of them are published in two or more languages. As in the case of Egypt, it is to be regretted that the character and tone of the native press are not very high, though there are notable exceptions. An excellent example is set by the English-language press in India, which is, on the whole, conducted on a very high level. Such a paper as the *Pioneer*, of Allahabad, would be a credit to any city.

The use of the printing press, together with the growth of education and of nationalist ideals, has led to something like a literary revival. At any rate, the output of magazines and books in native languages has become extensive, and coincides with a deliberate effort not merely to exalt the glories of the country's ancient literature, but also to emulate them. There has been a great deal of investigation and publication with reference to the history, literature, religion, and philosophy of ancient India. A considerable portion of these works has been published in English. India has not failed to produce some scientists of high ability, and it is reasonable to anticipate that such worthy examples as that of Sir J. C. Bose will not lack for emulation.

Very naturally, native journalism in India is closely associated with the nationalist movement, and tends to express in extreme rather than moderate manner its aims and interests. The vehement, even violent, nature of its propaganda has brought the native press into considerable conflict with the government. Since the anti-British feeling has produced in these papers expressions which are not merely critical of the government but absolutely subversive to it, it has been deemed necessary, as a matter of self-preservation, for the government to intervene by the enactment and the enforcement of penal statutes.

It is natural, in every reform or revolutionary movement, that there should appear those radicals and extremists who carry their activities beyond legal or even reasonable limits. Consequently, when they fall under the penalty of the law, they endeavor to arouse, usually with considerable success, sympathy for themselves and added hostility to the government they seek to subvert.

This situation is peculiarly unfortunate in India, because of the temper of the people, who, less readily than in most countries, can adopt an attitude of moderation or of suspension of judgment until all the pertinent facts in a case can be reasonably weighed. It is, indeed, this peculiar mental characteristic, which is apparently more clearly marked among the Hindus than among the Mohammedans, that makes western observers of India doubtful of the ability of these peoples successfully to develop and operate a system of self-government.

Representative self-governing institutions, as they exist in western countries, have measured their success by the degree in which the people concerned have been able to approach public questions in a judicial spirit and with a sense of fair play. The western observer fails to find in India what seems to him adequate evidence of the ability and readiness of its peoples to approach political problems in such a frame of mind. The people of India are able to see with great acuteness the arguments in favor of their own views and those which are disadvantageous to the other party, but they seem to lack the ability to see how these same arguments may look from the other side, or to consider other elements relevant to the case.

As has already been said, generalizations are always dangerous, and particularly so with reference to India, and when one makes such general statements as the preceding, one must, of course, recognize that there are brilliant exceptions to them. One must also recognize that the development of political-mindedness is, after all, a matter of slow growth, and comes with the practice of self-government. Fortunately, England has accorded to the peoples of India, in progressive measure, the privileges of constitutional government, and has been affording them the opportunity of political self-education.

To estimate the value of the result is extremely difficult. It is easy to point out certain obvious arguments both for the success and for the failure of the experiment. While one may conclude that the results have been as satisfactory as could have been expected, none the less, it is difficult to refrain from the conclusion that the results have been distinctly less satisfactory than is desirable. Political-mindedness, in the western sense, requires a peculiar combination of independence and individualism with the spirit of cooperation.

This may perhaps best be phrased by saying that in the matter of thinking and of cooperating in political life the individual must enjoy full freedom. He must be able to arrive at his own conclusions from the facts before him, without fear or favor, and he must be equally free to join with those whose conclusions are similar, in seeking the political attainment of his ends. Whenever institutions of a religious or social character, or conditions of an economic nature exist, which seriously interfere with this freedom of the individual, either in his thinking or in his action in political matters, self-governing institutions have not operated satisfactorily.

The peoples of India are subject in unusual degree to such constraints upon thought and action. The differences of race, of historical experience, of religion, and especially the existence of caste with its far-reaching social and economic significance, operate both to direct the character of the thinking and to restrict the freedom of action of the individual. If the people of India are to attain in satisfactory measure to representative self-government, they must develop ability to rise above these age-long restraints of race, religion, and social and economic order upon the freedom of the individual.

Each must be able to arrive at his own conclusions upon consideration of the facts and to combine freely, regardless of these old orders, with those of any class, race, or creed, which arrive at similar conclusions and seek aims corresponding with his own. If India is to develop as a nation and is to establish for itself a system of representative self-government, it must do so not as a utopian project, regardless of the past, but it must definitely rear the new structure upon the foundations of its history and of its present circumstances.

India proper and, to a much higher degree, the territory which now forms the Indian Empire, owe whatever unity they possess to the establishment and maintenance of British rule. Never prior to the nineteenth century were all the provinces of India itself united under one single government. There had always been many petty kingdoms and states, almost incessantly at war with one another; and the country owes absolutely to the establishment of British control the creation within its borders of a state of freedom from war, of internal peace and security, and of law and order.

Of the Indian borderlands, which have been brought within the empire chiefly since the Mutiny, only a small portion had ever been under the rule of an Indian state. Their presence within the empire is distinctly a novelty for which the British are entirely responsible. If the people of India, therefore, are to establish for themselves in India proper and much more in the empire as a whole, including the borderlands, a unified Indian nationality, they must build very carefully upon the foundations of unity which have been established under British authority.

Haste would result not merely in the falling away from the empire of some, if not all, of the borderlands, but would almost inevitably result in disintegration within India itself. For this reason, the success of the Indian experiment is dependent for a long period to come, until the welding together of races and the growth of identity of interests have progressed far, upon the persistence of a considerable degree of British control. This necessity for British control arises, moreover, not only from the internal situation of India, but likewise from the necessity of safeguarding India against aggressions from without.

It is unlikely at the present time, though it certainly was not true prior to the close of the World War, that there is danger that any European power would seek to replace England in India, but the situation upon the northwest frontier, as evidenced in a high degree during the past five years, shows that, even within Asia itself, India needs the protection of England's strong arm and the skill of its diplomacy. To no less degree must the people of India take into account, in the creation of their nationality, the necessity of laying the foundations upon the control exercised by the British in more or less of the country for a century and a half.

They must also recognize that it is solely from the British that they have derived the ideals both of nationality and representative self-government. It is the British who have not merely created an Indian nationality as a fact upon the map, but who have been responsible for the development of the idea as a mental and moral fact. India must confess, as does every country on the continent of Europe or anywhere else which at the present day enjoys or is endeavoring to establish representative institutions, that the whole system, with the ideal involved and the method concerned, was developed by England, and has been by them borrowed for their several uses.

It would be absolute madness for the people of India to overlook the fact that they have enjoyed the rare privilege of public training in these matters by the inventors and great masters of the art, or for them to reject that guidance until they shall have erected the new superstructure upon the foundations already laid. Nowhere so truly as in India does the old adage apply, that the more haste, the less speed.

There is the other side of the case, and that is the obligation upon England with reference to its future conduct. England must fully and heartily recognize the aims and desires of the people of India. England can lose India irretrievably by endeavoring too strenuously to maintain its hold. The preachings of the hide-bound Tories and of the reactionary Die-Hards, that England must save itself in India, can have no other result than the complete alienation of India.

Generous and sympathetic treatment of India, on the other hand, can result in the establishment of unbreakable ties of friendship, which will yield to the British Empire far more valuable results when measured in terms of political profit or of trade or of financial investment or of intellectual and spiritual usefulness, than can possibly accrue from any policy of forcible maintenance of authority. It is entirely possible for England to follow such a generous policy as might result in the loss completely of political control over India, and yet of conserving to England a relationship with that country and its peoples of infinitely greater value than has yet accrued. This great truth has already been demonstrated in the case of Canada and the other dominions.

These facts have a pertinent relation to an immediate problem. The Indian nationalist leaders, even of the more moderate sort, are demanding the prompt and thorough, though not necessarily complete, Indianization of both the army and the civil service. It may be readily conceded that a greater degree of Indianization of both is desirable, but the Indian people will seriously injure their own cause by undue insistence upon either of these policies, particularly the latter. The nationalist agitation has seriously damaged the morale of the British civil service in India, and has almost completely arrested the recruiting of that service.

The interests of both India and England require the continuance in India of at least as many English appointees, in both the civil service and the related services, as at present, and require that that personnel shall be of the highest quality. Any action, whether in India or in England, that interferes with such a result will be unfortunate to both parties. It is not necessary that the present distribution of the English civil servants and other officials in India shall continue, or that the powers exercised by them shall remain the same, but their presence as guides and councilors, as expert advisers and assistants is essential for a multitude of reasons.

One of these reasons is that India cannot become a nation unto itself. It must become a nation as a partner in the great society of nations; and if it is to do so, it must command the confidence of the other partners in the society. It may be humiliating to the pride of the Indian peoples, but it is a fact which must be reckoned with, that the continuance of such a group of British officials in India will be the most valuable contribution toward the creation and development of that confidence. The practice of Japan affords a clear example on this point.

The British, on their side, should take care to select only officials who will represent the best traditions of the service in tact and consideration for the peoples of India and who will conform to the growing demand for recognition of their political and social equality. There have been unfortunate examples of the harm that the acts and utterances of a tactless official can do. Objections have been frequently raised to the pensions paid from Indian revenues to British civil servants who almost invariably retire to England after the completion of their stated period of service.

If instead they should continue to reside in India after retirement, the drain of funds to England would cease and they might continue to contribute from their experience and wisdom to Indian national progress and welfare. It is perhaps worth while to add a few words with regard to the relation of the United States to this situation. It does not occur to most Americans that there is any such relation, but in the minds of the people of India the relation is extremely obvious. The very existence of the United States is a notable argument in support of their case. The States were once colonies of England. They declared their independence, successfully maintained it, and have grown great and powerful.

It is extremely easy for the Indian nationalist to draw comparisons from the American conflict with England in the eighteenth century, and he arrives without any difficulty at all at the conclusion that the separation of the United States from England affords an absolute parallel and a perfectly decisive argument for the freedom of India. It can, therefore, be understood that the Indian people naturally look to the United States for friendship and encouragement as well as example. Their feeling is that they are trying to do what the Americans successfully accomplished and that the Americans ought, therefore, to be friendly disposed toward the aims of India and ready not merely to sympathize but to assist in the achieving of those aims.

The American in India cannot fail to be impressed with the alertness of the people to detect an American, and the eagerness to enter into conversation with him, which promptly turns in the political direction, nor can he have failed to note the sudden change of attitude upon the part of an Indian the moment he discovers an individual is an American and not a British citizen. It becomes almost amusing, therefore, when one raises the question as to what would be the attitude if the United States should be substituted for Great Britain in relation to India, to find them answering with alacrity, "We would feel just the same toward you then as we do toward them now."

It would be unfair to omit one further point. There is, after all, a limit to the self-confidence of the Indians in their ability to succeed unaided in the achievement of their nationalist aims. When brought fairly to face the ultimate situation, they will almost invariably acknowledge that the continuance of British authority in India in some form and to some degree will be indispensable to them for a considerable time to come. Even Mr. Gandhi himself seems never to have been able entirely to free himself from such a conclusion.

The future of India, therefore, would seem to lie in the steady growth of self-government under British protection and guidance. The safety of the future depends not upon listening to the rabid doctrines of the British Tory or of the Bengali Brahmin extremist, but in the development of ever-deepening sympathy and ever-widening coöperation. As the unification of India under British rule was the greatest achievement of its sort in the nineteenth century, so the successful establishment of Indian self-government under British leadership may be the greatest fact of its sort in the twentieth century, and prove one of the most important steps toward preparing the world for an effective brotherhood of nations.

RECENT EVENTS

In Bombay, which may be taken as an illustration of progressive provincial administration, during the five years ending in 1923, compulsory primary education was inaugurated, model tenement houses were constrücted, improvements in sanitation were carried out, and work was started on an immense irrigation scheme at Sukkur in the Indus valley which is planned to open up for agriculture new land more extensive than the whole cultivated area in Egypt. An important labor reform affecting mining operations throughout India restricts the employment of women and children and limits the hours of work for men.

The commission headed by Lord Inchcape on the retrenchment of expenditures made its report in March, 1923, recommending a reduction of the estimates for annual general expenditures of £105,000,000 by £12,500,000. The government has proceeded with measures for a greater degree of Indianization of the army, and for the reduction of military expenditures. The decision to concentrate the government offices at Simla has been made with a view to further economies. Since the establishment of the new legislature under the Montagu-Chelmsford reforms, there has been a failure each year to balance the budget.

The government motion for doubling the salt tax made in order to attain that end was rejected by the assembly in March, 1923, on the ground that this tax would fall heavily on those least able to bear it. Lord Reading then exercised his prerogative as viceroy by "certifying" the salt tax. This procedure was the subject of serious denunciation, and in July the assembly passed a resolution favoring the restriction of the viceregal power of certification. In the earlier part of 1923 there seems to have been a subsidence of unrest.

There were a few sporadic disturbances and some bolshevist agents were arrested. The adjustment of difficulties in the Crown colony of Kenya in East Africa proposed by the British government was unfavorable to the claims of the Indian immigrants to that region. The Indian people regarded the arrangement as a measure of unfair discrimination within the empire and denounced it with remarkable unanimity. In August, 1923, serious disturbances between the Hindus and Mohammedans and between the Sunnite and Shiite Mohammedans began to occur and have since continued. In August also the Ali brothers, Lajpat Rai, and other important political prisoners were released.

Finally on September 12 the viceroy announced the dissolution of the legislative assembly. These circumstances were promptly followed by a special meeting of the Indian national congress at Delhi. The primary purpose was to allay the religious strife, and committees were appointed to investigate and report on the subject. With the approval of Mr.

Gandhi it was agreed that the nationalists might stand as candidates at the approaching elections to the legislative assembly. Contrary to the advice of Mr. Gandhi a boycott of British goods was proclaimed in protest against the Kenya arrangements.

A proposal to extend the boycott to American goods, because of a decision of the United States Supreme Court that Hindus could not become citizens, failed. A resolution declaring complete independence the goal of the nationalist movement was defeated by a large majority, but plans were approved for organized civil disobedience. At the end of December the regular meeting of the national congress assembled at Cocanada under the presidency of Mohammed Ali, whose utterances were criticized as unduly Mohammedan in tone. The actions of the congress were practically limited to affirmation of the decisions reached at Delhi in September, but friction over religious matters and between the different factions of the nationalists were ill-concealed.

Mr. Das and his followers held a conference at Lucknow and issued an ultimatum that they would refuse to coφperate in the work of the legislative assemblies to which they had been elected unless the British government announced the concession of full responsible government. Some nationalists declined to follow this course. The proceedings of the caliphate congress which met under the presidency of Shevket Ali displayed an ultra-Mohammedan spirit. On February 4, 1924, Mr. Gandhi, owing to his ill health, was released by the Bombay government unconditionally. The wisdom of this act has been generally commended.

In the elections to the legislative assembly the nationalists obtained 50 of the 105 elective seats in the house of 145 members. In the provincial elections they won an overwhelming majority in the Central Provinces, but nowhere else did they secure a majority, though in Bengal they obtained 49 of the 113 elective members in a house of 139. In the Bombay presidency they secured less than a third of the elective members and in Madras less than a tenth. In Bengal the governor, Lord Lytton, asked Mr. Das, the nationalist leader, to form a ministry, but he declined on the ground that it would be contrary to the policy of his party to undertake to conduct the government under the Montagu- Chelmsford plan of dyarchy which it considers impracticable, instead of attempting to defeat its operation as a step toward securing genuine responsible government.

In February, 1924, the newly elected legislative assembly adopted a resolution in favor of a round-table discussion of the working of the Montagu-Chelmsford reforms and their possible revision. This drew forth a statement from the MacDonald ministry in the British parliament disapproving hasty action in Indian affairs. Two months later the situation in India became a subject of extended debate in the British House of Commons. The MacDonald ministry rejected a proposal for a parliamentary commission to investigate the operation of the Montagu-Chelmsford reforms but it announced that ministerial investigations were in progress and matters were the subject of discussion with responsible Indian politicians.

The secretary of state for India created a commission of eight members including Indians and British residents in India under the chairmanship of Sir Alexander Muddiman, with the purpose of investigating the details of the operation of the Montagu-Chelmsford act, but not with the purpose of undertaking a general revision of the measure. This commission began work in April. At the same time announcement was made of the establishment of a national convention at Allahabad to unify the workers for Indian home rule.

The definitely avowed purpose of this convention was announced to be the securing of authority from Great Britain to summon an independent or nonofficial convention to frame a constitution for India as a dominion. This proceeding is an obvious rejoinder to the appointment of the Muddiman commission, an official creation with a circumscribed sphere of action. Meanwhile, the nationalists in the newly elected legislative assembly had mustered enough votes in March, 1924, to defeat the annual budget, which has since been "certified" by the viceroy. On May 27, the executive committee of the Indian national congress met in Ahmedabad, the home of Mr. Gandhi. In the opening discussions Mr. Gandhi was able to command a majority in opposition to Mr. Das.

The intransigeant behavior of the latter, however, led Mr. Gandhi to make concessions in order to avoid an open split. This weakness on the part of Mr. Gandhi resulted in an actual success for Mr. Das and his followers who, in contrast with Mr. Gandhi's teaching of nonresistance and noncoφperation, favor aggressive, though not violent, political activity, including participation in elections and accepting membership in the legislative councils but not coφperation in government until full responsible government shall be granted.

Nevertheless, conditions seemed to improve and even in the legislative assembly the moderate swarajists or nationalists coφperated with the administration and proceedings were carried on satisfactorily. More recently there have been some untoward occurrences which have accentuated existing causes for bitterness. A royal commission headed by Lord Lee of Fareham has been investigating the question of civil service. It appears that the compensation and other conditions are such that few satisfactory British candidates are now attracted and the possible effects are considered unfortunate.

The recommendations of the commission have been the subject of severe criticism by the nationalists and have been rejected by the national legislative assembly, but it is anticipated that they will be "certified." The assembly has constituted a commission with extensive powers to inquire into the taxable capacity of the people and the distribution of the burden of taxation. Religious conflicts between Mohammedans11 and Hindus persisted, notably in Delhi, and disturbances were still rife on the northwestern frontier. On September 18, 1924, in spite of his weakened health, Mr. Gandhi announced his intention to fast for twenty-one days as penance for the religious strife. He declared:

"The recent events have proved unbearable for me. My hopelessness is still more unbearable. My religion teaches me that whenever one is very distressed which one cannot remove, one must fast and pray. I have done so in connection with my dearest ones. Nothing evidently that I say or write can bring the two communities together. I am therefore imposing on myself a fast....As a penance I need not have taken the public into confidence, but publish the fast as, let me hope, an effective prayer both to the Hindus and the Mussalmans who have hitherto worked in unison, not to commit suicide. I respectfully invite the heads of all the communities, including the Englishmen, to meet and end this quarrel which is a disgrace to religion and humaraty. It seems as if God has been dethroned. Let us reinstate him in our hearts." In pursuance of this appeal representatives of the several religions, including Christianity, have been organized into a committee of fifteen, with Mr. Gandhi as chairman, to arbitrate all religious disputes.

3

Governance in India in the 1980s

It is tempting to view the "saffron wave" from the late 1980s onward as a logical outcome of decades of disciplined, well-planned organizational and ideological expansion of the Sangh parivar. This interpretation tends, however, to reproduce the RSS's narrative of its own history as an unbroken, consistent, and thus irresistible effort to "organize Hindu society" and to "awaken the Hindu." Such an interpretation excludes from view the specificity of the political space created by the broader societal transformations in the 1980s, which the Hindu nationalist movement and a multitude of other forces sought to occupy.

The "saffron wave" certainly had much to do with new and bold public strategies, including effective appeals to widely disseminated communal mythologies. Nonetheless, the successes of the RSS, the BJP, and other affiliated organizations in winning broad support in new areas and within new social groups remained crucially dependent on processes beyond the control of its organized effort.

The central argument here is that the "saffron wave" was made possible by the conditions of possibility offered in the political field: the emergence of a "majoritarian democracy," new forms of "populist governmentality," and proliferation of new demands and new identity claims in a process of "intensified democratic revolution." The success of the Hindu nationalist movement was far from inevitable, but it was able to expand and change the political common sense in India because it drew on already existing discursive registers, because it voiced broad-based if imprecise disgruntlements and anxieties, and because in large parts of India it could occupy the political space that opened up as the Congress party gradually disintegrated.

POPULISM AND THE TRANSFORMATION OF GOVERNANCE

Congress returned to power in 1980 and began to reconstitute its political power on the basis of huge electoral majorities in the elections in the following decade. It soon became clear, however, that the edifice of the "Congress Raj," as it had evolved in the course of the first three decades after Independence had changed irreversibly. The political upheavals of the 1970s had mobilized larger sections of the electorate than ever before, and had further spread a language of rights and a sense of entitlements vis-ΰ-vis the state among still larger groups in Indian society.

The Congress organization had been fatally weakened by Indira Gandhi's consistent attempts to deinstitutionalize the party, and her reliance on populist electoral techniques. At the same time, a still more self-confident, if heterogeneous, range of opposition parties had built constituencies in north India and in such states as West Bengal, Tamil Nadu, and Karnataka.

The classical Congress structure of the Nehruvian period was an intricate institutional mechanism negotiating power, resources, and mandates among districts and between the states and the center, distributing fiscal resources and arbiting social and political conflicts resilience was premised on the inclusion of most important elite groups within a structure of negotiation, bargaining, and aggregation of the discrete powers and constituencies of local elites upward to the center.

After the split of Congress in 1969, Indira Gandhi set out to consolidate her own weak position by creating a new parallel system of authority in the party based on loyalty to her personal leadership. The formal structures in the party were bypassed, internal elections were continuously postponed and stalled, and large groups of ambitious but inexperienced politicians made fast careers in the political apparatus by virtue of their unconditional loyalty to the central leadership. The other instrument was the institution of "electoral populism" and the search for unassailable majorities.

This method combined effective slogans and centrally organized lavish campaigning at rapidly increasing cost with recruitment of "winners" at the local level on Congress tickets. Locally influential businessmen and wealthy peasants who could finance a campaign and secure a seat would get Congress support. Prominent persons believed to be able to deliver electoral support from their specific community would also get on the ticket. The distribution of places on the ticket became commercialized and engineered from above, often bypassing the local party organization.

This generated considerable instability within the Congress party and within state governments, where factionalism was regularly encouraged by the central leadership in order to prevent state-level politicians from building large independent followings. By increasing the potential gains in terms of money and power in politics, the clientelist structures within Congress further accelerated the articulation of conflicts and the mobilization of new groups.

To prop up the electoral base of a still more deinstitutionalized Congress party, candidates from poor and marginalized communities such as Muslims, tribals, scheduled castes, and other lower-caste groups were promoted, along with flimsy promises of benefits and protection from a distant but benevolent state.

These populist campaigns often depicted the Congress as the ally and protector of all depressed groups in their conflicts with local elites and upper-caste groups.

The Janata party's tenure in power had in some ways broken the spell and self-evidence of Congress's mandate to rule. But more importantly, the Janata party represented a configuration of political and social forces in the old heartlands of Congress in north India that gravitated around large communities of upwardly mobile peasants. In the face of these challenges, Congress produced in the 1980s a new configuration of electoral and mobilizational strategies, as well as a new system of political bargaining, which has been characterized as "majoritarian democracy".

This new configuration was marked, above all, by a proliferation of agitation and popular mobilization based on symbols of community or on single issues. Such manifestations were no longer confined to election periods but became more permanent strategic devices deployed in conjunction with institutional bargaining and in connection with launching new high-profile policy initiatives or development schemes.

The very large majorities secured by Congress in the general elections of 1980 and 1984, and in many states during this period, however, could neither cancel nor coopt the growing demands from a still more assertive opposition and from active movements and interest groups.

Effectively banished from institutional politics at the national level as well as from general elections organized around a few overriding emotional issues, these proliferating demands were instead staged by social movements, in concerted campaigns and agitations, and in many cases also through the growing range of regional parties.

The practices of competitive populist mobilizations have been interpreted as effects of the ongoing institutional decay of the Indian state. This decay has rendered more and more people available for a host of extra-parliamentary agitations and political mass demands, and has further strained the crumbling capacity of the overloaded Indian state to deliver development results to groups outside the established networks of patronage presided over by the ruling elite coalitions. According to this influential analysis, clientelistic forms of distribution of resources and populist forms of political mobilization stand in a mutually contradictory position.

This argument seems, however, to underestimate the extent to which clientelist practices, factional competition, and the institutionalization of brokerage (*dalal*) have become naturalized elements in the political culture in modern India, and have acquired widespread legitimacy in what we may term quotidian forms of political common sense. The expectation that elected representatives will look after and favor their constituency, their faction, and their caste or community, and only incidentally work according to more Universalist standards, is probably one of the most common de facto "legitimate problematics" in Indian politics.

Politicians may be criticized for this type of "favoritism," for corruption, and so on, but ordinary voters do, at the same time, expect a local elected representative to be efficient as a broker, available for local complaints, and able to provide services to the constituency or group regardless of the strictures of formal rules. Obedience or submission to formal rules is not uncommonly interpreted as a sign of weakness. Populist mobilization, as it is exercised by virtually all parties in Indian politics, revolves around expansion of clientelistic networks by consolidating the position of the party, or a faction, in legislative bodies and government institutions, thus enabling it to accumulate more resources and control larger flows of resources.

Access to large resources is, hence, employed to conquer larger constituencies through expensive election campaigns and, through its promise of patronage, attract local "big men" and community leaders. Contemporary Indian politics is undoubtedly marked by such an expansive logic of competing "clientelist populisms." I wish to argue, moreover, that the majoritarian and plebiscitary democracy instituted and administered by Congress in most of the 1980s in fact created new forms of governmentality, that is, new forms of governmental technologies as well as new forms of rationalities informing governmental interventions.

New modes of high-profile framing and implementation of centralized programs were introduced, aimed at direct distribution of benefits and bypassing intermediate governmental structures, or at liberalizing access to foreign technology and capital for the numerous upcoming groups of parvenu entrepreneurs. These new techniques suspended a major part of the intricate but flexible institutional bargaining that had characterized the older Congress system, in favor of manipulative and covert strategies of undermining adversaries.

It also produced populist techniques of representation and overt manipulation of central symbols and "legitimate problematics" in the political field, such as secularism and national unity. Congress deployed these new techniques of government and representation to contain the many new forces and contentious issues unleashed by the intensified democratic revolution in the 1980s. The first years of Rajiv Gandhi's tenure as prime minister were marked by an initially successful staging of him and his group of young, "cosmopolitan" advisors as "modern," in the sense both of being westernized and of being dynamic, self-reliant, and self-confident.

Rajiv Gandhi blamed the degeneration of the party for having caused a general decline in popular faith in politics and politicians, and he promised to cleanse the body politic of these vices. However, neither internal elections in the party nor the long-overdue panchayat elections scheduled to be held all over the country in 1989 were ever implemented. Instead, the populist governmentality was further developed. Centralization of institutions and policy making continued, and the framing of policies seemed still more to be informed by short-term electoral rationales-consolidating constituencies as well as weakening potential adversaries-rather than by the pursuit of any consistent administrative practice aimed at producing more general effects.

The enthusiasm for advanced technology within the party leadership produced a peculiar technocratic mode of governance through communities. The party headquarters's extensive, centralized computerized mapping of the caste and confessional composition of every district and taluka in the entire country became an indispensable tool in selecting and fielding party candidates at all levels, but also in framing policies, special programs, symblic gestures, and so on. This governmentality rested on a rather unveiled arrogance vis-ΰ-vis democratic processes, as well as a peculiar computerized version of the objectified (colonial) knowledge of the electorate as a series of culturally defined communities that could be reached and mobilized through effective engineering of their respective symbols of community.

Within the agricultural sector, the Union government ignored the discretion of state governments in this area and launched a number of large and high-profile schemes such as the "Prime Minister's Massive Program," waiving loans and extending new credits through the district administrations without involving the state level. A series of employment-guarantee schemes launched by Rajiv Gandhi to commemorate his grandfather Jawaharlal Nehru bypassed state governments and was designed to maintain the dynastic aura of the Nehru family, and to prove the patronage power of the party. The fact that in several states this program actually did ameliorate the lot of landless poor and raise rural wage levels somewhat was one of the few substantial successes of Rajiv Gandhi's administrative strategies.

Throughout the 1980s Rajiv Gandhi developed TV coverage of his day-to-day activities to an extent that he, in the popular wit, had more screen presence than even the leading film stars. The national television station, Doordarshan, also launched major TV serials that were presented as beneficial to national integration, such as a semi-dramatized version of Nehru's *Discovery of India* and the more controversial but hugely popular serialization of the *Mahabharata* and *Ramayana* epics.

Circulation of newsreels, video machines, and satellite TV quickly went beyond the larger cities and the English-language audience, and spread to rural areas and provincial towns as well. This opened new opportunities and mass audiences to critical journalism and provided unprecedented opportunities for articulation of opposition, just as the introduction of regular TV coverage of parliamentary sessions deprived the parliamentarians in the ruling party of a good deal of their earlier aura. During the general election in 1989, electronic media were massively introduced in electoral campaigns with wide circulation of election propaganda on videocassettes, and video raths - trucks with huge screens and video equipment-were taken from village to village.

Although the effects of this escalation of media technology in election campaigns seemed of limited significance in terms of the electoral results, video circulation and heavily media-borne campaigns now became regular elements in the inventories of the electoral machines of all political parties in India. Introduction of advanced technology in the industry, the administration, and the media, and an incipient liberalization of the economy that made importation of technology, technical cooperation, and joint ventures with foreign firms easier, was favorite themes of the Rajiv Gandhi administration.

The much-publicized dismantling of the "License Raj" was, however, gradually played down in the face of resistance from parts of the large-scale sector, the public sector, and agrarian groups. The impact of the liberalization policies was limited to the expanding consumer goods sector which, aided by numerous joint ventures with Japanese and western firms, poured a host of new products into the market. Cars, electronic gadgets, computers, and a range of modern household items appeared and made the consumer goods sector expand rapidly.

The urban middle classes reaped most of the benefits of the results of the liberalization and modernization programs as they entered the brave new world of computers, electronics, and emulation of western consumption patterns and taste. But this "consumer goods revolution" also spread very fast to the rural areas and to minor towns. Soon, many of the symbols of urban modernity-two wheelers, electronic devices, VCRs, refrigerators, sunglasses-became available to the more affluent sections in many villages.

The designs and quality of a lot of the new products manufactured in India on a joint venture basis also exposed the poor quality and technological backwardness of many consumer products from the licensed industry in the country. In the automobile sector, the difference between the modern Maruti car and the traditional Ambassador or Premier cars reflected a technological gap of three decades.

The incipient liberalization in the 1980s gradually generated a widespread "foreign technology fetishism"-an obsession with the stereotyped symbols of modernity: Japanese efficiency, American ingenuity, German solidity, French sophistication, Italian taste-as these qualities were believed to be embedded in commodities. Commercial advertising underlined the nationality of the foreign technology behind the particular product. It showed rather interestingly that "commodity fetishism" in the age of globalization is linked not only to certain global styles of consumption but also to the imagined location of one's culture and nation in a global hierarchy.

Not surprisingly, the "foreign technology fetishism" generated a feeling of displacement of the Indian nation, especially vis-ŭ-vis the economically successful Asian countries. The success of China and the East Asian economies attracted considerable attention among educated groups in India, and produced a feeling of being somewhat left behind a dynamic economic development in neighboring areas. The exposure to new technologies and global media flows deepened the sense of India's gradual "sliding" downward in the global hierarchy of nations.

This imprecise but powerful frustration in the middle classes further depleted the credentials of the Congress party in its erstwhile core constituency. A more coherent policy of economic liberalization was, however, not implemented until 1991, when the Government of India, in the face of a rapidly growing foreign debt and an acute deterioration of Reserve Bank deposits, agreed to implement a comprehensive liberalization and reform package negotiated with the International Monetary Fund.

COMPETING POPULISMS

From the late 1970s on, the peasantry of north India began to emerge as a significant constituency in national politics. In these years, Delhi experienced for the first time hundreds of thousands of north Indian farmers staging rallies to express their support of the Janata party. Peasants in Karnataka, Gujarat, Tamil Nadu, and other states were organized by independent leaders not directly connected to the political parties. The common features of these rallies and agitations were their straightforward staging of economic demands toward the government, their social base that stretched across various categories of peasants but gravitated around a core of "middle peasants."

They employed innovative tactics and agitational methods, such as *rasta rokos* (road blocks), preventing transport of food to the cities; gavbands, sealing off the villages from outsiders such as politicians and officials; and disciplined dharnas (sit-in actions). The primary problem facing this large and amorphous group, whose production and economic strategies were fully integrated into monetized systems of credit and trade, was profitability of production in the face of state regulation of prices, infrastructural facilities, and inputs.

Compared to earlier peasant organizations that were often closely related to political parties, this "new agrarianism" represented, Dhanagare argues, a form of "apolitical populism" seeking direct influence on the formation and implementation of government policies. The movements revealed that a language of rights and entitlements-the right to articulate protest, the right to assert oneself, but also the entitlement to be heard and to be accommodated by government schemes-had become naturalized in rural India as processes of commercialization had transformed structures of class and status.

The gradual deinstitutionalization of Congress and the marginal influence of opposition parties had closed the conventional channels of negotiation and accommodation within the political field. Instead, farmers led by people like Tikait and Sharad Joshi took to the streets and staged large rallies in Delhi, Bombay, Bangalore, and many other cities in the first half of the 1980s. Paradoxically, the techniques of agitation employed by the movements led to an elaboration of the populist governmentality they opposed.

The movements actually caused a modification of agrarian policies in many states, and many of their demands soon became part of official political rhetoric. They demonstrated, in other words, that extra-parliamentary campaigns on simple agendas were able to produce results, as the Congress party found it relatively less complicated to accommodate such precise demands than to deal with larger issues of structural reform.

THE RISE OF THE OBC AS A POLITICAL IDENTITY

Whereas the 1970s were marked by a gradual political mobilization of the cultivating castes in northern and western India, and a rising assertiveness of cultivating and landowning nonBrahmin groups in southern India, the lower castes-squeezed between the scheduled castes and the dominant landowning groups-became politically mobilized in the 1980s. These groups were initially targets of Indira Gandhi's "garibi hatao" strategy, and a number of leaders from these hitherto politically docile groups were promoted by Congress as part of its endeavor to reconstitute its popular base after the split in the party in 1969.

The term "Other Backward Classes" (OBC) had been coined as a residual administrative category as early as in 1950, but it was only after the Mandal Commission in 1980 recommended the reservation of 27 per cent of all educational seats and governmental jobs for this social category that the OBC denomination gradually acquired political potency as a rallying point for a range of upward mobile groups falling within these categories.

In northern India the rather condensed congruence between socioeconomic status, political power, and ritual rank made the OBC formula a potent instrument in the hands of opposition parties. The Janata Dal sought to forge an alliance between dominant landowning castes such as Jats and Yadavs and a multitude of OBC groups on a platform of agrarian populism. The successful mobilization of middle farmers by the farmers' movements was simultaneously drawing support from the same moderately prosperous, socially ambitious, politically assertive, impatient, and politically highly "available" group in north India.

The growing social ambitions and life expectations of the cultivating middle farmers were directly related to the effects of agrarian commercialization and the general growth of the middle classes in the 1980s. The political articulation of this amorphous grouping as a distinct political identity through the employment of the Mandal Commission's categories were, however, largely conditioned by two powerful logics governing the "majoritarian democracy" of the 1980s.

One logic was the search for stable electoral majorities. The tantalizing promise of a potential 52 per cent share of the electorate made appeals to the OBC categories a central element in Janata Dal's vaguely socialist, antiestablishment rhetoric. Another powerful logic was that reservations of government jobs and education opportunities had developed into a widely used clientelistic device for securing electoral support from disadvantaged groups. In the southern states the reservation providing for a host of nonBrahmin groups had since the 1960s grown to cover more than half of all admissions to higher education.

The strength of nonBrahmin sentiment in the southern states had made this gradual development possible without attracting much political conflict. Gujarat was one of the first states in the northern and western parts of India to be affected by open conflicts over rising ratios of reserved seats and jobs. The reservation issue created serious disturbances in that state from the early 1980s onward, as an alliance of lower and scheduled castes emerged as a stable political constituency.

What today has become known as "Mandalization" of the political field in the late 1980s has often been interpreted as a watershed in Indian politics, as the beginning of a new phase in which the poor and lower-caste majority began to assert its rights against centuries of tyranny by the upper castes. The entire issue of caste-based reservations seemed, however, neither to upset nor challenge the logics of the majoritarian democracy. The promises of social uplift enshrined in the "Mandal formula" were in many ways premised on the populist governmentality developed by Congress policy making and implementation bent on high-profile symbolic action rather than structural reforms.

In fact, the expectations engendered by the Mandal agitations bore very little resemblance, or reference, to the realities of existing schemes of reservation and to the very limited number of jobs that could become available. The reservation of 27 per cent of all seats and jobs for OBCs as recommended by the Mandal Commission would in many states have only a marginal effect on the prospects for OBCs as well as for higher-caste groups.

What the Mandal formula provided was, rather, a focal point for diverse identifications, a label invented by a statistician that could provide a common ground for expressing and condensing multiple subtle exclusions experienced by ever more assertive and selfconscious groups of upwardly mobile peasants and others outside the social world of the upper-caste Hindus. The methodology used by the commission gave economic criteria a very limited weightage in the overall evaluation of the backwardness of a person or community. In keeping with the prevalent ranking of status, the most important criterion was whether a community was "considered backward by others."

Other decisive criteria were high frequency of manual labor, low age of marriage, and above-average percentage of working women. The criteria were perfectly suited for identification of culturally conservative peasant castes. The importance of status parameters over economic parameters in fact extended the OBC denomination to the significant number of dominant castes such as Jats, Yadavs, Lingayats, and Rajputs who rapidly emerged as the leading forces in this numerically strong vertical alliance of backward castes encompassing wealthy peasants and businessmen as well as marginalized landless laborers.

The Mandal Commission scrutinized communities and not individuals. It was assumed that in spite of singular examples of successful social mobility, the overwhelming majority of "backwards" shared modest living conditions and bleak prospects of life improvement, and lived, in the words of the commission, in "a climate of extreme social and cultural deprivation." The community approach reflected the widespread paternalist assumption entertained in the urban middle class world that "backwards" and rural people simply live in their caste world, and that individual assessment of educational and cultural needs was therefore superfluous and not applicable.

Besides, the community approach further entrenched and codified the longstanding knowledge-practice in the political field of representation, imagination, and self-objectivation of lower-caste groups. The commission thus codified the historical mode of production of the Indian people, and codified the prevailing political practices of democracy and accommodation between cultural groups-be they caste, linguistic, religious, or ethnic-objectified by the state and continuously reproduced by self-proclaimed representatives.

The endeavor toward objectivation of essential caste cultures, the trust in a symbolic enfranchisement and populist governmentality, and the belief in a "natural" solidarity among lower-caste groups were expressed in strikingly naive terms in the recommendations of the commission. Here it was clearly stated that the objective of reservations was to give OBCs "a feeling of participation in the governance of this country," while admitting that the effect would mainly be "a psychological spin off."

It was even anticipated that future OBC officers might be "a shade less competent" but that this would be outweighed by their "first-hand knowledge of the sufferings of the backward sections of society." Needless to say, this peculiar style of representation in the political field of the "backward community" had little resemblance to the widely dispersed and contradictory social, economic, and cultural practices within each of the categories depicted in the commission's report.

The emerging OBC identity thus gave voice and stage to an "intensified democratic revolution," as the 1980s became dominated by competing populist agitations-farmers, OBCs, regional formations- within the overall framework of "majoritarian democracy." The Mandal issue also played a crucial role in providing a distinct focus to the mounting resentment among upper-caste and middle-class groups (rural as well as urban) against the growing assertiveness of lowercaste and less well-educated communities. The urban middle classes (predominantly Hindu) had historically provided the backbone in Congress's construction of the Indian nation state.

For decades these groups had been confident that the future belonged to them as a socially, culturally, and economically dominant group, and only a fragment of this group had until the 1980s proved to be a receptive audience for communalist discourse. The growing responsiveness within these groups to Hindu nationalist discourses revolving around themes of the endangered nation was conditioned by what was felt as a sense of encroachment on their social world by ascending groups of peasants, traders, and entrepreneurs.

The feeling of encroachment had partly to do with sharpened competition over jobs and education because of the entry of newly mobile social groups. But it was also linked to a sense of "depurification of values" accompanying the increased visibility of lower-caste groups in the public realm, in institutions, government offices, and so on. This effect of social transformation and democratic revolution-belated in north India compared to the rest of the country-in turn challenged the sense of security, status, and competence in the middle classes, already shattered by the gradual retreat of the Indian state from the economic and regulative model of which it had been the main beneficiary.

The anti-Mandal agitations and self-immolations of upper-caste students in north India in 1990 must be understood against this background of an established middle class, haunted by fears of what was seen as a "plebeian" threat to its hitherto complacent way of life and social position.

CASTE AND THE IMPURITIES OF POLITICS

The political imaginaries and the imagination of the mechanisms of the political field were marked by deep ambivalences. On the one hand, politics was seen as corrupt and politicians generally denounced as dishonest and semi-criminal. The political field was depicted as an area marked by erosion of moral principles and proper behavior in favor of commercialized and criminalized behavior. In this upper-caste environment, the "decay" of the world of politics was unequivocally ascribed to the rising assertiveness of lower-caste politicians- depicted as "goonda types" or "uncultured types." Similarly, the ostensible decline in the quality of public administration was attributed to the influx of ever more officers from the lower castes.

Almost all the families denied that caste was an active factor in the community. The official discourse of caste as a thing of the past has become integrated into everyday language, not least in upper-caste educated families. But other discourses on caste did frequently break through these narratives, as remarks in passing on the essential character of certain other caste groups, on cleanliness, on the "atmosphere" of an area, and so on.

The parameters of caste were in a sense extended and transformed into an idiom of civic conduct and order: private purity was extended into public hygiene; Brahminical values into societal discipline, education, and culture; the notion of a Brahmin caste spirit into "modern mentality"; and erosion of caste boundaries became translated into erosion of morality and civic sense, wherein pollution became disorder (dangerous to women), noise, and dirt in public places. These changes seem to me to constitute genuine transformations, and not mere translations of perennial hierarchies into the idioms of urban modernity.

One might say that the conceptual grammar of caste seems to continue as the reproduction of logics of differentiation and hierarchical separation. The political organization of caste obviously contributes in numerous ways to the consolidation and simplification of castes into states of "sociological solidity." Confronted with the problematics of urban modernity, a competitive labor market, competitive electoral mobilization, the alphabet-or signification-of caste is constantly sliding. The meanings of certain practices, boundaries, and caste myths have within the last few decades increasingly become inscribed into changing surfaces of democratic competition between groups and communities, and of competitive access to jobs, business, and education.

As the signification of caste has changed, the signified-the hierarchy of differences-has also been transformed and extended from ritual purity toward civic conduct, Oxford degrees, or NRI (non resident Indian) status. It seems, nonetheless, that important dimensions of the conceptual grammar of caste-separation and hierarchy-tend to be reproduced again and again. To the middle-class professionals living in Pune and aspiring to become as "modern" as those in the Camp area, caste identities appear obsolete in their older forms.

Instead this logic of discreteness and hierarchization is reproduced in notions of the advanced stage of their own sophistication (as modern liberals) and as the natural physical and cultural distance of their community from other, less advanced groups. In the old city the Brahminical ethos is transformed and displaced into a sense of superior ability to capture and utilize the instrumental rationality of modern knowledge and to internalize the utility of civic order, without losing the ancient cultural heritage and the cultural groundedness one requires in the turmoil of urban modernity.

Communities placed lower in the hierarchy do not possess this shield of cultural sophistication, many Brahmins here argue. When exposed to the perils and temptations of urban life they become rootless, vulgar, dirty, and greedy for money and power. Most of the upper-caste people from these environments who dismissed politics as immoral were also intensely interested and engaged in politics, captured by the *jouissance* derived from the constant display of the "scandalous secret" of politics-corruption and naked power-that was an obvious drive for most of these persons.

But it was also broadly realized that without political connections and political brokerage it was next to impossible to conduct a business, to pursue a career, to see that one's children get a good education and a job, or to get proper housing, civic amenities, and so on. As if to disentangle those necessary practices from the "immoral" sphere of politics, both the "buyers" and "sellers" of dalal employed a rather depoliticized businesslike vocabulary to depict this sphere of life- "to get work done," "a small job," "everyday business," and so on.

Most traits that the families saw as repulsive in politics-corruption, dishonesty, and vote catching-were at the same time ethically neutralized as necessities in politics for "our party" to win, or necessary for "our work to be done." There was, especially among BJP supporters, an additional dimension to the *jouissance*, namely, fascination with and enthusiasm for the adroit management and maneuvering by "our people" in the immoral web of intrigues and games in the political field.

A tale of loss and declining ethics marked most of the narratives of politics among the middle-class families I interviewed in Pune. Bemoaning the loss of the "original effervescence" of independent India in the (golden) era of Nehru and lamenting the declining standards of politicians often seemed to serve as metaphors for a fuzzier sense of loss of community, security, predictability, justice, and meaning and direction of society. These narratives are, to my mind, intrinsic to modern political imaginaries and "symptoms" of the unfolding of the democratic revolution. Lack of order, lack of development, and the bemoaning of an immoral modernity threatened by "uncultured people" are all seen as results of a faulty and corrupt polity producing an excessively liberal, fragmented, and immoral society.

A Brahmin clerk said: "We don't need these silly corporators whoever they are, they are useless.... There should be a single person to decide. With a thousand persons thinking in all directions nothing will work out. Nowadays democracy only means 'by the political people, for the political people.'" A wealthy Marwari businessman stated: "Self-discipline is the core of democracy. We need a clean and tidy house-in elections the candidate must be learned, be able to think of a democratic way of functioning. I believe in the background of a person because education and culture must form the thinking of a person."

The narrative of loss of order and democratic ethics applies mainly to the realm of electoral politics. In the realm of everyday local issues, the rights to citizenship seem to be interpreted in more mundane terms as the entitlement to school admissions, "to get work done," to be looked after by the corporators-members of the Municipal Corporation. Also in this sense, the primary parameters of public justice seem to be equal entitlements and endowments of various castes and cultural groups.

The ostensible disorder and the loss of a civic equality (which only, if ever, has been extended to privileged groups) experienced by the upper-caste families in Pune was mainly attributed to a rising assertiveness and a growing will among hitherto excluded and marginal groups to use whatever channel is available- democratic or not-to get access to resources and entitlements. Although the rise of more resolute "plebeian" modes of politics among lower-caste communities is often framed as a way of winning social respectability, influence, and recognition, middle-class residents in Pune seem increasingly to dream of "a clean sweep," an imposition of an authoritarian moral order that would privilege those in possession of culture and status.

RELIGIOUS SYMBOLS IN THE POLITICAL FIELD

The increasing prominence of religious symbolism in Indian politics in the 1980s was in many ways initiated by the somewhat paranoid strategies pursued by Indira Gandhi and her sons in order to secure and consolidate a perpetual Congress majority in national electoral politics. The political manipulations in Punjab in the 1980s and the subsequent creation of a "Sikh menace" paid off in the massive victory of Congress in 1984 due to the wave of sympathy and national rage in the wake of the assassination of Indira Gandhi. To counter the growing assertiveness of the Janata Dal and regional parties in the 1980s, the Congress leadership embarked in the following years on a rather clumsy communal arithmethic, practicing a shifting accommodation of both Hindu and Muslim communal forces.

In April 1985 the Supreme Court in Delhi delivered an historic verdict granting divorced Muslim women (Shah Bano) maintenance from her former husband by applying a section under the general Criminal Penal Code to the case. The decision broke with the legal precedents of treating matters of family dispute under the special provisions stipulated in the Muslim Personal Law Application Act, which was interpreted by the members of the ulama appointed to the Muslim Personal Law Board (MPLB).

Muslim leaders influenced by conservative and fundamentalist currents in the Islamic world regarded the verdict as an infringement on the cultural autonomy of Indian Muslims and called for public protests. The agitation started as a cautious protest call during the Friday prayer, but quickly developed into a mass movement all over the country, to the surprise of both Muslim and non-Muslim leaders. Coordinated as a "shari'a protection week" by the newly formed All India Muslim Personal Law Board (AIMPLB), hundreds of thousands of Muslims gathered in October 1985 at rallies against the Shah Bano verdict and for upholding the status of Muslim personal law.

The size and spontaneity of the mass rallies-such as the 300,000 people who gathered in Bombay on a call by a handful of relatively unknown Urdu journalists on 20 November 1985-indicated that frustration and a sense of insecurity had been fermenting for a long time among the Indian Muslims, especially in the major cities.

The Shah Bano agitations provided an escape valve for this accumulated frustration, while at the same time it also propelled a new and more communally minded Muslim leadership into national prominence. In an attempt to align Congress with the most conservative elements of the Muslim leadership, which appeared to have a grip on the Muslim community during the 1985 agitations, a bill annulling the Shah Bano verdict was passed haphazardly in May 1986, in spite of massive protests from most quarters of political life. Seen from an electoral point of view, the strategy never worked properly for Congress.

Since the mid-1980s, the Janata Dal and the Samajwadi party in Uttar Pradesh emerged as major political rallying points for Muslims in northern India. Both these parties tried to articulate the interests of the large numbers of small farmers in the Gangetic area, among them many Muslims. Both parties also took a firm pro-Muslim stand against Hindu nationalist claims to the site of the Babri Masjid, the disputed mosque in the town of Ayodhya in eastern Uttar Pradesh.

The site of the Babri Masjid had been legally contested by Hindu and Muslim organizations since the nineteenth century, and had been sealed off for decades by the colonial authorities. The core of the dispute was a small platform (chabutra), inside the mosque, allegedly constructed on the site of Ram's birth, and worshiped by Hindus. In 1949, militant Hindus-probably militants from the Hindu Mahasabha- installed sacred Ramlila idols inside the mosque. Shortly afterward the masjid was again sealed off for worship, and a title suit was filed by local Muslims, demanding the removal of the idols and reopening of the masjid for worship. These had been left pending at the local court in Faizabad since 1950.

The Vishwa Hindu Parishad began its agitation in 1985 by filing a writ petition in the local court in Faizabad requesting a reopening of the "disputed structure" for Hindu worship. To everybody's surprise, a court order reopening the premises was issued within a week. There is little doubt that this swift action was promoted by the Congress leadership in another transparent attempt to accommodate the rapidly growing constituency for militant Hindu nationalism.

The Congress strategy in 1985-1986 thus displayed the shortsighted rationality of populist governmentality, now aimed at heightening communal tension, while hoping to reap the electoral benefits of the ensuing sense of insecurity among Hindus as well as the minority communities. In keeping with previous opportunistic election strategies, Rajiv Gandhi openly appealed to communal sentiments among Hindu voters. He started his electoral campaign in 1989 in Faizabad-the constituency in which the town of Ayodhya is located-with promises of creating a Ram Rajya ("rule of Ram") using language in several ways resembling that adopted by the BJP.

This strategy also failed, and in 1989 Congress was for the second time in independent India voted out of power at the hands of Janata Dal's anticorruption slogans, and by the Hindu communal campaign of the BJP deriding the "pseudo secularism" of the Congress. There is little doubt that these transparent maneuvers in the realm of symbolic manipulation aggravated tensions between Muslims and Hindus in north India in the 1980s. Congress's most decisive contribution to this process of "communalization," however, was its de facto authorization of a majoritarian discourse on democracy and a culturalist discourse on political loyalties. Furthermore, the continued depletion of the capacity, skills, and legitimacy of the party, especially at the local level, created important conditions for the subsequent emergence of communal politics at center stage of Indian politics in the late 1980s.

MUSLIM MINORITIZATION

Economic growth in the urban sectors and the steady commercialization of agriculture in large parts of India in the 1980s had relatively few beneficiaries among Muslims in India. The burgeoning urban and rural middle classes were overwhelmingly Hindu, whereas Muslims generally remained stuck in such economically marginal positions as selfemployed artisans, traders, and marginal farmers. Although a middle class of Muslim traders, and professionals was emerging in the urban centers of western and northern India, the consistently lower rate of literacy and the lower attendance in formal education among Muslims as compared to Hindus testified to the continued economic marginalization of this very large minority in the Indian state.

The virulent anti-Muslim rhetoric disseminated by the VHP and the RSS in the wake of the conversions to Islam of approximately one thousand scheduled-caste people in Meenakshipuram in Tamil Nadu in early 1981, made it clear that the Hindu nationalist forces were allowed a relatively free hand in public, whereas the Muslim community stood without powerful public leaders. In this vacuum, disparate leaders such as the populist Syed Shahabuddin who advocated cultural equality, and the conservative Imam Bukhari of the Jama Masjid in Delhi-previously Indira Gandhi's informal contact to the religious establishment-emerged as Muslim leaders on an outspoken and culturally conservative platform.

A brief glance at some of the transformations of this rather bleak horizon of many Muslims may, however, shed some light on the outburst of what appeared as "conservative radicalism" in the community. From the late 1970s onward, an increasing number of Indian Muslims (and Hindus) had gone to the Gulf countries to work as skilled workers, technicians, and domestics. They brought back money and status to their otherwise deprived communities, such as the Muslim Moplahs in northern Kerala. The apparent might and affluence in the Arab world strengthened the Muslim identity of many Indian migrant workers, though not without ambiguities born out of the generally brutal treatment of migrant labor in places like Saudi Arabia.

Simultaneously, the radical antiwestern and assertive rhetoric of Islamic radicalism in Iran and the Middle East impressed a new urgency of articulation and assertion of a distinct Muslim identity upon groups of younger intellectuals and journalists, as well as parts of the more conservative clerical Muslim establishment in India. The strong assertions of a Muslim identity in connection with the Shah Bano agitations in Bombay, Gujarat, and Kerala were undoubtedly informed by the newfound pride and the quest for recognition produced by this new flow of wealth and religious discourse. However, the development of ties between Indian Muslims and the Gulf countries and the conservative postures of Muslim leaders seemed to confirm all the run-of-the-mill stereotypes about inherently "antinational" Muslims.

This contributed in no small measure to making the Indian Muslims a perfect and demonized other in the Sangh parivar's subsequent mass production of communal stereotypes. A brief, but unexceptional, quote from an 1991 editorial in Shahabuddin's monthly magazine *Muslim India*, whose title signals the proposed hierarchy of loyalties of the Muslim community in India, certainly seems to indicate that the Muslim identity propagated here tended toward the same essentialist and totalizing construction of cultural and religious identities as those of the Hindu nationalists.

For a Muslim, at the personal level, his religious identity is supreme, rising above race, language, geography or political jurisdiction. Indeed he is not prepared to trade his religious identity at any price-bread, profession, vocation, political ideology or national identity.... By Islamic doctrine, the Muslim family code, to the extent it is based on his scriptures, the Holy Koran and the Traditions of the Holy Prophet, is universal sacrosanct and immutable, valid for all times and for all societies. No one has the authority to change it.... In short, for the Muslim, Personal Law is Religion.... Even a welfare state in a developing society, with an expanding role, cannot be permitted to change the Shariat, or to replace it with a man-made code in the name of unity or progress.

The growing Hindu nationalist visibility in the religious and political field made Shahabuddin's audience ever larger in the 1980s. The Sangh parivar's sustained anti-Muslim campaign and the rapidly escalating communal violence in many parts of the country, in which Muslims in most cases were targeted and attacked, produced anger and incipient radicalism among sections of young urban Muslims. A disturbing trend was that the long-term trend toward dispersion and "normalization" of the Muslim vote, that is, its distribution over a number of political parties according to social position and ideological inclination, was abruptly reversed in the 1989 and 1991 elections as Muslims in large numbers chose to vote en bloc against the BJP, or against Congress.

A HEGEMONIAL CRISIS

An effective hegemony in the Gramscian sense presupposes an effective historical bloc-a strategic alliance between dominant social interests-and a moral and political leadership capable of modifying institutions and reproducing societal cohesion through the governance of the state and by virtue of control over "civil society." In spite of the continuation of the historical bifurcation between a middle-class society and the uneducated communities of the "masses," the Congress party was in all these senses a truly hegemonic force in the first decades after Independence.

In the late 1980s the economic basis of this hegemony, the "License Raj," gave way to various attempts to liberalize the economy; governmental institutions crumbled under the weight of corruption and were transformed to ad hoc instruments in a new populist governmentality; the security apparatuses were unable, and unwilling, to retain law and order effectively; the political system of institutional bargaining gave way to competing populist projects; and the moral and ideological leadership of the secular state disintegrated as the dominant Hindu middle classes drifted toward Hindu nationalism.

Faced by these challenges, the chaos and the "plebeian" assertiveness thrown up by the democratic revolution in the 1980s, the majoritarian and populist interpretation of state and society promoted by the Hindu nationalists began to appear as a more effective guarantee of stability and continued privilege among dominant strata in Indian society.

4

The Politics of Hindutva

In South Asian politics, a polar contrast between national and communal politics has been assumed often enough since the 1920s, more complicated patterns of affinities and distinctions emerge when we consider majoritarian communalisms. Claiming to represent both a communal population and nation-Hindus in India, and Muslims in Pakistan and Bangladesh-majoritarian movements has appropriated the mantle of authentic nationalism. In the aftermath of December 1992, however, we need to look at the relationship between nationalism and communalism more closely.

Problematization has to go further, however, into a more basic questioning of the assumption that Indian nationalism and Hindu and Muslim communalism have comprised the entire meaningful world of political action and discourse. Such an assumption involves an uncritical acceptance of ideological claims by nationalism and communalism, which have tried to homogenize a variety of differences-of region, class, caste, and gender-through elision of conflicts and power relations conceived as internal to the community being constructed thereby.

Even radical historiography has seldom questioned the absolute priority of the anticolonial struggle, while emphasizing the role within it of organized class struggle or autonomous subaltern initiatives. Elision has been most powerful in respect of caste, which has figured remarkably little in general historical reconstructions of modern India. Yet it is precisely this dimension that has shot into unexpected prominence in recent days, with Mandal confronting mandir and a backward-dalit electoral combination halting the advance of the BJP in Uttar Pradesh state politics.

This chapter attempts a preliminary exploration of the ways that questions of caste - more precisely, lower-caste aspirations - have been handled in the constructions of *Hindutva* and Indian nationalism. Even a brief glance reveals major difficulties of incorporation and points to the presence of other histories not neatly encapsulable within narratives of anticolonial nationalism or religious communities, which dominate historiography.

Only very recently have a few efforts been made to explore the interrelations between such partially autonomous histories without postulating an a priori normative primacy of the nationalist, or anticolonial, "mainstream". The current Mandal-mandir dichotomy suggests that the construction of homogenized Hindutva should be considered in part as an effort to respond to and counter pressures from below in the form of lower-caste aspirations. One needs, perhaps, to recuperate and extend some aspects of the logic of the early *Subaltern Studies* scholarship, which has been largely abandoned by many of its present stalwarts.

A few concluding remarks would be warranted, then, about the intellectual assumptions that have sustained the relative silence trying to disrupt - a silence that still gives a title like mine a deceptive aura of naturalness. The enormous overlap in personnel, assumptions, and symbols between mainstream Indian nationalism and Hindu communalism is too obvious to need much elaboration. One can think of the "Bande Mataram" hymncum-slogan, central to much anti-British patriotism and at the same time a Hindu rallying cry, at least in Bengal, during confrontations with Muslims.

A more dramatic example would be the murder of the *Mahatma* by Nathuram Godse: both these protagonists in that total confrontation of January 30, 1948, could in some senses be called nationalists and pious Hindus, and for both Rama was a central icon. Nationalism and communalism, again, far from being definite and stable signifiers, can quickly change and even reverse their signifieds as one crosses the Indo-Pakistan border: Muslim separatism or communalism, pejorative terms in India, become, in Pakistan, laudable nationalism, with a reverse process operative with respect to Indian and Hindu.

Nationalisms grounded in religious identity have been hardly uncommon in history: one thinks of Iran today, Ireland, or even the concept of "God's Englishmen" in the making of patriotism in Protestant England. It is possible, therefore, to speak of Hindu or Muslim nationalism in place of the obviously pejorative communalism, provided one does not go on from there to make the historically absurd assumption that nationalism itself is somehow laudable (or always harmful to the same extent) and that distinctions cannot be drawn between various types of nationalisms in terms of objectives and consequences.

One way in which the ground for such distinctions is being undercut today is through the argument that communalism has been a mere labeling exercise that secular nationalists took over from colonial knowledge and used pejoratively to brand community identities, which perhaps need rather to be valorized as counterpoints to the tyranny of the modern, post-Enlightenment nation-state (which is one way of understanding Pandey 1990b).

Distinction is necessary, above all, in the context of the Hindutva logic that identifies the RSS-VHP-BJP combine uniquely with the Hindu community, and then, through a specious majoritarian argument, transforms it into the authentic voice of the nation. What this majoritarian argument deliberately ignores is the contradiction between the notion of a permanent majority, based solely on the census definition of a Hindu, and the democratic determination of changing electoral majorities and their governments.

Making appropriate distinctions becomes logically possible, once, in the specific conditions of a multireligious subcontinent, communalism is not taken to mean (as it often loosely and inconsistently has been) the construction, assumption, or deployment of more-or-less homogenized community identities claiming a religious basis. Developed communal ideology needs to be distinguished even from the politicization of such identities through demands for quotas in jobs or seats, or the use of religious appeals in election campaigns.

These have often contributed massively to communal developments but should be considered necessary, rather than sufficient, conditions. For a full-fledged communal ideology - as distinct from occasional, usually localized clashes between groups of Hindus and Muslims, which could have an enormous variety of causes and did not generate conceptions of countrywide, mutually opposed blocs before the late nineteenth and early twentieth century - two further assumptions seem indispensable. Conflict with a similarly conceived community Other has to be assumed to be both inevitable and overriding in the sense of being more crucial than other tensions or projects (such as ending British rule, before 1947, or alternative programs of national economic development and social transformations, after 1947).

A genealogy of Hindu communalism, in other words, would have to think in terms of two historical transitions. The first is a transition from a relatively inchoate Hindu world, without firmly defined boundaries, to the late-nineteenth-century construction of ideologies of unified Hinduism, in the context of integrative colonial communication, administrative, and economic structures. The second transition, roughly datable to the mid-1920s, is a move in some quarters toward an aggressive Hindutva postulated usually upon an enemy image of a similarly conceived Islam.

Distinguishing among Indian, Hindu, and Muslim nationalisms -rather than simply between nationalism and communalism - is helpful also because, in the specific conditions of subcontinental religious, linguistic, and cultural diversity, Indian nationalism did have to develop thrusts or tendencies (not more than that, and often reversed) that can be seen to be contradicted by the ideology and practice of Hindutva. Indian nationalism had to seek a fundamentally territorial focus, attempting to unite everyone living in the territory of British-dominated India, irrespective of religious or other differences.

Ways of building or maintaining that unity included efforts to create public spaces where religious difference would not be allowed entrance, and also included conceptions of composite or federal nationalism with religious communities as its building blocks. Thus the early, moderate Congress forbade the raising of any issue to which delegates from any religious community strongly objected, while in Bepinchandra Pal's ideal of composite patriotism, "Hindus, Muslims, Christians and tribals would each preserve distinctive features and by cultivating them contribute to the common national life".

By contrast, thoroughgoing projects of agnostic secularization remained a relatively minor strand. "Secular" in India, in other words, has meant, principally, "anticommunal," and this makes the argument that "hard secularists" are somehow responsible for the growth of communalism seem both curious and tendentious. Territoriality remains the starting point in developed Hindutva ideology, as epitomized above all in V. D. Savarkar's *Hindutva - Who Is a Hindu?* (Published in 1923), in which *pitribhumi* (fatherland) is immediately equated with *punyabhumi* (holy land), and the latter is unambiguously identified with "the cradle-land of...religion".

Only Hindus, therefore, can be true patriots, not Indian Muslims or Christians, with their holy lands in Arabia or Palestine. The edge of the entire argument is clearly directed against Indian Muslims and Christians, and not against British rulers, who never claimed India to be either fatherland or holy land. The logic proceeds here, as in the entire subsequent discourse of Hindutva, by using "culture" as an apparently innocent middle term invested with Hindu religious meanings and associations. A generation later, M. S. Golwalkar expounded the distinction with enviable clarity:

> The theories of territorial nationalism and of common danger, which formed the basis for our concept of nation, had deprived us of the real and positive content of our real Hindu nationhood and made of the freedom movements virtually anti-British movements. Being anti-British was equated with patriotism and nationalism. This reactionary view has had disastrous effects upon the entire course of the independence struggle, its leaders and the common people.

Two important corollaries, in significant contrast, that could follow from Indian nationalism's unificatory project were an orientation toward the future (the concept of a nation that had to be built, that was still in the making, as implied for instance by the title of Surendranath Banerji's autobiography; and a rejection or softening of hard, closed, impenetrable identities. Gandhi's philosophy of change of heart through *ahimsa* (non-violence) for instance, involved not just nonviolence but an assumption that human communication was possible across even the sharpest of divides and so efforts should be made to combine change with avoidance of total, violent ruptures. Gandhi tried to apply this philosophy to a whole range of contradictions: British and Indian, Hindu and Muslim, propertied and propertyless (in the concept of zamindars and capitalists as "trustees"), high and low castes, men and women.

There are manifold problems here for anyone who is not a Gandhian, yet perhaps a point can be made even by an unbeliever about the greatly varied degree of relevance of the strategy with respect to specific kinds of tensions. The Hindu-Muslim relationship, it seems to me, stands on a significantly different level from the others, in that it alone does not point toward any generalized structure of domination, as contrasted to colonial rule, caste hierarchy, class exploitation, and gender inequality.

It is not, therefore, accidental that leftist commentators - otherwise often sharp critics of Gandhian nonviolence and change of heart as ultimately fitting in with the interests of dominant groups - have generally been warm admirers of Gandhi's ideal (if not necessarily always of his specific methods) of achieving a "unity of hearts" among Hindus and Muslims even at moments of maximum communal strife - an ideal for which Gandhi sacrificed his life.

And the court statement of his murderer, Nathuram Godse, a self-acknowledged disciple of Savarkar who had had his early training in the RSS, indicates with equal clarity the nature of the divide. Godse rejected Gandhi's philosophy of ahimsa, not on the ground of its possible inefficacy and utopianism (the traditional leftist critique), but because it "would ultimately result in the emasculation of the Hindu Community". Emasculation - a word with significant resonances.

Yet the logical distinctions I have been emphasizing have been blurred repeatedly. It has often seemed important for even the most secular nationalists to derive sustenance and authenticity from an image of subcontinental unity (or what is called "unity-in-diversity") extending back into a glorious past. Because, except for brief periods of imperial unity (often excessively valorized), this image is difficult to substantiate at the political level, the tendency has remained strong to assume some kind of cultural or civilizational integration as the ultimate foundation of nationalism.

And then it becomes difficult - even for a Nehru, writing his *Discovery of India* -to resist the further slide toward assuming that that unity, after all, has been primarily Hindu (and upper-caste, often north Indian Hindu at that). The slide was made easier by the undeniable fact that the bulk of the leading cadres of the nationalist and even leftist movements have come from Hindu upper-caste backgrounds. The harsh words of a contemporary dalit writer thus indicate an important dimension, exaggerated and unfair though they might sound too many:

> The national movement was turned into a form of historical mythological movement and ancestor worship.... Those who ... did not want society to be democratic started eulogising history, mythology and ages gone by, because in those mythological and historical ages, they were the supreme victors and leaders. ...People such as Phule, Agarkar, Gokhale and Ranade who talked about misery and servitude of Shudras and Ati-Shudras ...were declared enemies.... The intelligentsia won, they succeeded in turning the Indian liberation struggle into a lop-sided fight, and in reducing the other movements to a secondary status.

The blurring of distinctions became qualitatively more powerful after 1947 and most blatant of all after the withering of Nehruvian hopes of sustained independent economic growth, socialistic change, and populistic alleviation of poverty. Transformed from inspiration for mass awakening into the official ideology of an increasingly bureaucratized and centralized nationstate, Indian nationalism has become more and more of an icon, with predominantly, though not invariably, Hindu lineaments. The dividing line between national and Hindu communal assumptions and values became increasingly porous, to the great advantage of Hindutva political forces.

The differential ways in which caste has entered the discourses of nationalism and Hindutva have certain paradoxical features. Mass anticolonial struggle obviously required the mobilization of large numbers of lower castes and dalits, and it was hardly accidental that the emergence of Gandhian nationalism roughly coincided with the incorporation of issues of caste discrimination, in however partial and tokenistic a manner, in the Congress agenda. Gandhi made ending untouchability one of the preconditions for the realization of his "Swaraj within one year" promise of 1921, and after the confrontation with Ambedkar in 1932, harijan welfare became for some years his principal activity.

Nor was there any logical difficulty in incorporating anticaste principles within programs of anticolonial nationalism in both its liberal and leftist forms. Hereditary caste inequality clearly contradicted both bourgeois-liberal principles of citizenship and socialist ideals of thorough egalitarianism. The characteristic left programmatic combination of anticolonial with antifeudal revolution could incorporate caste among its targets as a presumably feudal relic. Yet caste, along with gender oppression, all too often became issues of social reform less immediately relevant than basic questions of political independence or class struggle.

They could be postponed, would be more or less automatically resolved with changes in political and economic structures, and might be divisive from the point of view of anti-British struggle. The limitations of orthodox Marxism, on the whole dogmatic and economistic, evidently played a critical role here, blocking theorization from the realities of leftled mass action in which lower castes and dalits were often very prominent. R. P. Dutt's pioneering and still valuable Marxist study of modern Indian history and society did not include caste among its index entries, and contained only three references to "depressed classes".

Caste, in significant contrast, was both vital and embarrassing for projects of Hindu unity and Hindutva, and so, to some extent, has been gender. For some two thousand years, for instance, the characteristic high Hindu dystopia of *Kali Yuga*

- the last and most degenerate of eras that is always imagined as the present - has firmly located the sources of evil in the insubordination of *Shudras* to upper castes and of women to men. It has been next to impossible to think of Hinduism without some form of Varna and jati.

The votaries of Hindutva have tended to come in the main from high castes quite self-conscious about their status privileges, and yet the conflicts that tended to emerge from hierarchical rigidities needed to be resolved or kept in check if unity was to be achieved. Evasion through postponement, as an admitted evil that would be remedied in the future, was thus more difficult. There were, rather, uneasy oscillations between volubility and deliberate silencing through diversion, between projects of limited, integrative, Sanskritizing reform and aggressive assertions of hierarchy. The ebb and flow of lower-caste pressures seem to have played a critical role in these variations.

A convenient entry point and focus is provided here by the prominence of the concept of *adhikari-bheda* in mid- and late-nineteenth-century discourses leading up to the construction of unified notions of Hinduism, particularly in Bengal, which I take up here as a brief case study. Adhikari-bheda (literally, "differential rights, claims, or powers") conveyed the notion that each jati (caste) and sampraday (sect) has its own rituals and beliefs, in a unified, but hierarchically differentiated structure within which each knows its appropriate place.

Catholicity could thus be combined with conservative maintenance of norms appropriate to a group's location within the overall hierarchy. Louis Dumont's structuralist analysis comes very close to this basic Hindu-conservative principle through the much-quoted statement that "Hinduism hierarchizes and includes." What needs to be emphasized, however, is that classificatory devices like adhikari-bheda are not just innocent objective descriptions, but projects of specific groups for acting on social reality: having some relationship with it if they are at all effective, but never of a one-to-one, purely reflexive kind.

The historian needs to explore their undersides, as E. P. Thompson for instance did with concepts like paternalism and deference in eighteenth-century England. Thus adhikari-bheda, looked at from below, may point toward a relative openness to the emergence and survival of a multitude of practices and beliefs. Such catholicity may have been more or less inevitable under premodern conditions of undeveloped communication integration within a set of traditions - a "Hindu" world without firm boundaries, not yet "Hinduism" - which did not have an unitary textual base, centralized priesthood, inquisition, or consistent state backing on a subcontinental scale.

Diversities, in other words, were not necessarily perceived as building blocks in a Hinduism unified through a single, hierarchically differentiated order as is indicated by the difficulties modern observers have faced in classifying the Kabirpanthis or the Bauls, say, as Hindu or Muslim. Adhikari-bheda, as a formal doctrine, seems to have emerged in the seventeenth and eighteenth centuries as a Brahmanic way of accommodating and keeping within proper limits differences in ritual, belief, and philosophy.

By the late-nineteenth, adhikari-bheda tended to signify not fluidity and openness, but neat compartmentalization, the drawing-up of definite boundaries, and the arrangement of differences in a fixed hierarchy, to the obvious advantage of established power relations of caste and gender. Symptomatic here, perhaps, was a definite efflorescence in many late-nineteenth-century high-caste Bengali tracts, plays, and farces of the *Kali Yuga* dystopia of breakdown of proper boundaries, with Shudras and women on top.

Education and jobs had now become theoretically accessible to all, and there was much talk and a few concrete measures in the direction of what was called *stri-swadhinata* (emancipation of women). And so the *Kali Yuga* myth flourished in some quarters for at least a couple of generations after the entry, under colonial auspices, of clocks and modern notions of linear time, which could have been expected to erode a construction grounded in assumptions of cycle time.

The social contexts of the emergence of pre-colonial notions of adhikari-bheda and Hindu unity (like for instance the high Hindu conception of *smarta-panchapasana* (the equal validity of devotion to Ganesh, Vishnu, Shiva, Shakti, and Surya) remain unexplored. But we might speculate that the communicational linkages relevant and necessary for such conceptions would tend to be predominantly Brahmanic: learned contacts during pilgrimages, the wanderings of ascetics, centers of religious and philosophical discussion like Vrindaban, Nabadwip, or some south Indian temples, the courts of princes and zamindars dispensing patronage to Brahman pandits and offering sites for debates on such theological matters.

Biographical data about nineteenthcentury leaders like Dayananda Saraswati or Ramakrishna Paramhansa occasionally provide glimpses of this older world. Dayananda Saraswati's early years were full of acrimonious debates with orthodox Brahmans about the meaning of sacred texts (*shastrartha*), carried on in Sanskrit and organized by zamindars, merchants, and bankers of western United Provinces. The virtually unlettered Ramakrishna's religious training came from a succession of holy men who had passed through Dakshineswar on their way to the pilgrimage of Gangasagar.

Colonial rule both stimulated such unificatory tendencies and provoked them into existence through its exploitative and aggressive presence. Communications were qualitatively transformed through print, modern education, and new transport facilities. Orientalist scholarly constructions of Hinduism as being grounded essentially in ancient sacred texts like the Vedas and the Upanishads, missionary polemics denigrating Hindus for the absence of indispensable elements of true religion, and incipient patriotic sentiments, all contributed in diverse ways to unificatory projects.

And, crucially, the operations of the census from the 1870s onward insisted on firm definitions and boundaries for purposes of enumeration and control through classification. For instance, in 1911, Census Commissioner E. A. Gait rebuked the Bombay census superintendent for using the hybrid term "Hindu-Muhammadans" for some groups whose responses and customs refused clear identification: he should have relegated "the persons concerned to the one religion or the other as best he could".

It is important, however, to avoid bland, mechanistic depictions of the impact of late-colonial integration or of colonial discourse. Such depictions had been the pitfalls of much modernization theory, and one feels at times that the Saidian counterorthodoxy of today has run into similar problems through an inversion of values that retains implicit assumptions of passivity among the colonized.

There is need for greater specificity about the precise location, ethos, and strategies of the groups directly involved in the transitions from "Hindu" toward "Hinduism." That they were, overwhelmingly, upper caste and male would occasion no surprise, for alreadyexisting hierarchies of caste and gender played a critical role in determining early access to the new integrative networks. The predominantly high-caste slant of projects of Hindu unity, in other words, continued on an enhanced scale in the late-colonial era and beyond.

Schematically, it is helpful to make a further distinction between three groups participating in and/or responding favorably to constructions of Hinduism that were built up in the late nineteenth century around notions of adhikari-bheda. Many of the tracts relevant for our argument were written by fairly obscure men, high-caste and predominantly Brahman, with little or no connection with Western education. Colonial transformations within this world of traditional literati and religious specialists seem to have gone in several directions at the same time.

The initial British dependence on pandits and *maulvis* (Muslim learned men) in revenue and judicial administration as well as in the early accumulation of orientalist knowledge must have strengthened the traditional literati considerably. Confining ourselves (for reasons of manageability, as throughout this chapter) to the "Hindu" world, it is important to note in the first place that the influence of Brahmanic sacred texts and of notions of Varna hierarchy was being simultaneously extended and deepened.

These texts were now disseminated on a vastly enhanced scale through print and translation, and colonial administration of Hindu law in many domains of everyday life as interpreted by Brahman experts heightened the importance of high Hindu texts where notions of hierarchy had always been most clearcut. There are many indications - particularly in Bengal where Western education came earliest and had established fairly deep roots by the late nineteenth century among gentlefolk - of a considerable decline in the prestige of traditional literati sticking to older ways, and also of a drying up of their sources of patronage.

Both their continued or enhanced influence and a decline in their prestige and income could in different ways stimulate an emphasis upon conservative, hierarchized Hindu unity, where Brahman males would once again be firmly on top. This was all the more likely under conditions of an alien rule often suspected of encouraging Christian conversions and Hindu reform.

The crucial ideological and organizational initiatives in the formation of both Hinduism and, later, Hindutva, however, have come primarily from a new middle class produced by colonial education. It is widely recognized that this middle-class social phenomenon - like its contemporary counterparts in Indian Islam and communalism in general - is basically modern, colonial, and postcolonial. There is little need to rehearse once more the familiar narratives of both reform and revival that contributed in different ways to a new emphasis on Hindu unity among the middle class. The linkages between the late-nineteenth-century strengthening of such tendencies and growing middle-class disenchantment about British tutelage are also a much-explored theme.

Two aspects relevant for our argument, however, have been relatively neglected. That the Western-educated were for long almost invariably of high-caste origin is well known, but possible implications of this fact have not been sufficiently highlighted. Yet, focusing on Bengal once again, it is surely symptomatic that the terms *jat*, *jati*, and *jatiya* were used in Bengali from around the third quarter of the nineteenth century to indicate, indiscriminately, "caste," "the Hindu people" (*Hindujati*), "nation," and "national."

Theoretical Brahmo Samaj criticism of caste, to take another example, goes back to Rammohan Roy, yet even the radical social reformers among Brahmos did little in practice about it, barring the encouragement of intercaste marriages within their own community and symbolic steps like insisting that Brahmo preachers give up their sacred thread. The first substantial Brahmo tract systematically attacking caste, Sibnath Shastri's Jatibheda, came out only in 1884, and a Depressed Classes Mission for philanthropic work among Bengal's low castes and untouchables had to wait for its inauguration till 1909.

The Arya Samaj perspective on caste reform was much more limited, and here, too, the integrative, Sanskritizing device of shuddhi - through which lower castes were given the sacred thread, emblematic of the three high varnas, and purification was sought for their rituals and ways of life - became widely adopted as a strategy only from around the turn of this century. These dates are rather significant in terms of the relevance of partially autonomous lower-caste pressures.

The colonial middle class, in the second place, has been generally studied in terms of its prominent or successful men (and a few women) alone: well-known writers, lawyers, journalists, doctors, scholars, officials, politicians. But it also included an increasing number of humbler, though still overwhelmingly upper-caste folk, remnants of the traditional literati who had lost patronage in the new era, obscure hack writers, and humble teachers, clerks in government offices or predominantly British-owned mercantile firms, unemployed educated youth, high-school or college dropouts with highly uncertain job prospects.

This lower middle class, neglected in historiography (Mayer 1975; Crossick 1977 are notable exceptions) had certain specific features: the lack of an artisan element due to caste distinctions and, in Bengal (though not in northern India), the weakness initially of a small-trader-shopkeeper component due to British, followed to some extent by Marwari, predominance. Chakri (the clerical office job) thus became in Bengal the dominant signifier of this social group, in actuality and even more in imagery.

Despite great differences in living standards and ways of life, education (at least in the vernacular) and print culture helped to constitute a community of readers (and viewers, after the development of the public stage in Calcutta from the 1870s) that extended over both the successful and the obscure high-caste bhadralok (the gentlefolk or respectable classes, in Bengal); and increasingly, it also included a small but growing number of women.

As actual or target readers and audiences of cheap tracts, prints, plays, and farces, the world of genteel upper-caste poverty was able to set its distinctive mark on many of the vernacular texts that constitute our primary evidence. Bhadralok aspirations, lacking the wherewithal for their fulfillment, possibly made caste status even more vital and enhanced the attraction of ideologies grounded in adhikari-bheda. Kali Yuga, significantly, took on new modulations, with a reordering of its package of evils around clerical work (*chakri*).

This was often combined with a neatly gendered shifting of guilt. In many plays and farces, the insubordinate wife with her modern, Westernized, extravagant ways forces the husband to take up a clerical job that is depicted as peculiarly demeaning, a kind of *dasatya* (bondage), due to its association with a new discipline of clock time being imposed by alien bosses. The conversations of Ramakrishna - the saint of poor rustic Brahman origin whose first intimate disciples in the Calcutta of the early 1880s came mostly from a clerical milieu - regularly conjoined lust (always given a feminine form), money, and *chakri* as the triple evils of Kali Yuga.

Ramakrishna and many late nineteenth-century religious tracts argued that clerical work - governed by the rigors of clock time - left no time for complicated ritual worship or deep philosophical contemplation. The simpler ways of *bhakti* (devotional piety, which might consist of no more than recitation of the name of the deity) was therefore preferable. Ultimately, perhaps, what remained was little more than a sense of belonging or identity: this was becoming more indispensable than ever before, particularly for obscure newcomers to city life.

In twentieth-century Hindutva, one may note, the denudation of Hindu traditions of theological or scholastic argument has kept pace with increasingly aggressive assertions of Hindu unity, while despite many transformations, the social lineaments of the movement appear not unfamiliar. An urban or small-town, predominantly high-caste, lower middle class of professionals, clerks, and traders has been the principal and stable base of the Sangh Parivar. There has been a marked influx also, particularly in recent years, of the more successful and upwardly mobile urbanites; while simultaneously links have been established through the VHP with what remains of, or can be claimed to be, a traditional religious literati of holy men, heads of ascetic orders, sants and mahants.

There are discursive and contextual shifts here, however, that demand emphasis. Early printed tracts centering around adhikari-bheda, as well as the conversations of Ramakrishna, were primarily concerned with the justification of ritual and behavioral norms against Christian polemic and reformist attacks. There are no developed enemy images - not even of Christians, while Muslims are hardly mentioned - and adhikari-bheda is repeatedly combined with apparently wide notions of catholicity.

"All [forms of worship] are acceptable, to each according to his taste," says an 1845 tract, while Lokenath Basu's *Hindu-dharma-marma* (1858) similarly argues that "what is bad is to lose one's *dharma* [religious duty]; the possibility of salvation remains so long as any *dharma* is devoutly followed". One is reminded of Ramakrishna's wellknown parables of the mother cooking many dishes to suit the diverse tastes of her children, and the man getting to a roof by staircase, ladder, or rope, but falling if he did not stick firmly to any one way.

A second striking feature of these and similar nineteenth-century texts is the remarkable openness of assertions of inequality and hierarchy. "Remember that distinctions of *Varna* (*varna-vivedha*) are indispensable to *mukti* [salvation]. Parameswar has given different kinds of *shakti* [power] to different *jatis* - if one takes up the *dharma* of another, only harm can follow". And even the supremely catholic and gentle Ramakrishna became very angry when Vidyasagar asked him why God should have given varying *Shakti* to different people.

Defense of caste hierarchy possibly figured in the early adhikari-bheda texts of Bengal largely as a routine matter, for it was not yet perceived as under serious attack, unlike, say, in Maharashtra. Women's rights, in contrast, had become the central divisive issue in nineteenth-century bhadralok life, and it is significant that the explications of the Kali Yuga during these decades focused obsessively on the insubordination of wives and was much less concerned with any Shudra threat. It was primarily in this gender context, too, that the aggressive assertions of Hindu hierarchy and discipline reached a point of climax during the 1880s and early 1890s, particularly in relation to the virulent campaign against the Age of Consent Bill of 1891.

Discipline was glorified, in an almost sadomasochistic manner, precisely because of the suffering and pain it often admittedly caused. Thus a pamphlet by the leading conservative writer Chandranath Basu in 1892 categorically located the ultimate virtues and superiority of Hindutva in the "woman who cooks in her kitchen, all but burnt by the flames, suffocated by the thick smoke".

Such a note of near hysteria, however, could not be sustained or be effective for long, and men like Chandranath Basu were soon almost forgotten. Hindu unity, after all, needed the willing consent of substantial numbers of women and lower castes, and for that, it seems, adhikaribheda had to be softened through devotion (*bhakti*). A servant can never normally expect to sit next to his master, Ramakrishna once explained in another of his homely parables, but moved by the servant's devoted service, the master might one day elevate the servant to a seat next to him.

Medieval *bhakti* texts had already introduced significant modulations in the high-caste myth of Kali Yuga, through which that worst of times became in some ways the best, for simple devotion was now declared sufficient for salvation. Textual learning and complicated rituals, from which women and Shudras were excluded, were no longer necessary, and sometimes, paradoxically, the social categories otherwise held responsible for degeneration were even privileged. The humble, it was announced, constitute the ideal devotee (*bhakta*) and women and Shudras "can attain good simply through performing their duties" to husbands and high-caste men.

One notices a similar dualism in the portrayal of Kali Yuga in many late-nineteenth-century Bengali plays and farces. If evil is located in the insubordinate Anglicized wife who dominates her worthless husband, counterpoints are often found in figures of pure women (and, occasionally, good plebeians - devoted domestic servants, even one or two peasants), who act decisively, while always maintaining proper deference, to set right the disturbed moral order. A literary trope of what I have elsewhere called "deferential assertion" thus emerges, in which women are given an active role, going considerably beyond the traditional Sita model in the Ramayana of patient, entirely passive suffering that ennobles but does not modify the course of events.

The limits remain clear, however, as does, above all, the fact that such initiative invariably culminates in the restoration of proper patriarchal and Brahmanic order. And once again, it is tempting to find affinities: twentieth-century Hindutva has also oscillated between frank assertions of hierarchical structures and projections, principally through bhakti, of a softer, more populist, hegemonic face. The greatest success of Hindutva to date has been through the appropriation and development of the image of Rama, a central bhakti hero, in whom benign paternalism (udarata) and martial prowess (krodhita mudra) have been classically combined.

But there were major discursive shifts too between the 1890s and the mid- 1920s, when - with Savarkar's text and the foundation of the RSS, in 1925 - Hindutva became crystallized as an ideological-political formation. Fundamental here were certain well-known contextual changes, which for our purpose may be summed up as a transition toward qualitatively new kinds of mass politics, interrelated with institutional changes like extension of the franchise and safeguards for minority or backward groups, accompanied by spells of communal violence and the organization and proliferation, from around the turn of the century, of lower-caste movements and caste associations.

Bengal is not generally associated with the kind of caste politics that is most relevant for our present argument: it is all the more significant, therefore, to recall that a fairly large number of lower-caste movements developed even in Bengal around this time, particularly among the Mahishyas, the Namashudras, and the Rajbansis. A rough indicator of the extent of transformation is provided by the India Office Library classified catalogs of printed Bengali tracts. Only 24 entries appear under the heading *"Castes and Tribes,"* before 1905; by contrast, 140 titles appear for the period 1905-20.

The role here of British divide-and-rule and classificatory (specifically, census) strategies has been explored often enough: one might mention in particular the efforts of Risley and Gait as census commissioners to fix *jati* hierarchies and even determine whether or not the lower castes could be considered Hindus at all. The more important question, however, concerns the widely divergent ways in which incipient subordinate-caste movements and high-caste advocates of Hindu unity responded to such colonial moves and discourses. What was frankly accepted as a great opportunity by low-caste movements was a threat to high castes, almost on a par at times in some regions with threats posed by what was termed "Muslim separatism."

One consequence of the increasing presence of lower-caste groups in political life and as members of the vernacular reading public was that frank assertions of adhikari-bheda started becoming less common in the Bengali texts. The Kali Yuga theme, too, seems to have declined, and it is interesting that in one of the last farces that I have come across built around that motif, published in the early 1920s, caste mobility had become the major theme. The adhikari-bheda argument for Hindu unity, if used at all, is now increasingly given an abstract, philosophical color, detached from blunt avowals of caste (and gender) inequality.

One notices this ratification already in Vivekananda, and again, some thirty years later, in Radhakrishnan: both were engaged in projecting attractive and impressive images of Hindu unity before external audiences. In an argument, which to

Vivekananda's disciple Nivedita marked the transition from the "religious ideas of the Hindus" to "Hinduism", Vivekananda - at Chicago, in 1893 - located fundamental Hindu unity in a hierarchy apexed by Vedanta that pertained to philosophy rather than to ritual, belief, or social difference. In his Oxford lectures, *The Hindu View of Life*, in 1926, Radhakrishnan similarly assumed Hinduism to be unified by an "absolute.... Vedanta standard" that has been able to incorporate differences as "expressions of one and the same force at different levels".

Adhikari-bheda, alternatively, could be displaced by a new image of upper-caste leadership, formulated in terms of paternalist philanthropy and Sanskritizing reform that would uplift or purify the lower castes, an agenda that was now coming to be recognized as indispensable for building Hindu or national unity. Already in Vivekananda, passionate denunciations of caste oppression were combined with fear of Christian and Muslim proselytization, and emerging anti-Brahman movements of the south were criticized for being in too much of a hurry and encouraging "fighting among the castes".

The recent research of Pradip Kumar Datta has established the centrality in the development of this paternalist "reform for Hindu unity" argument of U. N. Mukherji, "the influence of whose *Hindus: A Dying Race* (1909) provides a convenient casestudy of the importance of such hegemonizing strategies ... as well as of their crucial limits". Mukherji interpreted some Bengal census data as indicating an inexorable decline in Hindu numbers relative to Muslims, attributed it to the wretched conditions of the lower castes as contrasted to the supposedly more virile, energetic, united, and prosperous Muslim peasants, and urged paternalistic upliftment at Brahmanic initiative as means to the end of Hindu survival, unity, and rejuvenation.

In a slightly later pamphlet, Mukherji posed as the key problem the question of "authority" in Hindu society: the upper castes could legitimize their ebbing authority only through initiating or helping processes of orderly social readjustment. Mukherji's pamphlet, which praised a movement of Malis in East Bengal to obtain with some support from upper-caste gentry the services of the slightly superior barber caste, contained a revealing extract from the Calcutta vernacular newspaper *Hitavadi. The Malis were praised for being devoted servants of high-caste gentlefolk (bhadralok), and the newspaper urged the latter to reciprocate such devotion on the interesting* analogy of Yudhishthira in the *Mahabharata*, who refused to enter heaven without his faithful dog.

Mukherji's influence is eminently visible in the pamphlets and activities of Digindranarayan Bhattacharji, who wrote copiously against the evils of caste, composed many histories of subordinate jatis, tried to spread high-caste customs among upwardly mobile Shudras, and was hailed in his lifetime by a lower-caste activist as comparable to Chaitanya, the Buddha, and Muhammad. Bhattacharji's *Jatibheda* carried an introduction by U. N. Mukherji and quoted extensively from his *Hindus: A Dying Race*.

Yet it also borrowed anticaste arguments from the identically titled 1884 Brahmo Samaj tract of Sibnath Shastri and in some passages went very much further than Mukherji in attacking caste oppression and its justifications in ancient texts like the *Manusmriti*. Interestingly, Bhattacharji's *Jatibheda* contains also a direct repudiation of adhikari-bheda: God has given "the same powers [*saman Shakti*] to all human beings, just as he has made the same sun for Brahman and *Chandal* [untouchable]". The theme of Hindu unity against external, primarily Muslim threat, central for Mukherji's *Dying Race*, is occasionally mentioned but has become a subsidiary motif in Bhattacharji.

Its further marginalization and, indeed, implicit rejection become clearer in tracts connected directly with the Namashudra movement, which from 1905 to 1912 distanced itself from the bhadralokdominated Swadeshi agitation against the partition of Bengal. We may take as examples two pamphlets, published within a month of each other, in 1911, but somewhat different in aims and style of argument. *Namashudradwijatattva* deploys historical arguments to establish claims to high-caste status, while at the same time making more radical attacks on caste oppression: untouchability, for instance, is contrasted to the care lavished by the bhadralok on their dogs.

Namshudra-Gyana bhandar adopts a milder tone and urges self-improvement efforts in education and agriculture. What the two tracts have in common, however, is a firm distancing from all forms of bhadralok politics, expressed at times through loyalist effusions to British rule. If such were the travails of unificatory projects in Bengal, the problems must have been far more acute in regions like Maharashtra and many parts of the south, where many lower-caste and dalit movements explicitly rejected Sanskritizing claims to higher status in the varna hierarchy and developed alternative versions of subcontinental history in which upper-caste Aryans figured as alien conquerors, neatly inverting both nationalist and Hindutva arguments of territoriality or pitribhumi.

Maharashtra appears particularly relevant in this context, as the land of low-caste political leaders Jyotirao Phule and B. R. Ambedkar - as well as RSS founding fathers V. D. Savarkar, K. B. Hedgewar, and M. S. Golwalkar. The crystallization of the ideology and organization of Hindutva in the mid-1920s in Maharashtra, despite the relatively weak presence in that region of the supposed Muslim threat, which was its overt justification, may become easier to explain through such juxtaposition. Nagpur, the birthplace of the RSS in 1925, had also been the site of the All India Depressed Classes Conference, in May 1920, when Ambedkar began wresting the leadership of dalits from more moderate groups associated with Vithal Ramji Shinde's efforts at reform from above under high-caste initiative.

And the RSS image of its own origins as embodied, for instance, in the official biography of its founder, K. B. Hedgewar, locates lowercaste assertion on par with the Muslim threat as the twin dangers that lay behind Hedgewar's initiative: "Conflicts between various communities had started. Brahman-Non-Brahman conflict was nakedly on view". U. N. Mukherji's emphasis on the need for lower-caste upliftment had played a significant role in the turn toward aggressive Hindutva in the early 1920s. Shraddhanand, who from 1923 had made removal of untouchability and Sanskritization through shuddhi the major planks in his drive for Hindu organization (*sangathan*) with an openly anti-Muslim thrust, acknowledged his debt to Mukherji through the title of his last tract: *Hindu Sangathan: Saviour of the Dying Race* (1925).

Savarkar, too, acquired something of a reputation as a social reformer by his support for moves to bestow the sacred thread and open temples to low castes. But the limits of such reformism were once again revealed when Savarkar advised Mahars to stick to their traditional occupations as village menials, against which they had started agitating under Ambedkar's leadership. Much more significant, however, is the silence about both lower-caste movements and reform efforts in Savarkar's crucial *Hindutva* text. This, as well as the whole the subsequent organizational practice of the RSS, developed yet another strategy for dealing with caste difference, distinct from both aggressive assertions of hierarchy and efforts at controlled paternalistic reform.

Savarkar's definition of the Hindu solely in terms of the *pitribhumi* = *punyabhumi* equation made caste differences and differences of ritual and belief among Hindus irrelevant: what mattered was not content or status, but authentic indigenous origin in *Bharatvarsha* (classical India). Caste (and gender) inequality became implicitly unimportant and could be more or less left alone, except when they specifically hindered Hindu unity and mobilization. Difference, in fact, could be celebrated as so many flowers making up the single garland of Hinduism, which was how K. S. Sudarshan, senior official of the RSS, eloquently described it in a recent interview. A space remained even for reassertions of adhikari-bheda, since that, presumably, would be as indigenous and authentic as anything else.

"Diversities in the path of devotion did not mean division in society," argued Golwalkar, in an essay that went on to justify Varna hierarchy. "Special concessions to scheduled castes and tribes [i.e., affirmative action], on the other hand inculcated a separatist consciousness". The central unificatory thrust of Hindutva ideology made autonomous lower-caste assertions appear inevitably divisive. This is made fairly obvious, for instance, by the notes kept by an RSS member attending an officer's training camp, which have been reprinted in a generally sympathetic history of the organization: "In the last thousand years, the bonds that linked society were broken. This led to selfish caste mentality that divided society. . . . The RSS was organised to prevent the further disintegration of Hindu society".

Another passage in these lecture notes predictably asserted that "NonHindus must be assimilated to the Hindu way of life." A construction of Hindu unity that evaded rather than sought to reform or even significantly ameliorate hierarchy needs for its sustenance the notion of the Muslim as an ever-present, existential threat, actualized and renewed, furthermore, in recurrent communal riots. (An identical logic has operated in the production and reproduction of Muslim communalism, with similar consequences in terms of subordinated groups, particularly women; the only difference, in postindependence India, has been its relative weakness and incapacity for influencing state policies and administration).

The theme of medieval Muslim tyranny - elaborated in numerous late-nineteenthcentury literary texts, like the historical novels of Bankim Chandra Chattopadhyay - was given new immediacy in the 1920s, and linked up, through the trope of the "dying Hindu" with interrelated counterimages of the Muslim as ever proliferating, sexually prolific, and lusting after Hindu women. Such assumptions have entered deep into middle-class Hindu common sense in many parts of the country, helping to constitute attitudes of approval or compliance about communal violence among many who would never actively participate in riots themselves.

Communalism here veers close to everyday racism, with the Muslim - like the black or colored immigrant - felt to be a biological danger, a threat simply by being born, giving birth - even dying. A highly respectable gentleman of South Delhi told a group of us investigating the Nizamuddin riot of 1990 that every time a Muslim died, a bit of Mother India's soil was lost through his grave, while the self-effacing Hindu is cremated and does not waste space.

But how different, it will be asked, was Indian nationalism in its handling of difference, and specifically of lower-caste assertions? Surely all nationalisms, with their projects of constructing modern nation-states, inevitably homogenize and repress internal differences. So is Hindutva in this respect no more than a particularly aggressive and crude variant of a far more general trend? The sincerity of Gandhi's indictment of untouchability is unquestionable, but his defense of a supposedly original and pure *varnasrama* (duties appropriate for every status in society) against later distortions was unacceptable to E. V. Ramaswamy Naicker, Ambedkar, and many other lower-caste and dalit activists.

The specific programs of harijan welfare and upliftment - the opening of wells and temples to them, and village-level constructive work - as well as the term *harijan* (god's children) itself, can be rejected as mere paternalism. They were perhaps not all that different from the projects of high-caste reform from above that we have already considered in brief, and that at times encountered similar difficulties. And the record of the non-Gandhian left is at first sight even more dismal, whether Nehruvian, Communist, or Socialist - with the exception of R. M. Lohia's movement.

The treatment of caste oppression as epiphenomenal to more basic questions of class struggle might even appear to a really harsh critic as not all that different from Hindutva subordination of the same issue to the higher requirements of Hindu unity. A closer look, however, would indicate some significant differences and make assessments of the kind I have just outlined unfair.

Crystallized Hindutva, since the mid-1920s, has on the whole kept away from even paternalistic caste reform, preferring the Savarkar argument of irrelevance; and it has worked, as the general RSS practice indicates, overwhelmingly in urban or small-town upper-caste milieus. This did change significantly, through VHP activity in the main, during the height of the Ram janmabhoomi campaign - but then there can be little doubt that it was the hysteria sparked off by V. P. Singh's decision to implement, after years of delay, the Mandal Commission recommendations that enhanced greatly the appeal of Hindutva among high-caste groups.

The provincial elections indicate the instability, at best, of gains among lower-castes by utilizing in vastly modified form the appeal of *Rama bhakti*. Signs of internal tensions and oscillations still beset Hindutva's relationships with lowercastes. The electoral reverses of late-1993 immediately produced a flurry of gestures directed toward regaining the support of subordinate groups, balanced soon after by an aggressive speech by the new RSS chief Rajendra Singh at a Delhi rally hailing the special role of the Brahman, warrior, and trader castes in safeguarding the entire country.

The Sangh Parivar nowadays makes occasional efforts at appropriating the memory of Ambedkar through stray quotations, but Ambedkar's call for the "annihilation of caste" through a direct onslaught on Hindu sacred texts and eventually mass conversion of dalits to Buddhism remain logically irreconciable with Hindutva ideology. Ambedkar, way back in 1936, pinpointed this contradiction through his polemical assertion that Hindu society is "really a myth" because "a caste has no feeling that it is affiliated to other castes except when there is a Hindu-Muslim riot".

Mainstream nationalism, in (partial) contrast and mainly at Gandhi's insistence, refused to consider caste oppression and particularly untouchability to be unimportant or irrelevant, thus moving away to some extent from the earlier Congress separation of political from social matters, which Tilak had crystallized by expelling the Social Conference from the venue of the Congress session in 1895.

Despite many bitter conflicts, a basis for dialogue and compromise with lower-caste and dalit movements therefore remained. In the 1930s, the Maharashtra Congress was able to absorb the bulk of the Non-Brahman Satyashodhak activists, and it is surely significant that the murder of Gandhi by a Maharashtrian Brahman was followed by widespread anti-Brahman riots in that region Gandhi and Ambedkar could, after all, agree in the end to the 1932 Poona Pact, which was bitterly denounced by the more aggressive orthodox Hindu elements inside and outside the Congress.

Ambedkar had a seminal role in drawing up the Indian constitution, as well as in preparing the earlier drafts of the Hindu Codec bill, and the postindependence Congress enjoyed a substantial harijan electoral base that has been eroded only in recent years. As for the left, it undoubtedly paid a high price in many regions for its long underestimation of caste as a possible form of subordinate assertion. But it would be quite unhistorical to deny the substantial gains achieved, in terms of human dignity and not just economic advantages, by lower-caste and dalit groups in other areas and times under leftist leadership and through exploring the mobilizing capacities of class. Caste identity, after all, is not a natural, given, unchanging, or hermetically sealed entity, any more than class.

It may be appropriate to end, as I began, with a consideration of historiographical silencing. Ambedkar's *Annihilation of Caste* includes a powerful section giving specific examples of caste oppression between 1928 and 1935, which he had taken from contemporary newspapers. Such incidents keep recurring even after nearly five decades of independence and, along with violence against women, probably on an ascending scale. Yet they find little or no place in most standards works on modern Indian history.

At a different, but not unrelated level, a large number of leading Indian intellectuals and social scientists denounced the extension of reservations to backward castes attempted by V. P. Singh in 1990 as "pandering to casteism." They included several scholars who had spent a lifetime writing in fairly sympathetic terms about Sanskritization: surely the kind of caste movement that is the most casteists, in the sense of encouraging narrow sectional loyalties through the quest for mere positional mobility on behalf of a caste group (*jati*), while maintaining and even strengthening the basic hierarchical order. Movements claiming to represent Other Backward Castes (OBCs) or dalits, in contrast, have to try to build new, wider, horizontal solidarities, overcoming narrow caste boundaries.

Fairly often, as notably under Phule, Ramaswamy Naicker, or Ambedkar, they have directly attacked caste. There are very obvious links between such silencing and the priorities of mainstream nationalist (or Hindu communalist) history writing that center around the building and maintenance of the nation-state. Less obvious, and therefore more worrying, are some recent tendencies that seem to be reproducing that silence precisely through what is accepted by many as the most radical and chic critique of all such nation-state projects.

The burden of this critique is no longer class or even elite domination, but the alleged root of the modern or postcolonial nation-state in Western, Enlightenment rationalism, successfully imposed on the Third World by colonial cultural domination. The logical corollary of this total concentra- tion on the critique of colonial discourse is that only movements or aspects of life demonstrably free of such Western or rationalist taint can be given the status of authentic, properly indigenous, protest, resistance, and culture. It then becomes difficult to study with any marked sympathy not only the history of the traditional Marxist left, but also figures like Phule or Ambedkar or the many movements that have tried to extend the rights of lower castes and women by selectively appropriating elements from Western discourses and even on occasion using colonial state policies as resources.

The fairly deafening silence of the bulk of *Subaltern Studies* historiography in these areas may be taken as symptomatic. Within such a framework, again, a critique of Hindutva can only take the form of presenting it as a Western or modern distortion of a basically pure and problem-free precolonial Hindu world. The first part of this proposition may be acceptable; the second is not.

The most lucid statement of these positions was made a decade ago by Ashis Nandy, in his admirably clear declaration of intent at the beginning of *Intimate Enemy*: "to justify and defend the innocence which confronted modern Western colonialism." The "innocence" here involves a deeply disturbing elision of centuries of caste, gender, and class oppression. Arguments like these threaten to leave us today with no language adequate for analyzing many of the most basic issues of contemporary Indian society and history.

5

Images, Mobilization, and Communalism

It is meant to be heuristic rather than comprehensive, providing basic information about Indian media and research materials. It is also far from conclusive: totalizing explanations of media effects are impossible to construct because of the complex ways in which media both shape and are shaped by larger social, political, and cultural structures. Though various methodologies can provide useful insights, any research on media and social outcomes is necessarily partial and tentative. Of many possible approaches, this chapter privileges an institutional, historical approach: How did various media genres develop in India? How did legislative, administrative, technological, and market forces combine to shape both message and audience?

And what are the connections between the evolution of these genres and expressions of communal violence? Through this approach, and using the destruction of the Babri Masjid and resultant riot-related deaths as a focal point, we will see that various genres lent themselves to very differing roles in expressions of communal sentiment. Some - such as cinema - largely avoided communalization, while others - particularly the Hindi press - were easily appropriated for communal ends.

One media genre in particular - television - emerges as most crucial in this analysis. Briefly, a confluence of technological, legal, and administrative developments created a window in the late 1980s - after unprecedented infrastructural investments in the mid-eighties and before the advent of transnational satellite television in the early nineties - during which the government of India held a monopoly over a vast television broadcasting system.

Because of this novel, hegemonic position, *Doordarshan* (Indian state television) programming decisions took on extraordinary salience. Since the late eighties, many, often well-founded, charges have been made that other forms of media were politically biased or promoted communal tension. However, these charges implicated a limited number of media professionals who stood accused of perpetrating communal violence. Such charges against *Doordarshan*, however, precisely because it was under centralized national control, have highlighted questions about the very legitimacy of the government's secular and democratic credentials.

SPECIFICITY, LANGUAGE, AND CAUSALITY

Before more details, let's take three brief methodological detours - on specificity, language, and causality - to help situate this discussion for those who are new to the study of media in India. First, examples in this chapter were chosen specifically for their communal content and do not comprise a representative sample of all Indian media messages.

Every day in India, thousands of newspapers, hours of television programming, a thriving cinema industry, video and magazine production, and a host of other media forms generate entertainment, advertising, education, and political persuasion. In the vast majority of these productions, communal issues simply do not arise or are studiously avoided.

Furthermore, the focus of this chapter on communalism in Indian media in no way implies either that Indian media messages are subject to some natural gravitational pull toward communal uses, or that there is something peculiarly Indian about the use of media for divisive ethnic, religious, or racial purposes. As David Ludden (1994) points out, cultural chauvinists are mobilizing their troops not only in South Asia, but also in Russia, Eastern Europe, and elsewhere. Particularly after the 1995 bombing of a federal office building in Oklahoma City, it is crucial to note that the United States is no more immune than other areas to the harnessing of mass communications technologies for violent parochial messages.

Second, language in India is not simply a neutral means of conveying political messages, but is itself a contentious political issue. While this issue is much too complex to be detailed in this chapter, two basic issues must be understood: Hindi is not universally used throughout India; and there is an important difference between commonly spoken Hindi, or Hindustani, and what has come to be known as "*Doordarshan Hindi*," a stylistically *Sanskritized* form of the language. While Hindi in the *Devanagari* script is constitutionally the official language of India (according to Article 343), some dialect of Hindi is the mother tongue of at most a third of the Indian population.

Furthermore, Article 351 directs the union government to promote the spread of Hindi, drawing for its vocabulary "primarily on Sanskrit and secondarily on other languages."Efforts to spread Hindi to non-Hindi-speaking areas, particularly through primary education, have caused considerable political unrest. Similarly, the use of Hindi on national television programming has rendered *Doordarshan* a focal point for regional linguistic discontent. Also, because television is controlled by the Centre (the national government based in New Delhi), charges that *Doordarshan's* use of Hindi constitutes cultural imperialism radiating from Delhi bring into question the legitimacy of federal rule in a way that is not seen, for instance, with respect to more market-driven Hindi cinema production.

The heavily *Sanskritized Hindi* used by *Doordarshan*, particularly for news broadcasts, renders television liable to charges of communalism as well. The communalization of Hindustani - by at least the minimal definition of a differentiation of linguistic and cultural markers that divide Hindu and Muslim Indians hierarchically - predates the advent of electronic media. It was institutionalized in radio shortly after independence. Under Sardar Vallabhai Patel, India's first Minister of Information and Broadcasting, and his successor B. V. Keskar, All India Radio promoted *Sanskritized* vocabulary over *Urdu* forms in spoken language and devalued Muslim musical contributions as well.

The use of Sanskritized Hindi - a type of language easily perceived as not only Hindi, but also as Hindu -further institutionalized this division. Clearly, then, language can be used as a method for lending communal interpretations to messages that otherwise carry no communal content. In other words, analyzing Indian media requires examining not only what is said, but also the language used to say it. While this may seem obvious, it has profound implications for media research.

One of the most highly developed methodologies in communications research is content analysis. Content analyses that consider only content, however, without taking into account the language used to convey that content and the implications of that language in the social context of its deployment miss by design the media messages - including communal messages - that are carried by the choice of language used. And because the codified data created by content analysts are readily quantified, it is easy for researchers who study content alone to generate seemingly scientific statistical data that can be claimed to prove media messages are free of communal implications.

This raises the third methodological issue, concerning causality. It is virtually impossible to prove causality in media studies. From a positivist social science perspective, adequate data simply do not exist. From more nuanced theoretical perspectives that are skeptical about empiricism, no amount of data would be conclusive. Because of this, wildly differing interpretations of the connections between media and communalism have been presented by a variety of analysts, ranging from those who posit (but cannot prove) that media images promote communal violence to those who argue that there is no connection whatsoever between media and communal antagonism.

The very insolubility of the causality puzzle connecting mass media images and political mobilization has rendered mass media a resilient scapegoat. In the vicious communal polarizations of the last decade, concerned writers have sought to pinpoint causes and isolate feasible solutions, and the media have come to be counted as culpable in many accounts of the recent conflicts. On the other hand, the absence of correlative data supporting cause-effect hypotheses about the media's role in communalism has also opened terrain for arguments that mass communications do not have measurable social effects, but simply reflect a traditional ethos or national identity (in the cultural variant) or consumer taste (in the market variant).

From this perspective, for example, it can be argued that Rama is a cultural and not religious figure, and that Doordarshan's serialization of the *Ramayana* is therefore devoid of religious - and thus communal - connotations. Such perspectives are at best naive, however, particularly given that the state-run communications systems are predicated on inculcation of a national identity; and often, on closer examination, such arguments prove to be self-serving normative assertions regarding society, culture, and nation. As Richard Fox notes below, one popular but misguided way to discuss communalism is to see it as "an excrescence of Indian tradition, an atavism or primitivism." With respect to mass media, though, we must ask what these arguments teach us, what is hidden?

These smoke screens mask agency, funding, and the content of media imagery by neglecting the mobilization of both communications hardware and media imagery. Overly deterministic cause-effect models, rigid content analyses, and broad assertions differentiating realms called "culture" and "religion" all neglect what is coming to be called the study of "media ecology," which concentrates on the way media imagery shapes viewers' values and conceptions of society.

TELEVISION AND COMMUNALISM

The relationship between media and communalism with the most farreaching political implications is the connection between television programming and communal mobilization. This is because, even though no explicit cause-effect linkage between television imagery and violence can be clearly demonstrated, the broadcast of programming widely perceived as having communal undertones has highlighted and focused criticism on the legitimacy of the government's secular stance.

The core of these accusations concerns the serialization on state-controlled television of two Hindu epics, the *Mahabharata* and *Ramayana*. Though, communal violence and civic unrest were certainly not an intended goal of these programming decisions, the broadcast of the *Ramayana*, in particular, inadvertently promoted Rama-related imagery that was easily appropriated by Hindu nationalist leaders of the Sangh Parivar, especially by L. K. Advani.

Rama existed in India long before television was invented, and Doordarshan was not the first to attempt a hegemonic *Ramayana* narrative. Nonetheless, many scholars have come to the conclusion that the serialization of the *Ramayana* on Doordarshan was fundamental to the project of fundamentalism, creating a shared symbolic lexicon around which political forces could mobilize communal praxis. Perhaps the greatest evidence of the effects of the serialization of the epics has come from scholars in the humanities. One scholar, for example, noted that when people were asked about Ayodhya in studies done before the *Ramayana* broadcast, they would answer that Ayodhya is the birthplace of Rama, but they would leave its location vague.

Maybe Ayodhya is a mythological place, maybe it exists wherever God exists; Ayodhya could be in one's own backyard, or at the local temple. After Doordarshan's *Ramayana* and contemporary BJP mobilizations, however, people responded to questions about Ayodhya by defining it precisely as a town in Uttar Pradesh (V. Narayana Rao, personal communication). In 1991, Anuradha Kapur analyzed the "new," post-Doordarshan, iconography of Rama in popular posters, in which Rama as a militant warrior, poised to use his bow, is depicted more often than other iconographic possibilities. She wrote:

> The transformation of the Ram image from that of a serene, omnipresent, eternally forgiving God to that of an angry, punishing one, armed with numerous weapons, wearing armour and even shoes, is truly remarkable. Where does this new Ram, laden with all manner of martial gear, come from? He appears to come from television epics - Ramanand Sagar's *"Ramayana"* and B. R. Chopra's *"Mahabharata."* The *"Mahabharata,"* especially, feeds upon the escalating notions of a militaristic and virile Hinduism.

Barbara Stoler Miller devoted much of her 1991 presidential address to the Association for Asian Studies to a discussion of the serialization of the epics, noting that "it is the religious intensity, linked with politicized communal feelings, that has made the Ayodhya situation so compelling. The way militant Hindus have structured the narrative of Ayodhya's sacred history and bent the epic universe to their definition of Indian national identity is a striking example of how vulnerable the past is to the passions of the moment".

How did this state-sponsored depiction of Rama come to be? An answer requires an examination of the history of Doordarshan. Television in India began, as had radio, through the urging of Western companies seeking markets in India. It took many years from the first broadcast in 1959, however, for television to develop into a mass market media. Stations outside India's capital city were not set up until the early 1970s, and significant expansion of television did not occur until the 1980s. This hesitancy to expand, based on the high cost of television as compared to radio, was overcome by linking television and national development.

The 1966 Chanda Committee report on radio and television argued that difficulties in implementation of India's five-year plans could be ameliorated by using electronic media to promote understanding of and compliance with planning. Simultaneously, Vikram Sarabhai, in one of his initiatives to promote India's space program, argued that television could be used to "leapfrog" India into sustained economic development. This argument, combined with a commitment to rural development, culminated in the Satellite Instructional Television Experiment (SITE) of 1975-76. This experiment in rural development, however, did not prove to be the basis for the subsequent evolution of television.

The major impetus for the growth of Doordarshan was a political decision made after the phenomenally popular telecast of the Ninth Asian Games in 1982, during which color television was introduced in India. Realizing the enormous potential influence of television, Prime Minister Indira Gandhi's government decided to embark on a major expansion of television in time for the 1985 elections. S. S. Gill, who had overseen the creation of stadia and other infrastructure for the Asian Games, was appointed Secretary of the Ministry of Information and Broadcasting. Under his guidance, the number of transmitters rose from 39 to 140, increasing potential coverage from 23 per cent to 70 per cent of the population.

Transmitters were produced with indigenous technology, massive schemes were launched to train engineers, and import laws were liberalized to allow the production of more television sets. Commercially sponsored serials were introduced, partially became Doordarshan was simply unable to produce the amount of programming that would be required as broadcast time increased, and also became it was felt that sponsored programming would be more lively and popular, building the audience necessary for effective political communication. This new programming included commissioned serialization of the epics.

These initiatives led to a spectacular increase in the percentage of the population that could receive Doordarshan signals. The rapid pace of expansion from 1983 to 1985 slowed thereafter, mainly became further increases became more difficult, requiring low power transmitters to be installed in geographically remote areas. Current estimates are that Doordarshan signals are available to 83 per cent of the population; the percentage is this low only became of difficulties in reaching very remote and mountainous regions.

In 1983, the comparable figure was 26 per cent. In 1983, there were less than three million television sets in the country; in 1992, there were nearly thirty-five million. Mrs. Gandhi did not live to reap the benefits of her investment in television, and the sympathy vote for Rajiv Gandhi after her assassination overwhelmed the salience of television in the election process. Nonetheless, she had opened the door to a nexus linking state control of television for electoral ends with commercial pursuit of profit through advertising.

This decision was no doubt facilitated by her knowledge that eroding support for Congress in the early 1980s would require increasingly persuasive forms of electioneering, since more forceful measures - particularly blatant press censorship - had been largely delegitimated by her imposition of emergency rule. Furthermore, legislative precedent had rendered television a tool easily appropriated by the incumbent party. Technological innovations are seldom anticipated through the creation of new administrative and legal infrastructures to govern them. Instead Indian television evolved within a legal structure whose genealogy can be traced to the 1885 Telegraph Act under British colonial rule.

The act stated that "the Central Government shall have the exclusive privilege of establishing, maintaining and working telegraphs." "Telegraph" was defined to include virtually any communications technology, and so in the 1920s, radio also came under direct governmental control. An initial attempt to create an independent broadcasting corporation failed, in part because licensing fees allowable within colonial legal structures were inadequate. Although initially reluctant, the state agreed to protect radio-related capital by settling radio under the protective wing of the British Raj.

This hegemonic role of the state in broadcasting was embedded in the 1935 Government of India Act, which reserved broadcasting for the Centre. It also stated that the Centre should not unreasonably prevent provincial governments from creating transmitters. After independence, the 1953 constitution incorporated many features of the 1935 act, including the reserving of broadcasting for the Centre. The constitution did not, however, include even the minimal provision for decentralized, provincial control of broadcasting found in the 1935 act. The legal basis for centralized control of broadcasting thus continued, and in fact was strengthened, across the 1947 watershed of Indian independence.

At independence, Prime Minister Jawaharlal Nehru did argue that broadcasting should be made autonomous from direct governmental control, but he also maintained that this was secondary to more pressing issues of political stability and sovereignty. Calls for media autonomy accompanied by the political inability to implement change have since become a defining feature of the administration of mass media in India. The two most coherent policy initiatives toward media autonomy from central government control - the 1978 Akash Bharati report (by the Janata government) and the 1990 Prasar Bharati Bill (by the National Front government) -both succumbed to political paralysis.

To this day, no political initiative has successfully altered the administrative and legal infrastructure governing Indian electronic media that was created under colonial rule. Furthermore, in the late 1980s, state-controlled television faced no competition. Before transnational satellite television became available in India in the 1990s, Congress was free to televise its conception of the Indian nation. The crosscutting tensions of state centralization, development policies, and commercial sponsorship resulted in an array of programming that conflated national development goals and popular cultural traditions.

Increasingly through the 1980s, television was used as a tool for cultural engineering and electoral gains through creation of an "Indian" national character closely identified with the ruling party. Commercial interests had no reason to counter the attempt to create an Indian market - defined by the state and nationalized cultural forms - provided that laborious historical and political documentaries did not supplant more popular programming on TV. The Doordarshan epics are examples of an array of programs that arose from the triadic nexus of a growing middle-class, increasing commercial advertising, and the use of television as an election strategy.

What was depicted inside the public sphere created by Doordarshan, therefore, included a fuzzy conflation of state authority, Hindu legitimacy, Hindi supremacy, cinema tunes (*filmi geet*), and commercial promotions. Identifying what is absent from or marginal to this television public sphere is more difficult, but protests against specific Doordarshan presentations do indicate some boundaries. For example, *Tipu Sultan* - a story about an eighteenth-century Indian Muslim ruler who tormented British armies for decades before being conquered - did not fit easily into Doordarshan's nationalist paradigm, because it depicted the Muslim, Tipu, as being modern and progressive, and it was broadcast on Doordarshan only after lengthy arbitration.

The result of the court battle was that a disclaimer was aired before each episode to say that the story was fiction, not history, thus marginalizing *Tipu Sultan* as a historical figure and contributing to a nationalist history in which Muslims somehow become non-Indian. Other struggles over the electronic media have spilled beyond institutional confines into violent confrontations by some anti-Centre groups, in which Doordarshan and All India Radio personnel and infrastructure have been the target of terrorist actions. This has occurred when antisecessionist programming - typically dramatic presentations in Hindi, set in a timeless Punjabi or Kashmiri village, depicting primordial communal harmony -has been unaccompanied by actual decentralization of control over programming policies.

Broadcasting language policies have become a focal point for regional demands; and violent assaults on and assassination of Doordarshan personnel continue today. Serialization of the *Ramayana* was not the only Doordarshan attempt to create a centerpiece for national culture that would be comforting to the Indian, mainly Hindu, middle classes. As Romila Thapar notes, one of the functions of nationalist depictions is to locate cultures, usually by defining a national culture that selects some aspects of history and symbolism, but sidelines others. The television serial *Chanakya*, set in the Mauryan Empire and aired on Doordarshan in 1991, is a good case in point.

This empire, during the fourth to second centuries B.C., consolidated its control over more of the subcontinent than any other force until the British Raj. Chandragupta Maurya, who became emperor in 321 B.C., first gained control of the Ganges River basin, then moved northwest into a power vacuum created by the departure of Alexander the Great, and finally accepted the trans-Indus territories of the Greek Seleucid dynasty after a battle in 303 B.C. The empire reached its greatest extent when Chandragupta's grandson, Ashoka, conquered Kalinga, in present-day Orissa; in 260 B.C. Ashoka erected numerous stone edicts throughout the extent of his empire.

The existence of Ashokan edicts as landmarks in many Indian cities renders Ashoka a commonly, evoked name in many contemporary and popular histories. But Doordarshan's serialized drama about the Mauryas did not focus on Ashoka, who converted to Buddhism, but instead depicted his Brahman adviser Chanakya as hero of the Mauryan Empire. Numerous additional examples could be presented of the ways in which mass media have constructed images that have been or could have been appropriated for communal ends, but I do not mean to imply that these images were consciously constructed to promote communal strife. S. S. Gill felt it necessary to defend his decision to promote serialization of the epics as examples of Indian culture, rather than Hindu religion, through an editorial in the *Indian Express*.

In an interview in 1990, he also expressed his view that the decision to serialize the epics was based on their encapsulation of pan-Indian, and indeed universal, values. With chagrin, he noted that "these idiots gave it a religious gloss! If I'd been there, I'd never have let them do this! *Ramayana* and *Mahabharata* are not religious epics!" No doubt L. K. Advani, probably the most media-savvy figure in Indian politics, would also argue for the universal cultural significance of the *Ramayana*. It is certainly clear that he was able to capitalize on the availability of Rama imagery as a tool for communal mobilization. What is less clear is what would happen if the BJP were to gain control of Indian television.

While Advani argued vociferously for media autonomy from government control during the 1989 elections, similar arguments made during that campaign have gone by the wayside. For example, in a 1989 interview with me, he downplayed the Sangh Parivar's emphasis on Hindi as the national language, emphasizing the need for linguistic flexibility for effective communication. Nonetheless, in early 1995, after winning control of the government of Delhi in local elections, one of the BJP's first actions was to declare Hindi to be Delhi's official language.

Similar discrepancies can be found between the BJP's 1989 free-market sloganeering and current Sangh Parivar efforts to undermine an agreement for the Enron Corporation to invest in a power plant in *Maharashtra*. This economic nationalist stance has now been institutionalized through the formation of the *Swadesh Jagram Manch* (SJM), The Forum for National Awakening, a wing of the RSS that is devoted to driving multinationals out of India.

THE PRINT MEDIA AND CINEMA

Connections between communal mobilization and the print media do not carry the same ominous political implications as do connections between television and communal violence, mainly because communalist messages in the press do not automatically call into question the state's secularism. While it is not difficult to uncover instances of political interference with the press, the roots of the robust and multilingual print media are found in the struggle against colonialism, providing the press with the lingering aura of an oppositional, civil, and fundamentally legitimate media. Direct state intervention in the print media is not easily sustained and is hotly contested in political discourse.

Nonetheless, the communalization of print media during and after the Ayodhya conflict had severe effects on India's social fabric, civic discourse, and individual lives. When Mohandas Gandhi mobilized nationalist opposition to British rule by leading the Salt March in 1930 to protest the colonial salt tax, the effectiveness of this symbolic statement was enhanced because "the press reported the daily progress" of the march. The press served a similar role in Hindu fundamentalist mobilizations of the last five years - it is perhaps not coincidental that Advani likens his *rath yatras* to the Salt March.

And, at a rally organized by the SJM in Delhi in August 1995, former BJP president M. M. Joshi launched an economic nationalist campaign by addressing demonstrators arrayed around a statue of Gandhi on the Salt March. It is now widely accepted that the Hindi press in particular was crucial in propelling the: transition from Hindu symbolism to communal violence. The Press Council of India conducted an investigation of the role of the Hindi press during the late 1990 communal crisis. Its resolution states:

There is little doubt that some influential sections of the Hindi Press in U.P. and Bihar were guilty of gross irresponsibility and impropriety, offending the canons of journalistic ethics in promoting mass hysteria on the basis of rumours and speculation, through exaggeration and distortion, all of this proclaimed under screaming, banner headlines. They were guilty, in a few instances, of doctoring pictures (such as drawing prison bars on the photograph of an arrested Mahant), fabricating casualty figures (for example, adding "1" before "15" to make "115" deaths), and incitement of violence and spreading disaffection among members of the armed forces and police, engendering communal hatred.

Journalist N. Ram wrote that, "through its coverage of the OctoberNovember 1990 events in Ayodhya, a considerable part of the press - indeed the overwhelming part of the mass-circulated Hindi press - turned *kar sevak* in response to the crisis. The problem has clearly recurred during the much graver crisis of 1992". N. Ram does not let the English press off the hook entirely; the first half of his article focuses on the way in which journalists reported communal incidents as they occurred, without adequately theorizing them as part of a unified process.

This "episodic framing" as Shanto Iyengar (1991) terms this journalistic style, tends to isolate readers from broader understandings of political structures and processes. Ram implies that English-language journalists similarly succumbed to a myopic view of major transformations. Zoya Hasan and others at Jawaharlal Nehru University in New Delhi have also analyzed the role of the English press in communal mobilizations. Nonetheless, it is clear that the Hindi press was most directly culpable media genre in fomenting communal rioting. In her study of the press, Radhika Ramaseshan wrote,

> The [Hindi] press was directly responsible for causing most of the communal riots that erupted in UP after the masjid was attacked, resulting in a death toll of over a hundred. By carrying out a sustained, feverish campaign highlighting the alleged 'bloodbath' in Ayodhya, caused by police firings on November 2, against the "police repression" of *kar sevaks* lodged in different jails, especially the one in Unnao, and against the pro-Muslim bias of chief minister Mulayam Singh Yadav, this press has achieved three objectives: it has whipped up emotional fervour for the "cause" of the Ram temple even among a large section of disinterested and apolitical Hindus, and as a corollary, completely polarised the Hindus and the Muslims, since the shrine ultimately symbolises Hindu animosity against Muslims. Lastly, it has seriously undermined the moral authority of Mulayam Singh Yadav, who by steadfastly maintaining that he adhered to the letter of law in this dispute, came to represent the voice of moderation and sanity. Although Yadav has reiterated that he will not allow the temple to be constructed on the disputed site, the critical dependence of his government on the support of the Congress (I), which has not only loudly condemned the alleged "atrocities" committed on the *kar sevaks* but has also demanded that the temple be constructed on the

contentious site, the passage of the Vishwa Hindu Parishad (VHP) and its allies towards their ultimate goal - that of breaching the shrine and erecting a temple - has been rendered that much easier.

Charu and Mukul (1991) offer similar assessments in *Print Media and Communalism*, while providing examples of media distortion in the original Hindi, and broadening their scope to important issues outside of Ayodhya, including protests of the Mandal Commission report. In a seminar discussion of her paper in this volume, Zoya Hasan offered one extremely interesting explanation for the communal propensities of the Hindi press. She found that Hindu priests and mahants will pay sometimes up to twelve thousand rupees for the clout that comes with being a stringer for Hindi newspapers, thus gaining access to their audiences.

While space does not permit a full discussion of other resources that are available for the analysis of the print media, interested scholars may want to consult Dhawan (1987) for the history of laws pertaining to the press; JPRS Report (1993) for a compilation of press clippings related to secularism and Hindu nationalism; and Olsen (1994) for an analysis of "Economic and Political Weekly articles" about communal riots.

The cinema, while not devoid of political content, appears to be less implicated in recent communal mobilizations than do television and the print media. This is remarkable in it, and may be related to the paucity of research on recent Indian cinema. Additional research may uncover complex linkages between cinematic imagery and popular conceptions of the state that could have implications for the study of communalism. The avoidance of explicitly communal themes in the commercial cinema may also result from a form of self-censorship on the part of film producers, who must face inspection by the Indian government's Film Censor Board.

As K. Hariharan (1994) argues, while producers engage in numerous battles over specific pronouncements by the Film Censor Board, there is little mobilization to fight the concept of the board, since the board obviates the need to create industrywide mechanisms for selfregulation. More importantly, though, it may be that the market-driven and capital-intensive nature of film production has steered cinema away from communal divisiveness.

If so, further research is called for on the driving forces behind both television and the vernacular print media to ask why these media more than others generated communally incendiary messages. Future researchers will have to examine whether or not cinema continues to be an industry relatively free of communal violence. A foreboding omen of possible future trends occurred in July 1995, when Mani Ratnam, director of the controversial film *Bombay*, was injured in a bomb blast in Madras. *Bombay* explored the love of a Muslim girl and a Hindu boy, and was briefly banned to placate Islamic fundamentalist protestors.

NEW MEDIA FORMS

Technomarket trends, in the context of state-run communication infrastructures that controlled television and radio, stimulated a boom in alternative media, especially audio- and videocassettes, but also including vernacular media. These forms facilitated the expression of two additional and more fundamental trends, which are less easily disentangled: increasing opposition to the Congress Party and Congress Party governments, first at the state levels but increasingly at the Centre; and the rise of the middle classes, in an increasingly consumerist milieu.

Burgeoning new media outside state control allowed the BJP's pragmatic emphasis on communication to thrive; the BJP's dramatic use of public spectacles was disseminated and enhanced as a multimedia extravaganza, including audio- and videocassette tapes promoting Hindutva (Davis, above, and Manuel, below). One video, for example, depicted Rama's "miraculous" 1949 appearance in the Babri Masjid; an excellent discussion of this video and use of clips from it is available in Anand Patwardhan's documentary film *Ram ke Nam* (In the Name of God).

Ironically, the importance of videocassettes to communal mobilization arose in part from government policies. Strict governmental control over television resulted in lackluster entertainment shows and the manipulation of news reports, which became particularly severe before the 1989 elections; this fueled markets for videocassette entertainment, for independent video news programs, like *Newstrack*, and for the VCRs on which to play them.

A 1990 *Economic Times-Pathfinder* poll found that 36 per cent of metropolitan families with monthly incomes of twentyfive hundred rupees or more possessed a videocassette recorder or player and a 1991 National Council of Applied Economic Research poll found that low-income households with up to twenty-five thousand rupees in annual income purchased 33 per cent of all VCRs sold in India. Viewing videocassettes had become a common practice in India and the BJP disseminated its messages by distributing cassettes and providing mobile video viewings from video raths.

The BJP, and especially former Information and Broadcasting Minister L. K. Advani, make sophisticated use of new media technologies. The Sangh Parivar has far surpassed other political groups in media manipulation. The setback suffered by the BJP in the 1993 legislative assembly elections shows that its one-issue message may not be adequate for electoral success, but the mobilization it fostered for the destruction of the Babri Masjid was clearly assisted by calculated use of various media forms, particularly those that are outside of state control.

The proliferation of new communications technologies may allow the forces of *Hindutva* new ways to broadcast their messages. For example, cable television systems have been created throughout urban India in the last few years. Cable operators can transmit programming throughout a neighborhood using either a VCR or air signals. For the 1993 elections, the BJP created a publicity committee to use cable systems as part of a media-based election strategy. Videocassettes of party leaders' speeches were provided to cable operators. The Delhi Pradesh BJP president, O. P. Kohli, noted, "We know our operators. On an average we have one out of every two cable operators operating from a colony that has party leanings and they would be ever obliging to play the tapes for us".

It should be noted that the BJP did win the legislative assembly elections in Delhi, although there is no way to calculate the contribution of their media strategy to their success. The BJP also plans to distribute videos to rural homes that have VCRs and to facilitate public viewings in other areas. In the party's assessment, the most important feature of the cable network is that it reaches sections of society that neither attend public meetings nor read newspapers, particularly women voters and senior citizens. As Amrita Basu (above) notes, the BJP seems to have been particularly successful in mobilizing women; this media strategy may help communal parties build on these gains in the future.

Additional media developments bear examination, though it is again too early to understand their implications. There is a rapid proliferation of new satellite television channels, also to be broadcast through these cable systems. One, for example, was the idea of J. K. Jain, BJP member of the Rajya Sabha, the upper house of Parliament. The project is being launched by Joint American Indian Network (JAIN) Satellite Television, and promoted by Jain Studios.

It will broadcast religious, moral, and spiritual programming. Also difficult to measure is the impact of new communications systems on grass-roots sympathizers rather than official BJP leaders. For example, in mid-1993, a colleague told me of asking the cable operator in a posh Delhi neighborhood to provide a few hours of Pakistani television as one of many offerings. The operator said this was impossible; he had received threats when he had briefly aired Pakistani television in the past. This operator indicated that it is apparently common knowledge that an operator broadcasting Pakistani television would have his cable lines cut by BJP activists.

Technological innovations have allowed electronic communication to be tailored for specific target audiences, and state control of television has provided the fillip to create a market for these technologies. One outcome is that electronic media outside state control, like the print media and notably unlike television, have been able to develop the ability to tailor communication for India's diverse linguistic areas. Activists devoted to using new communications technologies for social empowerment of traditionally disempowered groups herald this capability, and many exciting projects are underway to create development programming.

While these schemes generate much enthusiasm, however, it is also important to note that these new technologies are not inherently liberating; small is not always beautiful. Hierarchies of oppression are at least as easily replicated as they are overcome at more local levels of social organization. Localized programming can be used for myriad ends, and, as with all media forms, political organization and funding skew the outcomes. Two questions arise from this examination of Indian television. First, if we limit our examination solely to the serialization of the epics, it is relatively easy to jump to conclusions about a media-communalism nexus.

Putting the television *Ramayana* in the context of broader programming decisions, however, reduces the sense that the *Ramayana* was an overwhelming presence on the airwaves. It instead becomes the center of a sphere that extends into many peripheries. In the context of Indian federalism, this center-periphery imagery is translated into center-state relations; secessionist movements in Punjab and Kashmir loom very large. We may want to ask if our emphasis on Hindu-Muslim relations, propelled by the brutality of their consequences, have blinded us to broader issues. To what degree was the communalism of the last decade a symptom or by-product of increasing centralization and state control of cultural production and economic distribution?

In other words, if an explanation for recent communal outbreaks could be devised, could this be done without simultaneously explaining secessionist movements? Are these phenomena unrelated, or are they both outcomes of political institutions created in independent India? Second, it does seem clear now that serialization of the *Ramayana* created a symbolic lexicon that aided Hindutva mobilization of communal praxis. However, an examination of the history of Doordarshan also shows that this serial was televised because of an explicitly political decision, and that both this decision and its salience for communal politics rested on the identification of Hindus as a majority target for both electioneering and advertising.

This emphasizes the need for studies of communalism to examine closely both the class basis of political mobilization and the effects of India's current rapid economic transformations on these class formations. Will liberalization increase the sense of economic insecurity-what Barbara Ehrenreich (1990) calls the "fear of falling"-among the middle classes? And could this insecurity be politically manipulated into increased communal tensions?

Or will a more competitive economic climate foster a rejection of communal politics that will be deemed too costly not only in human lives, but also in business profits? For example, Mushirul Hasan, in a seminar discussion on this volume, noted that when the BJP recently turned its attention to mobilizations around the Kashi Vishwanath temple in Benares, the head of the Benares VHP publicly denounced the BJP, because he feared harm to his business interests from local BJP mobilization. To rephrase the question, might Rama as political symbol be surmounted by an even more effective Indian symbol: the newly convertible rupee?

In a final note of guarded optimism, it should also be emphasized that the promulgation of the Rama imagery so easily appropriated for communal ends by the Sangh Parivar occurred during a unique political moment. As noted above, the serialization of the epics resulted from a political decision made by leaders of an insecure Congress Party, during a moment in which it held uncontested control over a powerful new medium. Such media imagery is unlikely to prove as potent in a fundamentally altered media and political landscape. Or so we may hope, given that, as of the writing of this chapter, the Sangh Parivar has announced plans for more *rath yatras* during the 1996 Lok Sabha election campaigns.

6

India Day-to-Day

The Congress leaders were arrested on August 9, 1942. Since then many well known Indians and Englishmen, including the Bishop of Calcutta and Metropolitan of India, attempted in vain to get permission to interview the jailed leaders in an effort to reopen negotiations. While the British Government stuck to its alibi of Indian disunity, they refused to allow Jinnah and others to communicate with Gandhi and Nehru. Permission to visit the jailed Congress leaders was also denied William Phillips, President Roosevelt's personal representative to India. Trade unions, both in Britain and the United States appealed to the Government to release the Indian leaders and reopen negotiations on the basis of a Provisional Indian National Government for the duration of the war.

On April 22, 1943, Chief Justice of India Maurice Gwyer delivered a judgment of the federal court declaring invalid Rule 26 of Section II of the Defense of India Act, under which some 8,000 Indians, including the Congress leaders, were imprisoned. The decision held that the rule "went beyond the powers which the Legislature thought fit to confer on the central government." Quite undismayed, Viceroy Linlithgow validated the arrests by decree. As the threat of a Japanese invasion receded, the British Government seemed content to sit complacently while India seethed with indignation.

India today remains a colonial country, and Mr. Churchill has said that the British Government means to hang on to it. What is Britain's stake in India? Not so very long ago it was customary to observe that India had a heavy Public Debt, owed to Britain. Hence it was unfair to expect the British Government to pull out of India at a financial loss. A glance at the origin and growth of this Public Debt would in part explain what India has meant to Britain.

The origin of this debt lay, in the first place, in the costs of wars and other charges debited to India. Besides conquering her at her own expense, Britain chalked up against India every conceivable expense that could be remotely or even fantastically connected with her. "The burdens that it was found convenient to charge to India seem preposterous," writes L. H. Jenks. "The costs of the Mutiny, the price of the transfer of the Company's rights to the Crown, the expenses of simultaneous wars in China and Abyssinia, every governmental item in London that remotely related to India down to the fees of the charwomen in the India Office and the expenses of ships that sailed but did not participate in hostilities and the cost of Indian regiments for six months' training at home before they sailed-all were charged to the account of the unrepresented ryot.

The Sultan of Turkey visited London in 1868 in state, and his official ball was arranged for at the India Office and the bill charged to India. A lunatic asylum in Ealing, gifts to members of a Zanzibar mission, the consular and diplomatic establishments of Great Britain in China and in Persia, part of the permanent expenses of the Mediterranean fleet and the entire cost of a line of telegraph from England to India had been charged before 1870 to the Indian Treasury." The annexation of Hongkong did not benefit India, and Indians did not aspire to the conquest of Burma. British trade, and not Indians, profited from the opium wars of China.

According to recent reports India has wiped out her Public Debt, and it is expected that she will emerge after the war with an accumulation of sterling credits in London. This is not a cause for optimism. A truly National Government of India might have utilized this credit for the benefit of the Indians. But these assets are now on blocked account, and the decision over their disbursement rests with the British Treasury. What the Treasury will do has already been indicated by Sir A. J. Raisman, Finance Member of the Viceroy's Council, as reported in the London Economist of March 6, 1943. Raisman has suggested that, first of all, a substantial amount would be deducted to set up a capital fund to enable the British Treasury to pay out sterling pensions and provident funds which amount to an annual transfer of 20 to 24 million dollars.

The Government would not be permitted to draw freely on the remaining credits, either; these would be considered as a longterm loan granted to Britain, repayments to be made only to the amount of the interest and in the form of British exports to India. In the words of the Economist, "the sterling resources in question must be regarded as blocked until such time as they can be freed for financing British exports to India."

Since the Public Debt is no longer a subject of controversy, what else is there that impels Britain to hold on to India? Lord Halifax is wont to say that, for the "material benefits" India has received "from the British connection ... she pays not a cent to England except the interest earned by British loans and ordinary commercial investments." It is true that India does not pay a cent directly to the British Treasury; but the "interest earned by British loans and ordinary commercial interests," which Lord Halifax casually tosses aside as of little significance, contains the crux of Indo-British relations.

The British Government represents the dominant economic interests of Britain, and India is preserved as a field of exploitation by these interests. Investments of British capital in India have earned fabulous profits. Coal mines have paid

160 per cent while paying a daily wage of 16 cents; the dividends of one of these mines averaged over 80 per cent throughout the period 1901-29. British-owned jute mills have paid as much as 100 per cent, and seldom less than 20 per cent. In 1940 the amount of British capital invested in India was estimated at about 5 billion dollars, or one-quarter of her total overseas investments.

Modern business cannot be conducted without credit. Most of the large banks in India are either Government-controlled or are branches of British and other foreign banks. As a result, Indian industrialists find it difficult to finance industrial enterprises of which the British do not approve. By the device of the Managing Agency system, which is a cross between a holding company and an investment bank, a small number of managing agency firms control and to some extent finance a wide variety of commercial enterprises?

These agents, mostly British, dominate the coal, jute and tea industries, cement, engineering, insurance, lime, oil, mineral, paper, stone and sugar production, as well as the shipping industry. No matter how many shares are held by Indians, "the managing agents run the whole show," wrote Herbert L. Matthews in the *New York Times* of Jan. 2, 1943. The Government of India today also supplies highly remunerative positions to Britons as well as to a few Indians. Extravagant salaries are paid to the Viceroy, the Governors of Provinces and the cabinet members, to mention but a few.

The Viceroy is paid considerably more than the President of the United States. In America the salaries of the Governors of States vary from $3,000 to $25,000; Governors of Indian provinces are paid anywhere from $12,000 to $40,000. In the United States government cabinet members receive $15,000 a year; members of the Viceroy's cabinet are paid $27,000 a year. Other salaries are proportionately higher. The enormous salaries of British officials and the super-profits garnered by British companies operating in India are not spent in India but go to Britain, and the income tax levied on them swells the British exchequer.

All these handsome salaries and profits are screwed out of the Indian workers, whose condition can be seen by the fact that between 1842 and 1922, while wages were quadrupled, the cost of rice alone rose eight times: in other words, the workers' real wage was halved in eighty years. Lord Halifax piously states that since 1858 Indians have obtained "a heightened standard of living"; on the contrary, whatever may have been the economic condition of the people in pre-British days; it is obvious that since the middle of the 19th century, at least, the standard of living of the vast majority of the Indian people has consistently deteriorated.

It is estimated that in normal times at least 750 million dollars are annually transferred from India to Britain in one form or another. Apart from this, India is important to Britain in other ways. Her exchange has been manipulated to serve British interests. Her population constitutes three-quarters of the total population of the British Empire and nearly ninetenths of its colonial population. She is of immense strategic value as a source of troops, supplies and funds, and base of operations for the control of Suez, the Persian Gulf, the Middle Eastern Empire, routes to the Far East and Australia. The power and prestige that is derived from the possession of India can hardly be minimized.

Lord Curzon knew it at the turn of the century. Lord Rothermere pointed out in the *Daily Mail* of May 16, 1930 that "many authorities estimate that the proportion of the vital trading, banking, and shipping business of Britain directly dependent upon our connection with India is 20%... India is the lynch-pin of the British Empire. If we lose India the Empire must collapse first, economically then politically." And even the liberal Manchester Guardian admitted editorially on January 3, 1930 that "there are two chief reasons why a self-regarding England may hesitate to relax her control over India.

The first is that her influence in the past depended partly upon her power to summon troops and to draw resources from India in time of need. This power will vanish when India has Dominion Status. The second is that Great Britain finds in India her best market, and that she has one thousand million pounds of capital invested there." India today is publicized by British Government spokesmen as ranking seventh among the industrialized countries of the world. This, however, is no indication of the industrial development of India; on the contrary, this merely shows that a high degree of industrialization is confined to less than half-adozen countries.

India today is producing large quantities of goods-mainly textiles, leather goods, puttees, tents, gunnysacks, etc. Some chemical products are being turned out, and a few simple machine tools are being manufactured. But today India cannot manufacture a single internal-combustion machine. A long catalogue describing the increase in the mere number of factories and the quantities of goods produced looks impressive but does not necessarily imply a continuously higher standard of living; this requires the ability to produce the machines which in turn will supply an increasing flow of consumer goods.

An agricultural community can never provide as high a standard of living as an industrialized one; the latter requires the development of basic, heavy industries; and this is where the government sits tight, protecting British interests. Only a progressive National Government, in a position to lend political and economic aid, can promote such industrialization. British rule brought India internal peace only in the sense that there was no longer warfare among the Indian princes; but the relationship between the Government and the people has hardly been a peaceful one. Railroads and highways were built, but only to the degree necessary for the defense of India and the proper exploitation of her resources.

In the United States there are 18 times as many miles of railway per capita as in India, and 30 times as many miles of highway. The present government of India spends 18 cents per capita on education, as compared with about $6.50 in Great Britain and about $20.00 in the United States. Even this minute sum is doled out grudgingly, mainly to turn out a corps of clerks and a disproportionate number of lawyers who thrive on the litigation which inevitably grows out of the land system. Technical education is practically nonexistent.

Even after the war began, the Government resolutely kept aloof from interfering with the technological backwardness of the Indian people. Not until 1941 did the Government takes a gingerly step in this direction. Then a scheme was hatched by British Minister of Labor Ernest Bevin, by which, beginning in February 1941, batches of Indians at the average rate of 50 every quarter, have been sent to England to learn industrial methods. These are the much publicized Bevin Boys. Though they were inaugurated for the economic exploitation of the country, the railroads and highways, the uniform postal and telegraph and the single monetary systems, and the government machinery have nevertheless been beneficial to India.

They have knit the country closer together, given her greater unity and have supplied the foundation for a higher standard of living through industrial development. But by its very nature British rule can go no further. In fact, it is obliged to be a handicap to the betterment of conditions in India. The Government of India is a tool of the British industrialists and financiers, is controlled by them and is maintained for their benefit. Every so-called constitutional reform up to the present has actually given an increasing amount of power to the Viceroy and the Provincial Governors to safeguard British economic interests. It can no longer perform an even objectively progressive role.

Since the arrest of the Congress leaders, constructive work was undertaken only by the leaders and members of the Trade

Union Congress, the Communist Party and the Kisan Sabha. Tirelessly they worked to keep anti-fascist sentiment alive and to rally the people to the war effort, even without government support. In April, 1943, the Kisan Sabha, under the presidency of Bankim Mukherji, held its annual conference in Punjab, where 60,000 Hindu and Moslem peasants-men and women - from all parts of India met and discussed current problems, national as well as international. They resolved to grow more food, called for an invasion of Western Europe, demanded the release of Congress leaders and the establishment of a National Government, and pledged all possible help to smash the Axis.

Young and old alike stood patiently in line before tents exhibiting Soviet posters telling of the war against Germany and of the Soviet social accomplishments. In May, 1943, the All-India Trade Union Congress, at its session at Nagpur, adopted by 424 votes to 192 a resolution demanding "the immediate release of Mahatma Gandhi and all other political prisoners, and the transfer of power to a National Government, so as to organize effective defense of the country against the Axis," and urging "all patriotic parties to accept selfdetermination of nationalities." But they faced the difficult task of rousing a starving population who did not have even the incentive of fighting a patriotic war under their own leaders. Soon their efforts had to be diverted to meet a long-foreshadowed disaster-famine.

As early as May, 1942, Indian leaders were warning of an acute food shortage, verging on famine, but the government paid no attention to it. By the Fall of 1943 prices rose as much as 1500 per cent, while wages remained low. Some staple foodstuffs were unobtainable even in urban centers. Famine raged from Kashmir in the north to Madras in the south. In November, 1943, in the province of Bengal alone, at least 50,000 men, women and children were dying of starvation every week. Even in the city of Calcutta conditions were appalling.

Mothers clawed through rotting garbage and hunted in the gutters for scraps while children with bloated bellies plucked feebly at their garments.

"Disposal trucks" roamed the streets, picking up the gaunt bodies of the dead. Death from starvation in Calcutta took the lives of more than 1500 a week, and the toll mounted by hundreds when cholera broke out in the wake of the famine. That British rule in India is totally bankrupt and monstrously incompetent is most glaringly proven by its handling of the present famine. It began during the Viceroyalty of Lord Linlithgow, who, more than anyone else was in a position to foresee its approach and to take preventive measures. From 1926 to 1928 Linlithgow was chairman of the Royal Commission on Agriculture, which gathered voluminous evidence on the critical agrarian problem of India.

The Commission's 675page final report, signed by Linlithgow, presented a vivid and comprehensive picture of the economic decay of the countryside. It laid the main responsibility for initiating measures leading to urgently needed improvements squarely on the shoulders of the Government of India. No steps were taken by the Government even to halt further deterioration of Indian agriculture, much less to improve it. Linlithgow became Viceroy of India in 1936, and was replaced by Lord Wavell in October 1943. Linlithgow the Viceroy found it convenient to ignore what Linlithgow the Chairman of the Agricultural Commission had previously recommended.

India was declared a belligerent in the war in September, 1939. Her backward economy was called upon to cope with the demands of modern total warfare. This required government planning as well as the full mobilization of the Indian people. The British Government failed miserably in both directions. Congress Ministries in the provinces resigned in protest-they had no power to introduce fundamental reforms anyway. It was soon obvious that the food situation, normally acute, was reaching dangerous proportions. The increased armed forces stationed in India had to be fed. Grain was also shipped in large quantities to the forces in the Middle East. Still the Government, under Linlithgow, did nothing.

In the spring of 1942 Japanese troops occupied Burma, cutting off the supply of Burmese rice to India. The rice which Burma normally supplied to Ceylon had to be replaced by exports from India. In addition, India was faced with the task of feeding nearly half a million refugees from Burma. The Indian leaders' plea to arm the people of the country went unheeded; instead, more troops poured into India from abroad, putting additional strain on the already depleted food stocks. The Government took no other measure than to exhort the peasants to grow more food. In July 1942, the Kisan Sabha pointed out that food production could not be increased by slogans, that it must be made "profitable and feasible for the poverty-stricken peasantry to undertake the cultivation of food crops."

They recommended that the government hand over available land now lying fallow to the poorer peasants and landless agricultural laborers for cultivation, and that no land revenue or rent be collected from such newly cultivated land. Furthermore, they asked that a moratorium be declared on all revenue and rent arrears; that excessive rents be scaled down; and that the peasants be furnished with cheap credit and guaranteed a fair price for their produce. They also demanded the establishment of a price policy that would bring food within the reach of the population, compulsory storing of grain in public warehouses to break the monopolistic control of wholesalers, and the full use of available means of transportation.

The Government did nothing to cope with the growing food crisis until the end of 1942. Then it began a series of conferences and released eloquent statements about price control and penalties against hoarders. But the Government's idea of price control was to put the ceiling high enough to coax the hoarders to release their stock; when that did not work, price ceilings were entirely eliminated. The Government opened a few relief kitchens in Bengal, providing one scanty meal of watery gruel a day. "The relief kitchen," remarked P. C. Joshi "is thus not a stepping stone for going back to the farm, but a halting station on the road to death."

In the summer of 1943, when people were already dropping dead in the streets of Calcutta, Secretary of State for India Leopold Amery coolly told the House of Commons, "There is no famine and no widespread prevalence of acute shortage in India." Later, when Amery was compelled to admit the existence of famine, the responsibility was put on the provincial governments.

Toward the end of the year, when the death toll from starvation was conservatively estimated at 100,000 a week, the Government of India presented an astonishing spectacle of passing the buck. For justification abroad the Government presented itself as the helpless victim of provincial autonomy and selfgovernment. It was explained that if people were suffering it was the fault of the Indians in the provincial governments. No mention was made of the fact that, since the Congress ministries resigned, the provinces have been governed either through the autocratic rule of appointed British officials or through ministries of corrupt politicians representing the big landowners.

While millions starved it was also argued that the Viceroy could not interfere with the internal affairs of the provinces, much as the Federal government of the United States did not interfere with the affairs of the States. It was conveniently forgotten that during the great depression the Federal government of America did not sit idly by and tell the people of the States to die of starvation for the privilege of protecting states' rights. In any case, the Government's alibi falls to pieces when it is remembered that the Viceroy and the Governors have the power to dismiss ministers and to suspend constitutional government in case of emergency.

In the case of rounding up and jailing the Indian political leaders in all parts of India, Linlithgow could throw overboard all pretense of provincial or even civil rights, but when it came to India-wide famine relief the Viceroy was reluctant to consider it an emergency. The Indians, on the other band, showed an amazing unity in the face of this crisis. Hindus and Moslems, trade unionists, Communists and peasant unionists organized people's food committees, collected grain from provinces which were comparatively better off and distributed it in the provinces which were hit harder by famine, and appealed for funds at home and abroad.

Members of British trade unions and cooperative societies immediately responded by setting up Indian famine relief organizations, and the CIO in the United States promptly donated $100,000. Thus, while the British Government hunted for scapegoats and alibis, the people of India, with the help of the British and American people, did what they could to relieve the situation. It is not quite correct to say that the British Government did nothing. It did-all the wrong things. Millions of acres of land were available, and millions of farmers were unemployed. During four years the Government had ample time to organize and encourage the growing of more food: through tax concessions, subsidies, guaranteed prices, crop loans, etc. Basic industries could have been greatly expanded.

The Government found it a better policy to limit its efforts to oral exhortations and shooting down hunger marchers who rioted for food. It could have made a systematic effort to prevent large scale hoarding and to control prices; instead it winked at the hoarders and set the prices so high that people could not afford to buy food-in effect trying to solve famine by discouraging consumption! The Government could have gained the whole-hearted cooperation of the entire population of the country by allowing their leaders to establish a National Government, but decided instead to put these leaders behind prison bars.

Late in 1943 it still had a chance to work together with the people's food committees set up by the Indians themselves, but preferred to either ignore them or actively persecute them. In addition, the Government had the unmitigated brass to announce that the rise in prices was due to too much money in the hands of the peasants, and to launch a campaign to collect seven hundred million dollars in war savings. This was the remedy the Government posed before Indians who had been driven to eating locusts and leaves. And to carry to its logical conclusion the theory that the peasants were wealthy, the Government arrested foodless and nearly naked Indians as vagrants!

This is by no means the whole story. Lately American newspaper reports have brought out additional facts which expose the whole sordid basis of British rule in India. At the Atlantic City conference of the United Nations Relief and Rehabilitation Administration, aid to India was quashed by the adamant opposition of Col. Llewellyn of the British delegation, though such aid was supported by many other delegates, including the Chinese. Worse still, it is now known that Australia had a surplus of four million tons of wheat and a large surplus of meat which she was willing to send to India, but the offer was turned down.

The Canadian Government offered 100,000 tons of wheat, which was also rejected. The excuse given was lack of shipping space. Yet American government officials in Washington agreed that there was sufficient shipping space available. The Canadian Government's offer of wheat was accepted by Wavell, the Viceroy of India, but was rejected by the British Government in England through Leopold Amery, and Wavell, himself an appointee of the Crown, was powerless against Amery's decision. At the CIO convention in Philadelphia on November 5, 1943, Harry Bridges of the International Longshoremen's Association stated that a year ago the CIO had pointed out to the United States and British governments that if certain things were not done, millions of Indians would starve.

The CIO at that time offered a plan for proper utilization of shipping space by which India could have been fed. "We were turned down," Harry Bridges told the convention, "and I want to tell you why we were turned down by Adm. Land of the U. S. Government and Sir Arthur Salter, representing Great Britain. They said, 'Look, you are getting into some deep social questions here; you are starting to disturb things,' and it meant that the Indian people and our ideas that we put forward to help win the war might have cost a few more pennies a week."

The British Government has often differentiated between itself and the Government of India, but the difference is a myth. For the sake of publicity a brown-skinned gentleman has been installed in Washington with the imposing title of Agent General and Minister Plenipotentiary for India. But this gentleman did not open his mouth at the UNRRA conference, leaving it to Americans to plead for Indian famine relief. When queried about the Indian famine the British Information Service in New York and the Ministry of Transport officials in Washington referred American newspapermen not to the Agent General and Minister Plenipotentiary for India nor to the Government of India, but to the Government in London.

The food crisis in India is not due to wartime conditions, destined to disappear when the war would be over. The diversion of the transport system to cope with military needs, the loss of rice from Burma, the necessity to export Indian wheat to the armies in the Middle East, are the reasons usually given for the famine in India; but these are only part of the picture. Uneconomic agriculture, fragmentation of holdings and lack of industrialization are the roots from which periodic famines spring to plague the Indian people.

Even in normal peace times India suffers from acute food shortage, with more than 60 per cent of her population living at a semi-starvation level. Death by starvation today is not a product of wartime dislocation alone, but of a primitive, overburdened agrarian system which yields only the most meagre living to the millions who have no means of livelihood but their tiny strips of land, and who must pay the greater part of their earnings to the government as tax, to the landlord as rent, and to the moneylender as interest, leaving them with only the barest margin of subsistence.

Unparalleled poverty of the peasants and the minute size of their holdings make the use of modern methods of cultivation impossible, with the result that yields per acre are low, the fertility of the soil is decreasing, and land is actually going out of cultivation because the peasants are too poor to maintain, much less increase their holdings. If the country's total food production were distributed with meticulous equality, it would not suffice to feed the people even on the far from generous scale adopted in Indian prisons.

The food problem of India cannot be solved by boasting about the 42,000 miles of railroad and the less than 52 million acres under irrigation; these did not help solve it in the past, nor are they preventing famine today. It requires the immediate distribution among the landless peasants of some of the 140 million acres of cultivable land now lying idle, and the adoption of the rest of the program recommended by the Kisan Sabha. But these can only be temporary measures; permanent solution requires a thoroughgoing revision of the entire system of land tenure, and the development of industries which will absorb the unemployed now overcrowding the land.

Only a National Government, composed of the trusted leaders of the people, can remedy the present situation. The British Government is powerless to take any constructive measures to alleviate the catastrophe in India. Importing food into India from abroad will threaten the wholesalers of grain and a moratorium on debts and taxes will antagonize the landlords. Indian provincial ministers have been accused of profiteering in grain, but the Government has taken no action against them, though it has the power to do so. Many Indians who remained in Government service after the Congress ministries resigned have since then left their posts in disgust.

It is significant that in the Fall of 1943 the Food portfolio in the Viceroy's Council was handed over to Sir J. Srivastava, a big landlord and mill owner. The Government dare not move against the wholesalers, moneylenders, landlords and the remaining corrupt ministries; for, if it loses their support, it will no longer be able even to say that some of its best friends are Indians. As a matter of fact the true color of the Government of India is revealed by the friends it has made among the Indians. As far as those Indians themselves are concerned, it only goes to show that economic interests transcend national loyalties in India as in other countries of Asia and Europe.

India today is urgently in need of fresh political and economic air, not for her own sake alone but for the sake of all the United Nations. The dead are leaving behind a legacy of bitterness which is augmenting the anger of the living, and anti-Government feeling is being transformed into anti-British feeling. It is true that this feeling has so far manifested itself only in isolated cases of attacks on police patrols and government grain depots. But the British Government has no reason to think that the comparative calm is due primarily to police clubs, whipping posts and machine guns.

Am equally important factor in the Indian scene has been the heroic effort of the trade and peasant unionists and other leaders to keep alive the larger issues involved in this war. These genuine anti-fascists are carrying on a tireless campaign of education and economic relief against the heavy odds of government repression, and Japanese propaganda in the shape of a puppet Indian Government in Singapore headed by Subhas Bose. The British Government in its relation to India stands thoroughly discredited in every way. While Indians die of starvation it has the unbelievably bad taste to boast of having given India "a heightened standard of living and of health."

It keeps itself in power in India by terrorizing the people and catering to the most reactionary elements, for whose support it is willing to sacrifice millions of Indian lives. By destroying the feudalistic economy of India and by introducing the rudiments of modern industry, the British Government once upon a time was an objective tool of history. But that time has long since passed, and it has been more than amply repaid for it. Today it is unqualifiedly a weapon of oppression in India, and can prolong its stay there only by force.

Among the Indians there is more political unity today than ever before; the demand for a National Government is universal. Significant of this common demand is an editorial in the Morning News, influential Bengal organ of the Moslem League, which declared: "Long ago the Moslem League expressed through M. A. Jinnah its willingness to work with its Congress colleagues in forming and running a national government at the center... The most obvious manner in which the Government can help the situation is to declare a political amnesty for all prisoners and release them without delay...so that they can hammer out an agreement."

Reflecting public opinion in Britain the conservative Sunday Observer admitted that "somewhere we took a wrong turning, probably when we failed to realize that Indian political parties were more proChinese and more anti-Japanese than we were, and had been anti-Nazi and anti-Fascist when we were appeasers. Their desire was to feel that the war was their war, but it still figures as a war to help Britain and save her Empire." Nevertheless, in November, 1943, the British Government kept behind prison bars such great anti-fascists as Jawaharlal Nehru and Abul Kalam Azad, but released the fascist Oswald Mosley from detention because of "improvement in the national fortunes!"

While 71 year old Mrs. Kasturbai Gandhi remained ill in jail, Mosley was let out for medical treatment. To the protests of the British people, Home Secretary Herbert Morrison sanctimoniously replied that a new law had to be passed to try Mosley, which would be "an act repugnant to every principle of British justice"; but it was quite agreeable to British justice for Viceroy Linlithgow to legalize by retroactive decree the illegal arrest of Gandhi and other Indian leaders.

7

Divisions in Society

Society in India is riven with divisions so deep that sometimes it stretches one's credulity to think of it as one country. But one country it very definitely is and its internal contradictions are responsible for the dynamic which is India at any point in its history. It is far too easy to think of the major divisions of society as if they generated completely separate units or were based upon separate issues, rather than thinking of the units or issues in isolation as topics in their own right. If one goes along that path, one finishes up with nothing more than trite and touristic commentaries about India being a land of contrasts.

India has to be taken as a whole and it needs to be appreciated that the lines of cleavage define the way that society is at any juncture; this means that opposing groups and interests define themselves in relation to each other and each other in relation to themselves. They do not have essential characteristics beyond this. Inden (1990) is at pains to demonstrate that many commentators have been happy to see India as a land of essences (postulating essentialist views of religion, the caste system, regions, etc.).

This is a largely western and brahmanical construction, which suits a particular use of knowledge as power; it is not something which captures any absolute reality. Of course, the construction is itself an interesting phenomenon which demonstrates the world view of a small, but very influential, section of contemporary Indian society. Acknowledging connectedness makes for a more nuanced understanding of India, but it also means that one has to forego the simple explanatory structures which are generally offered.

COMMUNALISM

The idea of membership by birth of separate ascribed groups, based on caste or religion, each with supposedly inherent characteristics, is very much a part of Indian life. Unfortunately, this idea in its 'communalist' form becomes the basis of a political reality in which communities present themselves as having not only clear identities, but also separate and conflicting interests. It has become as ingrained as racism is in many societies. In its Indian usage, the term 'community' invariably cuts across neighbourhood and locality; one would not normally think of a village as a community comprising people with different caste and religious characteristics, rather one would think of those characteristics constituting communities which extend beyond and divide villages.

Like racism, communalism is built upon illogical beliefs in innate characteristics, reinforced by selective observation, evidence-building and pseudo-science. Also like racism, the illogic is based upon a desire to maintain or achieve unfair advantage, or, as Tambia (1996) indicates, *jati* and ethnic groups with 'self- proclaimed collective identity' seek preference in the name of equality. This chapter will consider the nature of communalist politics and also the 'secularist' opposition to it.

Everything that is socially constructed can also be deconstructed and we find that increasing numbers of Indian intellectuals are turning their attention to the historical and philosophical underpinnings of European fascism in their quest to theorize the new forms of communalism emerging in the conditions predicated upon liberalization and globalization. There are certainly similarities, but theory cannot be imported wholesale.

Communalism is such an important issue in contemporary India that some of the very highest quality academic work is being done in this field, none better than Achim Vanaik's excellent study of religion and secularism, *The furies of Indian* communalism. Much of the analysis of communalism in India deserves a far wider readership than just people interested in the sub-continent since it is at the forefront of the theorization of the sub national divisions which bedevil so much contemporary politics worldwide. Vanaik writes of Hindu nationalism that one should see:

> The principal danger not as residing in something that lies behind Hindu communalism or as residing in some fascist core contained within or hidden in Hindu communalism, but as Hindu communalism itself as the specific manifestation of the politics of cultural exclusivity and right- wing reaction.
>
> The long term and ... more basic focus would not be on its potential or likelihood for a 'fascist' suborning of the state but on politicized Hindutva's deep roots and growth in civil society well beyond its capacity to appropriate the state. In a sense the phenomenon is more deep rooted than fascism, more enduring and more difficult to completely or comprehensively destroy.

Here he is referring to an ideology which requires the total suffusion of society with a single idea and a single value system. This is power well beyond government, ingrained into the constructed Hindu 'tradition', with no need to consider the structures as anything other than self-evidently right and pre-ordained. This is the ultimate communalist dream.

CASTE AS A COMPLEX

There have been numerous western/brahmanical accounts of the caste 'system' as the key to understanding the Indian society. The most influential of these in modern times has been the work of Dumont (1970) whose structuralist imperative caused him to believe that there was a pan-Indian hierarchy of jati arranged like a squash ladder (if one goes up another has to come down). His influence caused caste to be represented as a closed system, based around the concept of ritual purity as laid down in the Vedic scriptures. Whilst structuralists see internal positional flexibility as possible, they represent the system itself as having a constant shape.

Partha Chatterjee (1993a and b), however, emphasizes that caste should be seen as fragmentary and dialectical, agreeing with Gupta's (1984) claim that, though notions of inequality are certainly important, a simple linear hierarchy is not the determining principle. Dialectic generates a very different sort of whole from a closed system. There is nothing systematic about it, although it suited earlier western intellectual fashions to think otherwise.

Caste is, rather, a complex -a loose assemblage of practices, rules, ideas, relationships, beliefs and prejudices, which forms around hereditary membership of corporate 'communities', together with a recognition of inequality of rights. Often it is convenient for those who wish to maintain the status quo to represent this with all the power of a logical system, but this complex assumes very different forms and characteristics when experienced from different subject positions in society. There is not even any agreement about the shape and nature of inequality. Jati are groups which act for the mutual advantage of their members.

Since they are also endogamous, virtually all kinship and interpersonal ties of friendship are concentrated within them. They are obviously a powerful form of social organization and it is not difficult to see why they persist, changing form and function with different modes of production and political systems. There is no reason why modernization or globalization should be assumed to be intrinsically liable to erode caste.

Obviously there have always been more representations of caste from the point of view of the Brahmin*s* (the occupational specialists in literacy and the management and control of formal knowledge) than from any other social group's perspective and add that here people not mean individual born.

Taking the view that caste is a complex, we can distance ourselves from any sense that the way in which caste is configured in present times is a perversion of a former ideal system. It becomes axiomatic that caste will always be the manifestation of the current modes of inequality of power, prestige and wealth. It was not, somehow, more logically 'perfect' in the past when there were feudal systems of land tenure and division of labour, or trapped by the rigidities of British imperialist classification or liable to degenerate under globalized systems of capital accumulation - all of these forms echo and amplify their times.

Caste has always been political; most of the classic accounts of it demonstrate the forms taken under feudal economic and political systems, where the complementary forces of landownership and ritual laid down the dominant principles of profane and sacred (Kshatriya and Brahmin). Today's political systems take account of new configurations of caste, some of these based on economic change, others on new mobilizations in relation to the state. Kothari (1970) warns that to decry the involvement of caste in politics is naove, since caste, as an important social principle in India, is bound to be politicized. By 1997 Kothari argued that caste-based politics is not just a matter of the protection of privilege but that it can also become the basis of resistance through both political parties and new social movements, since it can offer a basis for minority mobilization against 'majoritarian' forces.

UNTOUCHABILITY

The term 'untouchable' was unsayable by all but the most insensitive until a few years ago, but the people at the bottom of the heap have started confronting the rest of society with the full implication of their status by challenging them with the word. Gandhi employed the term harijan (children of God) but was naovely unmindful of the fact that in the villages this word was used pejoratively for the children of devadasis. Of late, the favoured term is dalit, which translates as ground-down or oppressed. It is only with a sense of anger and self-recognition that 'untouchable' can be appropriated.

There has been a long, but largely unrehearsed, history of dalit resistance, including the bhakti tradition, going back as far as the seventh century. Mendelsohn and Vicziani quote Kabir, the fifteenth-century bhakti poet, who rejected caste hierarchy:

Pandits sat and read the law

Babbled of what they never saw

And

Pandit, look in your heart for knowledge

Tell me where untouchability came from, since you believe in it.

An early modern example is the conversion of Keralan 'untouchables' to Christianity in the nineteenth century which resulted in high rates of literacy, through attendance at mission schools, consequent rural development and left-wing State government. Prior to this, Malabar (as it was then known) had some of the most vicious and degrading devices for separating 'untouchables' from others. In the late nineteenth century there was a *bhakti* revival in northern India; gaining ground among urban 'untouchables' in the early twentieth century, it offered an organizational structure for the development of explicitly anti-Brahmin ideology. In the South it was parallelled by Phule's inversion of the caste hierarchy and rejection of Brahmin interpretations of religion.

The important Non-Brahmin Movement in the Madras Presidency (Tamil Nadu) in the 1920s led to the very first instances of government reservation and Periyar's Self-Respect League. Best known are Ambedkar's Independent Labour Party and Scheduled Caste Federation of the 1930s and 1940s with their opposition to Congress as 'a Brahmin-bourgeois party'. At Independence, positive discrimination in favour of the Scheduled Castes was continued and extended. It was initially assumed that this would be a transitional phase and that, by conferring access to government employment and preferential treatment in rural development, there would eventually be a collapse of the division between the caste Hindus and others. This has not been the case.

The majority of members of Scheduled Castes have seen none of the benefits of reservation but remain not just trapped in dire poverty but still on the receiving end of the contempt of the those who believe themselves to be their superiors. However, individuals and sometimes whole communities have been able to take advantage of reservation to acquire education and high-status jobs; there are significant numbers of *dalit* school teachers, doctors and bureaucrats. Even more important, *dalits* have been able to organize themselves into political units and have become a force to be reckoned with.

With the exception of the Republican Party of India, formed in the 1950s, *dalits* have mostly operated in organized politics through the established political parties; the regional parties in Tamil Nadu and Andhra Pradesh have strong *dalit* elements and Congress continues to pay lipservice to the *dalit* cause. The phenomenon of seat reservation gave *dalits* a good basis for recognition within the parties. However, with the development of the *Bahujan Samaj* Party and the growing power of Paswan in the *Janata Dal* in the 1980s, *dalit* politicians became significant players in the Hindi belt of northern India. Mendelsohn and Vicziani (1998) write of 'A new untouchable politics that is radical and assertive but also ruthlessly pragmatic.'

For the first time across large parts of India the *dalits* have to be taken seriously rather than viewed as a vote bank to be exploited by their social superiors'. There is certainly plenty for these politicians to fight for. Practices of 'untouchability' are most obvious in the rural communities where people have personal knowledge of each other and where any individual's caste status is known to all. A routine practice is to debar 'untouchables' from using the same water source as caste Hindus and to force them to live in separate settlements.

It may seem trivial, but in 1999 in Tamil Nadu there has been a fair amount of publicity given to the 'two glass' phenomenon at village tea shops. It is a common (and illegal) discriminatory practice for the people who run tea stalls to keep two sets of vessels, one for serving 'clean' castes, the other for 'untouchables', who are served separately and must wash their own receptacles. Pro-*dalit* politicians have been descending unannounced on tea shops to catch the owners out (of course it is a publicity stunt in the run up to an election). Trivial? In the same villages *dalits'* homes are being burned down and pitched battles are being fought between other castes and untouchables.

There has been a ban on naming bus concessions after 'caste heroes' - this because the concessions were granted by MLAs to their supporters who often showed their gratitude by naming them after leaders of their own community, publicly flaunting their relationship with powerful forces. There has also been a ban on casteist graffiti because it inflames violent reaction. These are feeble measures in the light of the fact that in Tamil Nadu, as in the northern States like Bihar and Uttar Pradesh, caste-based armies with both home-made and purchased weaponry are taking control of the rural areas.

In Bihar no one is striking poses outside tea shops - there is war between the *dalits* (here still called *harijans*) and the landowning castes, as the latter try desperately to cling to their feudal privileges. In the late 1970s, caste-based atrocities started to come to light whereby *dalit* men who were deemed to be getting above themselves were reminded of their lowly status by premeditated blinding with acid. With the passing of formal political power into the hands of the Other Backward Classes in the 1990s, new levels of caste violence have emerged.

Marginalized landowners, distrustful of the State government, are setting up alternative local structures of 'law and order', raising their own 'armies' (*sena*), often with the deliberate indifference or unofficial support of the police. To provide a counterweight, Naxalite guerrilla groups offer protection to the Scheduled Castes, whereupon the excuse given for attacks on villages becomes the need to flush out Naxalites.

In the past, caste-based violence and caste insults generally went unreported; today there is more publicity and this is a measure of progress, however limited. Though it is a relatively small shift, the media is increasingly representing *dalit* people as individuals with whom readers can identify, rather than as a category to pity or despise, though, as Kothari (1997) cynically remarks, this has become something of an empty show of concern.

On 16 July 1999 *Frontline* published a story about routine insults to *dalit* women in Tamil Nadu in which a woman is quoted as saying 'I am a midwife who helps their women. In the same issue was a report about the Mallahs of Bihar claiming back their fishing rights? Deepak Bharti, their leader, draws attention to the fact that *dalits* are not omy becoming organized but are also gaining a sense of self-worth, saying that they now call government officials *bhaijee* (honoured brother) rather than *huzur* (lord) and sit in chairs in waiting rooms rather than cowering on the floor.

That these are considered to be significant advances shows just how far there still is to go, but it is not long since it would have been hard to interest English readers in the insults borne by the people at the bottom of the social ladder. Of course, the greatest symbol of *dalit* pride was the appointment of Narayanan as President of India. Broken people, a Human Rights Watch report (1999), is essential reading for anyone who doubts the depths of the continuing neglect, exploitation, indignity and brutality to which dalit people are routinely exposed.

It reports upon a series of cases from around India, including the atrocities of house burning, systematic rape and butchery in Tamil Nadu in 1998 when caste Hindus turned upon *dalits* in a series of incidents. The details read like something one might think of in the context of war crimes, not actions which even the most depraved members of the same society could contemplate against the neighbours in conditions of peace.

'Why are they driven to this extent? Because for them *dalits* are nothing. They give more respect to their animals', said one woman. It considers the rioting in Bombay in 1997 which escalated, fuelled by the enthusiasm of the *Shiv Sena*, when 10 *dalit* young men, protesting against the desecration of Ambedkar's statue by caste Hindus during Independence anniversary celebrations, were shot dead by the police. It gives details of the many massacres perpetrated by *Ranavir Sena*, one of the landlords' armies in northern Bihar.

It also looks at the routine callousness against *dalits,* revealing the plight of the manual scavengers, the people from the bhangi (sweeper) caste whose hereditary role it is to remove human excrement. Exposed to disease, whether they are working for municipalities, businesses or private households, they are paid a pittance but are so despised by virtually everyone that it is near to impossible for a bhangi to get other employment. The absolute degradation of dalits is an essential part of caste differentiation as it secures the status of caste Hindus in terms of the distance they can put between themselves and these stigmatized people.

It is arguable that if dalits could achieve effective, not just legal, citizenship, the hierarchical aspect of the complex of caste would unravel. It is certainly not only the members of the highest ranking jati who have an interest in maintaining the depressed position of the dalits. In the case of the Tamil Nadu atrocities referred to, the perpetrators were members of OBC groups who resented the fact that dalits were moving out of their oppressed position. This had happened as a consequence of a combination of increasing educational achievement under reservation and remittance income from relatives working abroad.

In a single incident in 1998, 400 dalit homes were destroyed, young women raped and murdered, and the old people beaten as a consequence of OBC resentment of dalits with money trying to bid in a government auction for village assets. Human Rights Watch reports that in 1996-97 there was a 34 per cent increase over the previous year in reported incidents and that in by far the majority of 282 cases; the violence was between OBCs and dalits. Not only were some dalit groups becoming economically more advanced, they were also organizing themselves into new and challenging political units. Established politicians, the police and the bureaucracy had much to gain from attempting to maintain the status quo.

In the 1999 general election campaign, dalit politicians announced a new regrouping to take on what they perceive to be the degeneration of the Tamil politics which has discarded the core principles of the non-Brahmin movement for a populist form of Hindutva. It should not be assumed that caste animosity stops at the 'line of pollution'; there can be considerable conflict between Scheduled Castes on the basis of entitlements granted to them.

The Scheduled Caste quota at national and State level does not differentiate between different jati - technically it would be possible to fill the quota exclusively with members of one group. In Andhra Pradesh in 1998, a controversial new ordinance allowed for the generation of subquotas to represent the divisions between malas, madigas, rellis and adi andhras. Other states have similar problems.

NEO-KSHATRIYA

Although all anthropologists are brought up on the importance of Sanskritization (emulating the behaviour of the Brahmins as a strategy for a jati to improve its status), it is noticeable that in India today a new social mobility is forming around the principle of usurping the roles of the ruler/landowner groups. The Other Backward Classes (OBCs) are the castes which are deemed to be above the (totally unsanctioned) 'line of pollution' in which the majority traditionally had a low standard of living.

They are generally classified as *shudra* but increasingly apply the term *bahujan* (.ass/majority) to them. In several regions, particularly in northern India, significant numbers of members of cultivator *jati* moved into positions of relative power and wealth when old feudal systems of land tenure gave way to independent farming. The 'Green Revolution' further transformed the lives of farmers, often in receipt of considerable government subsidies and assured a controlled market. In what is popularly referred to as 'the forward march of the backwards', new political configurations emerged in the 1980s, campaigning for reservations in government and education which would allow them to catch up with the old ιlites in terms of political influence.

In 1992, under pressure from the new political parties of the OBCs such as the *Janata Dal* and the *Samajwadi* Party, the Union Government accepted the recommendations of the

Mandal Commission on extending reservation categories. The new 'bullock capitalists' of Uttar Pradesh are busily establishing neo-feudal modes of interaction with their employees and bonds of kinship and patronage with local administration as they reap the benefits of newly deregulated markets for agricultural produce, particularly sugar cane.

There is no doubt at all that the rise of emerging capitalists from these communities goes hand-in- hand with corruption, violent crime and sabotage of democratic processes as new informal power structures emerges. The success of the affluent sections of the OBCs subverts what Vanaik sees as the 'natural centre of gravity' of Indian political life, the numerical strength of the mass. This subversion takes place because people are enticed to vote according to caste loyalties, even though these cut across their class loyalties. There is a trite, but true, saying about no longer casting a vote but voting a caste in the newly restructuring India.

However, OBC politics has to retain some vestiges of populism. This is frequently manifested in direct patronage (in Bihar it is joked that one can map the home areas of Members of the Legislative Assembly by observing the distribution of tube wells). As always, there is built-in caste-based favouritism, but it is undeniable that in its new form the largesse is being distributed further down the social scale as in the past. The ılitist English- medium press often delights in snobbish criticism of the 'vulgar' style of politicians such as Laloo Prashad Yadav of Bihar and Mulayam Singh Yadav of Uttar Pradesh, both members of the upwardly mobile yadav (milk producers) caste. Even Deve Gowda was mocked as Prime Minister for his country ways (particularly his language problems and his attachment to his large extended family). The sneering is a mark of the anxiety of old ılites in the face of emerging new forces they cannot easily control.

RESERVATION

When it was announced in 1992 that the recommendations of the Mandal Commission would be implemented, there was considerable consternation amongst Brahmin and *kayastha* university students, particularly those from lower middle class backgrounds that feared that their anticipated employment in the clerical ranks of the bureaucracy would be threatened. Many took to the streets; wearing black armbands, they burned copies of the Mandal Commission Report. There were even suicides.

Mandal's recommendation of extending the principle of reservation to include the OBCs meant that, taken together, the three reserved categories would control about 50 per cent of all places, more in those States where the government, for reasons of popular support, chose to interpret the legislation generously. Since these three categories constitute more than 50 per cent of the population, one can understand the logic. The Mandal Commission Report showed that, though they formed only 15 per cent of the population, the 'most forward castes' held almost 70 per cent of all government jobs and 90 per cent of the Class I positions. Reservation was the obvious way of breaking this exclusion of the caste majority.

As Ilaiah (1996) is at pains to demonstrate, a typical Brahmin socialization emphasizes the avoidance of manual work, but encourages the specialization in knowledge-based employment, including administration, teaching and research as well as priestly functions and the liberal professions. Government posts had long been an important preserve, but access to college places was even more crucial. Higher education was the gateway to the modern professions and had been virtually monopolized by young Brahmins, brought up in literate households and taught from their infancy the importance of learning how to pass examinations. Mandal threatened this domination.

Many members of the upper castes criticized Mandalization on the grounds that places should be awarded on the basis of 'merit' alone (Shah 1991), but this championing of excellence was far from impartial, since their upbringing, contacts and everything about their culture ensured that they could command the highest levels of 'merit' (which, of course, they defined). Reservation has a range of outcomes and even those who support it in principle have misgivings. Most obviously it gives the chance of self-improvement to individual members of 'backward' communities, who would otherwise be held back by their birth and rearing.

It also extends dignity to whole groups when it is perceived that their members can achieve prestigious positions and, additionally, it gives the dispossessed sections of society networks of contacts into power and influence. Less beneficially, reservation has resulted in the creation of the 'creamy layer' (the language of caste is full of ugly terminology) - those affluent people who, having used their deprived caste status to rise to the top, and then distance themselves from others. It is impossible not to notice that, for some individuals, reservation has been a matter of jumping onto a 'gravy train' rather than a means of diffusing advantage through the community.

Reservation for OBCs is supposed to exclude its 'creamy layer' from job quotas on grounds of parental income; however, scaling down one's declared income is routine. The first ' Mandal' intake into the prestigious Indian Adminstrative Service in 1996 showed a marked intensification of a trend towards increasing numbers of recruits coming from the small towns. This reflects what was already realized, that it is the ılites of the OBCs - the people who have moved into the marketing and processing of agricultural produce - which are cornering the gains ostensibly intended for mass 'uplift'. The descriptive lists of the new trainees showed remarkably small parental incomes for such sophisticated young people.

Reservation has had the effect of changing the status of government employment and all but the most competitive of state-funded higher education, both of which are perceived by the ılites as having declined in prestige. The extra concessions to the formerly excluded sections of society were made close on the heels of the New Economic Policy. There was no direct causal link, but the backward sections came to a significant position in administration just as the power of the state was being questioned and society was becoming more orientated towards the market and privatization. There is a very real sense in some sections of society that the bureaucracy is now no longer significant in its own right but has become the plaything of politicians and their related business interests.

THE TWICE BORN

Shashi Tharoor said of the super ılite, of which he is a member, they are 'able, but not electable'. With the decline of feudal landlordism and brahmanical bureaucratic hegemony, combined with the organization of mass political parties, the upper castes can no longer expect to dominate Indian politics, even though they have a good deal of influence. Though still important players in Indian affairs, we find that the upper castes are aware that their best chances are in terms of finding a niche in the international realm.

For the most accomplished and best connected members of the upper castes this implies foreign higher education and employment overseas; for others it means private higher education, through fee-paying colleges and foreign-franchised courses in India, followed by the scramble for managerial positions in private companies; for the middle-class majority there is relentless studying to get the unreserved places at university and networking to gain acceptable employment which would recently have been seen almost as a matter of right.

Coinciding with 'the forward march of the backwards' in the public sector, we can witness the parallel development of an upper- caste domination of the corporate private sector, a new twist to caste-based division of labour. Thus, in a situation of radical restructuring, the ılite sections of the upper castes are still to be found where the real influence lies, but they now have a vested interest in weakening the power of the state, devaluing the status of the bureaucracy and thinking globally. This does not always mean working for an international firm; there is also a noticeable gravitation of members of the upper castes into the international organizations and the newly fashionable NGOs, given the mushrooming of possibilities for well-paid research and consultancy. An interesting new class of urbane upper- caste report writers and international conference attenders is emerging in the new globalized India.

But not all members of the *dvija* - the supposedly 'twice born' upper castes - are affluent, highly educated and cosmopolitan. The people who once dominated the clerical posts in the public sector - the functionaries who moved files painfully slowly in government offices, banks and railway booking halls and resented serving those they considered to be their inherent inferiors, the mediocre school teachers and State college lecturers - now find themselves excluded by both the policies of Mandalization and the competitiveness of globalization. Lower middle class members of the upper castes, like the mass of the lower castes, are finding themselves squeezed into new configurations. Out of these new caste alignments a new politics is being forged which shakes the former certainties of many people.

RELIGIOUS COMMUNALISM

In the same way as caste formations constantly change, the larger identities based around religion are not essential, despite the insistence from more entrenched Hindus that one is born to a religion and conversion should not be possible. A friend offered to compile a map for this book showing the distribution of membership of religions; I refused it, explaining that the very act of mapping not only perpetuated outsider perceptions of India as riven by clear-cut religious oppositions but also constituted a small reinforcement of the divide.

The data available on religion never addresses the question as to who is a Hindu, and divisions, once unambiguously assigned, become very difficult to transcend. This is not to say that identity based upon membership of religions is not important to a great many people, or that religion is not the basis of powerful groupings - it is simply that one can refuse to help strengthen the construction. The social politics of religion is intimately involved with the social politics of caste and, just as caste is in a state of radical transformation, so is religion.

HINDUTVA

Out of all of the churning, an old idea has emerged with a new significance - the vision of a Hindu rashtra, a nation built around the principles of Hindu culture, not just a nation where the majority of people are Hindus. The view of Hinduism taken by the proponents of Hindutva has to be seen as firmly grounded in hierarchical ideology, that is, one cannot understand Hindutva if one tries to divorce it from caste, even though it purports to be inclusive of all Indians.

The underlying philosophy is nationalist and the aim is to construct a monolithic culture regulating the values of all Indians. This may seem a strange claim in the face of the multiplicity of strands within Hinduism, but Praful Bidwai catches the contradiction perfectly when he writes that 'Polytheism may have helped Hindus accommodate to other faiths, but it did not make them tolerant'. Other religions are acceptable so long as they become a part of Hinduism, not if they remain 'other'. Bidwai quotes Joshi as saying, 'Hindu Rashtra is the basic culture of this country.

All Indian Muslims are Mohammadiya Hindus; all Indian Christians are Christi Hindus. They are Hindus who have adopted Christianity and Islam as their religion,' and Sudarshan as saying, 'If Muslims have to stay in India, they will have to submit to the Indianisation of their religion'. Bidwai also demonstrates the way in which contemporary militant Hinduism tries to claim that Buddhism is no more than a sect of Hinduism, whereas in truth it was one of the many breakaways from the tyranny of caste- based Hinduism.

THE RSS

The Rashtriya Swayamsevak Sangh (RSS) (National Association of Volunteers) had been the custodian of a dream of nationalist Hinduism since it was founded in 1925. Godse, Gandhi's murderer, was a part of a Sangh-based conspiracy and the RSS never made any secret of the fact that it believed that Gandhi had betrayed Hinduism. After a period in which it was banned (and went underground) the RSS rehabilitated itself and gradually built up a strengthened web of influence. In 1996 it even felt confident enough to hold a public 'felicitation' of Godse's brother to which it invited the widows of his co-conspirators, just to show it had no regrets.

The RSS is a powerful and efficient organization which works on a cell structure. It recruits its members at a young age and has a policy of sponsoring them to gain places in all professions and major organizations, including trade unions and the media. This allows the Sangh to conduct effective propaganda work and gather information, but, most of all, it creates powerful interpersonal networks. In some ways it is rather like freemasonry. Its aim is nothing less than the unification of the whole of India under a common culture. Romila Thapar explains that this has required the invention of a new form of Hinduism to fit contemporary conditions - a new, codified, inflexible, 'syndicated Hinduism' in imitation of the Semitic religions. In a study focusing on the significance of Ram in this process she maintains that:

Characteristic of the Semitic religions are features such as a historically attested teacher or prophet, a sacred book, a geographically identifiable location for its beginnings, an ecclesiastical infrastructure and the conversion of large numbers of people to the religion - all characteristics which are largely irrelevant to the various manifestations of Hinduism until recent times. This has largely been achieved through the work of the RSS in spreading a northern Indian, brahmanical version of the religion which elevates Ram, as the king *avatar* of Vishnu, into an equivalent position to Christ.

As Thapar mentions, the popular television serialization of the *Ramayana* was influential in reinforcing the adoration of Ram and propagating a single version of the story which imposed a knowledge of heroic, masculinized Hinduism, the authority of the Vedic scriptures, and Ayodhya - Ram's birthplace and capital - as a place of origin. All of this fed back into the RSS project. The RSS also undertakes a considerable amount of welfare work, disaster relief and fundraising and runs its own chain of schools. It is famous for its practice of bonding its members from youth into *shakhas* - local assemblies which combine consciousness-raising with physical fitness.

There is early morning drill with prayer, lectures and nationalist sloganizing to establish a sense of discipline and group; this emphasizes praise for the motherland and the quasi-military nature of these defenders of the faith. In addition to the local daily assemblies it also holds uniformed mass rallies. The gatherings particularly appeal to lower-middle-class males who have few opportunities for group solidarity and there are obvious parallels with the scouting movement.

Outsiders sometimes ridicule them as paunchy old men in gym shoes and khaki shorts, but it should be remembered that the RSS adopted its ideology of discipline of mind and body at the same time as other 'Aryan' groups in Europe. Their embracing of a virile image of Hinduism under the warrior god Ram, along with emphasis on purity and control, is a chilling combination when one remembers that some of the chubby knees belong to men in very influential positions and boys who will rise fast.

THE SANGH PARIVAR

The RSS is the core organization; clustering around it are the associations which form the *Sangh Parivar* (the *Sangh's* Family). The most significant of these is the political wing, the *Bharatiya Janata* Party (BJP) which came to power in 1998 as the majority member of a coalition government. In Atal Behari Vajpayee, the RSS has its first Prime Minister. The exact relationship between the RSS and the BJP in government is never made clear, but it is acknowledged that Vajpayee is not a free agent as Prime Minister.

Other members of the *Sangh Parivar* are various youth and student movements, women's groups, development associations, policy committees, groups committed to establishing policies of swadeshi, groups with a briefing for education, the thuggish Bajrang Dal and the sinister Vishwa Hindu Parishad (VHP) (World Hindu Council). As Ahmad (1996c) clearly shows, the RSS works through the formation of 'distinct but overlapping mass fronts' which he lists as being: '(1) the front of students and intellectuals, (2) the fronts that help it cement ties with the traditional sector for religious legitimation, (3) the fronts which connect it with the urban lumpen elements and (4) the crucial parliamentary front'.

Through these fronts it has influence in virtually all of the socially and politically significant arenas in India. The Sangh uses direct propaganda, distributing its own publications, tapes and videos, but it has also gained a considerable footing in the print media and television which helps to establish its ideology as mainstream. It has a website too. Basuet al. emphasize 'the attempt of the VHP and BJP to dominate the oral culture by means of the audio-visual media', using propaganda videos which offered depictions of heroic confrontations with marauding Muslims or popular television stars appearing in 'amusing' anti-Muslim sketches.

There was free distribution of inflammatory speeches on audio-tape, calling for sacrifice and martyrdom. In a country with low levels of functional literacy the tape cassette is an ingenious means of establishing hegemony. The Sangh combine manages to be popular and ılite; to back both the khadi industry and the construction of big dams; to offer a spiritual home to statesmen and peasants. Some of its component groups are fervently *swadeshi*; others (like the BJP) attract members of the globalizing business ılite. It masterminded the campaigns against Kentucky Fried Chicken and for testing the nuclear bomb.

It has enlisted the support of the *sadhus* and appropriated the fervour of major religious gatherings like the *Kumbh Mela* (though Pinch maintains that many of the *sadhus* came to feel that they had been used in the Ayodhya movement). It claims to *be* India and it can seem very persuasive. The *Sangh* is able to offer a sense of security to people who felt that their world was being turned inside out. By stressing the wholeness and virility of Hinduism it was able to give an illusion of potency to weak people. In its VHP incarnation it stresses that, though there are many forms of Hinduism ('one garland, many flowers'), to be Indian is to be unambiguously Hindu, since Hinduism is the Indian way of life in its entirety.

This sounds like the epitome of tolerance, but it means that to be Indian is not to be Muslim, Christian or Buddhist (it is ambivalent about the status of Sikhism, which it claims as militant Hinduism). It is crucial to *Sangh* ideology that all who accept Indian nationality must accept *Hindutva,* which can only be defined circularly as not not-Hindu. The VHP has sought to establish a degree of uniformity within Hinduism, focusing on Ram, the ruler of an earlier Hindu rashtra, and establishing common core symbols, including the use of the colour saffron, in an attempt to invent the fundamentals of a non-fundamentalist religion.

PRAGMATISM

Although the ethos and the higher level leadership of the Sangh is upper caste, it has had to attract support from the masses, particularly in terms of its political wing, the BJP. It cannot ignore the voting power of the lower castes and uses a mixture of alliance and inclusion to gain power. Perhaps the most blatant piece of cynical pragmatism on both sides was the coalition with the dalit party, the BSP, in Uttar Pradesh in 1995 and power sharing in 1998, negotiated on both occasions in order to frustrate their mutual enemy, the OBC Samajwadi Party.

In the Madhya Pradesh Assembly elected in 1996, the BJP representation not only contained more SC/ST/OBC members than the Congress Party, but these outnumbered its own upper caste members (Jaffrelot 1998). None of this implies any compromising of Sangh principles - it depends upon recruiting members of the lower castes who are personally ambitious and have a popular following.

Securing this following requires the delivery of concessions. In the run up to the 1998 General Election, the incumbent Punjab administration - consisting of an alliance between the Sikh Party, the Shiromoni Akali Dal, and the BJP - extended free electricity to the households of poor members of Scheduled Castes and OBCs and handed out senior citizens' pensions. In the same campaign the Election Commission banned State governments from extending the lists of communities classified as OBC - such classification, with all its built-in entitlement to quotas, being an obvious way of establishing group loyalty to the ruling party.

WOMEN AND THE HINDU RIGHT

Whenever there is a patriarchal system, the control of the honour of women becomes a primary symbol for the strength of social units, whether we are looking at the family or at the state. The most reliable form of control is always self-discipline, the internalization of the rules by the subjects themselves, and, in the case of female honour, this means that women develop a reverence for such concepts as chastity, fidelity, maternity, humility, self sacrifice and domesticity. Women's values then form around ideals constructed in the light of the relationships within the patriarchal family and they become the custodians of such value systems, ensuring the piety of the household.

In the conventional wedding ritual, the example of the long-suffering Sita, the consort of the hero-god Ram, is presented to the bride as one she should emulate and she is told that she should bow to the 'wisdom' of her husband and see virtue in duty. Bacchetta (1996) demonstrates the way in which the Sita story is incorporated into the ideology of the Rashtra Sevika Samiti (Women's National Service Association - the women's association within the Sangh Parivar) Women who have internalized these values and shaped their lives around them find their very self-esteem threatened by the economic, political and social changes of the present.

They resent the new images of women being presented in the media, the devaluation of their homely skills, the western fashions, the 'brazen' behaviour of young middle-class women, the threat to arranged marriages and extended families. It is not surprising to find that they are attracted to the conservative ideology of Hindutva, especially since the Samiti offers these womanly values up in an aggressive and militant form.

It glorifies the warrior Rani of Jhansi and, using the symbol of the conquering form of the goddess, Durga, it gives women the opportunity to be strong and angry at the same time as being very virtuous. Basu (1995) recounts the way in which Hindu nationalism has created new spaces for women's activism. It has done so partly by creating an aura of passionate commitment to a cause that demands tremendous sacrifices of its followers. Urban middle and lower-middle-class families - who tend more than others to practice female seclusion - have allowed women considerable freedom.

She explains that people permitted their daughters-in-law to take part in riots, when they would not normally have allowed them out at night, because they were 'safe in the midst of the Sangh Parivar'. As is observed in situations where there are deep social divisions, the protection of 'our' women from the rapacious intent of the 'other' is placed at the centre of the maintenance of normality. In India one finds numerous examples of the assumed predatory intent of Muslim men in relation to Hindu women. Similarly, higher-caste women are assumed to be vulnerable to lower-caste men. Kannabiran, in a paper on rape and the construction of communal identity, argues that

The upper caste Hindu sees himself as threatened and under attack on two fronts, from the outside by 'immoral minorities' [Muslims] and from the inside by 'unclean' castes; and women form the core target in both the perception of this threat and the use of violence to suppress it. Bacchetta refers to the way in which the RSS uses the Partition as a 'recurring theme'; 'Muslim rape of Hindu women' constantly repeated alongside 'Muslim pillaging of Hindu property'.

Mani Ratnam's film Bombay, which was made in the aftermath of post-Ayodhya rioting, found it symbolically necessary that the husband should be Hindu and the wife Muslim in the inter-communal marriage which stood for communal reconciliation. Had it been otherwise it could have been used to perpetuate the fantasy of the Muslim desire to possess the women of the majority. The prominent women on the Hindu Right are few in number and very varied in style and appeal, but common to all of them is an emphasis on personal strength.

Sadvi Rithambara is probably the best known, a passionate and violent orator whose audiotapes urged the storming of the *Babri Masjid*; in contrast there is Vijaya Raya Scindia, a gracious aristocrat; the tough and glamorous Uma Bharati (Minister of State for Human Resource Development in the BJP government); and the vulgarian Jayalalitha who has managed to introduce principles of *Hindutva* into the party which is the descendant of the Tamil Non-Brahmin Movement. All, like their supporters, are convinced of the need constantly to be vigilant against the Muslim and Christian foreign menace.

MUSLIM SCAPEGOAT

Islam is the obvious target, but Muslims, as the most numerous minorities, are primarily a scapegoat which permits the forging of a corporate Hindu identity. In his study of Hindu/ Muslim rioting in Hyderabad, the psychoanalyst, Sudir Kakar, refers to the Hindu 'cultural memory' of Muslim tyranny under rulers such as Tipu and Aurangzeb, saying that 'cultural memory is the imaginative basis for a sense of cultural identity ... for isn't imagination a memory of vital moments of life freed from their actual, historical context?' As Basu *et al.* (1993) show, this means unifying Hinduism, when formerly it was unorganized; it also means giving preference to the religious forms of the upper castes in the Hindi-speaking 'heartland'.

Whatever anyone might say about Muslims receiving special treatment, reproducing too fast or plotting with enemies of the state, India's Muslim communities are on the whole deprived, politically cautious and very aware of their minority status. This does not make them any less suitable for demonization by the forces of Hindu chauvinism, for the goal is not so much the defeat of a threatening minority as the establishment of the power of a Hindu force for its own sake. Hasan (1996) warns against thinking of India's Muslims as a homogeneous group and shows that Muslim intellectuals have often, to their own cost, built upon a British notion of Muslims constituting a separate nation.

Ideas about *Hindutva* were becoming more popular through the 1980s as the VHP doggedly worked at encouraging Hindu households to fly a saffron flag, to display *Om* stickers on their crash helmets and posters of Ram in heroic mode in cafıs and other public places. It staged pilgrimages and organized group projects to increase solidarity. In 1990 the senior RSS/ BJP figure, Advani, embarked upon a rallying *rath yatra* through northern India to Ayodhya in Uttar Pradesh, the supposed birthplace and capital of Ram, the god king.

The translation 'chariot pilgrimage' does not quite do justice to the dignity of the symbolism of the vehicle of the conquering hero, Ram, but neither did the truck, decorated with a chariot cut-out and bearing an ageing politician, unless one were a devotee. There was a call for the demolition of the small sixteenth-century mosque, the Babri Masjid, which enthusiasts claimed had been built on the exact site of the birthplace of Ram at Ayodhya? When a new wave of international influence combined with the rumblings of Mandalization in the early 1990s, the hour of Hindutva had come.

On 6 December 1992, in an act of collective vandalism, RSS storm troopers tore down the mosque whilst the police looked in other directions. This date is taken as a milestone in the development of communalism in contemporary India. It provoked waves of communal violence across much of India, notably in Bombay where the attacks on Muslim citizens were co-ordinated by the ruling Shiv Sena. (I am using the old name Bombay in preference to Mumbai, since that was still its name. The change of name in 1995 was yet another sign of the Shiv Sena's authority.) Bal Thackeray, the leader of the Shiv Sena, said that the Muslims in Bombay had acted like the Jews in Nazi Germany and should not, therefore, be surprised to receive the same treatment. Mani Ratnam's film Bombay, banned and then released in 1995, is a sentimentalized but powerful treatment of the events.

As Ludden (1996) explains, Hindutva forces construct Muslims as foreigners - outsiders, invaders, infiltrators - and there is a constant discourse of 'othering'. They complain that politicians outside the BJP 'pander' to Muslims, who receive too many concessions, particularly their right to retain Islamic personal law instead of accepting a common civil code. (This came to public attention in the infamous Shah Bano case, in which the Supreme Court upheld a decision under Islamic law that a man was not required to pay alimony to his elderly divorced wife.)

They use sleight-of-hand to present Indian Muslims as Pakistanis, never more so than during the Kargil confrontation. Marqusee (1996) demonstrates the way in which Hindus checked Muslims for their reactions to India's win over Pakistan at Banglore in the quarter-finals of the cricket World Cup. They become disturbed by illegal immigrants coming across the porous Bangladesh border, deporting Indian Muslims who cannot prove that they are not Bangladeshi. Muslim-majority Kashmir is, of course, a constant source of anxiety. The military might of India, including the nuclear bomb, is constantly poised to repel attack from Pakistan, the Muslim state whose birth demonstrated the separability of India.

The same forces encourage routine harassment such as defiling mosques with pig carcasses or ransacking the studio of M.F. Husain, one of India's most eminent artists, on the spurious grounds that he had painted the goddess Saraswati irreverently. There is no justification for the pretence that Islam is anti-Indian or does not have a place in contemporary India. As Hasan (1990) demonstrates, there are plenty of historical precedents for peaceful co-existence of Hindu and Muslim people in India. If one thinks that pedigree is important in conferring rights of citizenship, the majority of Muslims are the descendants not of invaders but of *dalit* converts, attracted by the egalitarian ethos of Islam.

India has the second largest Muslim population in the world (after Indonesia); even though this constitutes only 12.1 per cent of the total, it is still a significant share. In any case proportions are irrelevant; there is no justification for demonizing a minority, whatever its size. The events of 1992 have served to make Muslims - always conscious of their minority status - feel ever more beleaguered. There is no doubt that fundamentalist forces within Islam gained increasing support. The election of a BJP majority in 1998 did nothing to calm their fears, especially when extracts from a 1995 article written by Vajpayee for the RSS journal, The Organiser, were published. Vajpayee (who became Prime Minister) maintained that the solution to 'the Muslim problem' was that Muslims should be 'changed and then restored to the mainstream after providing them with the right samskaras'; his alternative to this was that they should be rejected as compatriots (The Hindu 1998a). During the election campaign a bomb had devastating effects in Coimbatoire; it was planted by Islamic militants. In June there was rioting, with loss of life in the old city - the Muslim quarter of Hyderabad.

Their organizations protested that Muslims were full members of the nation and that their loyalty should not be questioned. They complained that Muslims were underrepresented in all governmental institutions and that the small number of Muslim MPs and MLAs in the secular political parties did not actively represent their interests, leading to a campaign for the regionalist Muslim parties to merge into a national party. They did this in November 1998, forming the Milli Jamhoohri Mahaz. Its first assembly passed resolutions demanding the reconstruction of the Babri Masjid on the same site, proportional representation in the State legislatures and Parliament, and quotas in the government services (The Hindu 17 November 1998) - one further step in the deepening of communalization in Indian politics.

AYODHYA

The demolition of the Babri Masjid was not a single finite act. The dispute had rumbled on for centuries, sometimes lying dormant, erupting in times of communal strife, acting as a symbol and a catalyst. Ramachandra Gandhi (1992), writing before the demolition, used Hindu philosophy and local mythology to argue that a narrow interpretation of the literal birthsite of Ram diminishes belief, confines the spiritual to the physical. 'The zone as a whole is Rama's birthplace; and every part and portion of it and every point on its surface.

Any number of birthplace shrines can be established there'. He explains that a far wider area is known in local mythology as ' Sita's Kitchen' and assumes that this must have been the site of a pre-Hindu sacred grove, leading him to argue that 'a deeper understanding of the site's significance can not only resolve the Ayodhya dispute but also help dissolve the pervasive dualism of "self" and "other" which is hurling civilization headlong towards annihilation'. The point is not to know who came first on the site but to understand why some people choose to rally around its ownership as a symbol of their own conflicts.

Archaeologists starting from different ideological positions have long found evidence to back the claims of their 'side' and the sequencing of the accumulation of supposedly objective scientific facts makes a fascinating story. The latest round in the struggle for the ownership of this history occurred in 1998 when the BJP Government, as one of its first actions, purged the Indian Council of Historical Research - the main historical research institute - of secularist historians who had questioned the archeological evidence for a Hindu temple below the mosque.

After the demolition, people all over India were urged to send money and bricks, inscribed with the name of Ram, for the construction of a new temple, giving widespread symbolic ownership of it. When it was revealed that pillars were being carved in Rajasthan for assembly in Ayodhya, *The Hindu*

(1998b) commented that 'The construction-related activities establish beyond doubt the continuing agenda of the Sangh Parivar to systematically erode the secular spirit of the national polity.' The control of sacred geography and history continues to be of the utmost importance in the maintenance of communal conflict.

In 1997 the VHP launched another initiative in Utter Pradesh which never gained the same emotive following as Ayodhya. This was the *Krishnajanbabhoomi* agitation, aimed at liberating Krishna's birthplace at Mathura from under yet another mosque; its initial rally was timed to coincide with the Muslim festival of Bakrid. Lest anyone think that this 'religious' movement was not a political gesture, one of its organizers told a *Frontline* reporter, 'We would like to see how SP leader Mulayam Singh Yadav opposes an agitation dedicated to liberating the birthplace of the principal deity of his community'. (The yadavs' traditional occupation is cattle rearing and milk production. The god Krishna was a cowherd. More importantly in today's politics, Mulayam Singh Yadav is a leading secular politician and former Chief Minister of Uttar Pradesh.)

CHRISTIANS

The Christian minority is tiny - just 2.34 per cent of the population - and though it is highly concentrated in the north-eastern States and Kerala, elsewhere it consists of small pockets of converts of *dalits* or tribal people who have used Christianity as a strategy for escaping caste status. The Syrian Christians of Kerala claim a lineage stretching back to St Thomas the Apostle, asserting that their ancestors were Brahmins who wished to escape from the matrilineal descent system. They are an ılite and exclusive category of people with very high levels of education, professional skills and business acumen; they have little in common with the Keralan *dalit* Christians who are more recent converts and are more typical of Indian Christians. Clark (1998) and Massey (1995) both emphasize the *dalit* identity of the majority of Christians and the ways in which this is not obliterated by membership of the church.

As part of the paranoia of *Hindutva,* Christians have come to be seen by right-wing elements as an enemy and conversions are regarded as a subversion of the power of the Hindu rashtra. Calls were made for a law to be passed banning conversions, on the grounds that, since Hinduism was a broad enough religion to contain any faith, conversions by force and trickery must be taking place. Administrators working in areas with Christian minorities say that they had seen the violence brewing for the five years beforehand, but it erupted in late 1998. Churches were burned in the Dangs district of Gujarat; nuns were raped in Bihar and RSS officers suggested that they had only themselves to blame.

In January 1999 in Orissa, Graham Staines, an Australian missionary, and his two young sons were burned to death in their vehicle. With remarkable lack of sympathy, the VHP Vice-President said that Staines' work with leprosy patients was a mere 'facade' for conversion work (Muralidharan 1999). Many explained the current upsurge of opposition to this politically inconspicuous community as a device to emphasize that to be Indian is to be Hindu, stressing that the Congress Party had disloyally selected a leader, Sonia Gandhi, who was foreign by faith as well as by birth. (So much for the idea of the loyal wife and the sanctity of mothers of the nation.)

An India Today article quotes an RSS member as saying of missionaries, 'They are not only changing the religion but converting nationality'. Because of the presence of foreign missionaries it is easy (and often justifiable) to make the link between proselytizing Christianity and western imperialism. Against all of this there were forcible 'reconversions' of Christians to Hinduism, even though tribal people generally were not Hindu before conversion to Christianity and the issue of dalit Hindu status is unclear. It is reported that, in the first two weeks of 1999, 1 200 members of the *Bhil* tribe in the Dangs district were reconverted. There was also violent 'liberation' of Christian institutions like schools which were seized in order to be run by Hindu organizations.

The leading figures in carrying out the atrocities were members of an organization of young men known as the *Bajrang Dal* (Bajrang is another name for Hanuman, the monkey god who was famous for his devotion to Ram). It is generally seen as the unruly but passionately-devoted wing of the *Sangh Parivar*. Halarnkar and Mahurkar (1999) show that there is paranoia amongst poorly qualified men of the upper castes about the way in which dalits and tribal people are able to gain education through adherence to Christianity.

They cite an interview with a youth from the Bajrang Dal who had taken a leading part in a raid on a kindergarten in an Ahmedabad slum and who felt that seizing it for the VHP was a noble act. It is obvious that the Dal offers the chance of the glow of heroism to people with few prospects. Although the battle is presented in religious terms, it is fairly obvious that we are also looking at a caste and class struggle in which religion is being used, on both sides, as a rallying point.

EDUCATION

Much of the most prestigious schooling in India is in the hands of the Roman Catholic Church. 'Convent educated' is a term often used to describe the English-speaking ιlites. This domination is not surprisingly resented by many people, as an educational system lays down the value system of a country. Virtually all of the teachers are Indian nationals and by no means are all of the staff at these schools nuns and priests or even Christians. Direct proselytizing is absolutely forbidden, but religious symbols and texts are everywhere. The RSS complains (and who can blame them?) that the church is influencing the ιlite.

Government schools are supposed to be religiously neutral, in keeping with the principles of the secular state. Schools usually interpret this by employing ecumenical devices, addressing an unspecified god, pruning out sectarian symbols, but it is very obvious that Hindu motifs creep in as uncontroversially 'Indian'. The current BJP Government, however, with the RSS constantly prompting it, has attempted a stealthy Hinduization of civil life in general and education in particular. The RSS has long complained that Hindu values are underplayed in formal education.

In 1998 at a conference of State education ministers, convened by the Human Resource Development Ministry (Minister Uma Bharati), the Vidya Bharati, the educational wing of the RSS, made a series of proposals for school education to be 'Indianized, nationalized and spiritualized', with the teaching of 'the essentials of Indian culture'. Everyone knows that this meant Hindu education. Things were deemed to have gone too far when the Uttar Pradesh Government made it compulsory to start the school day with renderings of the Hindu songs Vande Mataram (Praise to the Motherland, a freedom song which, to the resentment of many, has been appropriated by the Hindu Right) and the Sarawati Vandana (the hymn of praise to the goddess of wisdom, the arts and learning).

The Muslim League forbade Muslim schoolchildren to join in the worship. Besides maintaining its own schools, which often offer the only functioning education in rural areas, the Vidya Bharati demands the teaching of Sanskrit (the language of the scriptures) in all schools. It sponsors the revision and adoption of school textbooks which give a Hindutva construction of history and use Hindutva examples in grammar and comprehension exercises. With a BJP government in power, its project has greater power than ever.

It has already been mentioned that uncongenial historical research is being stifled. There is a similar trend in all academic disciplines which gains respectability by dressing in the clothes of anti-imperialism, which western scholars, mindful of their own imperial guilt, frequently take at face value. A recent example is Singh's paper entitled 'Rethinking development in India' in the collection edited by Simon and Narman; it asks seemingly innocent questions like, 'Is it possible to discern any sense of sacred in the "alternative development" strategy?' and builds up an argument full of the sort of 'tradition' which rests upon old divisions of caste, religion and gender.

SECULARISM

Many commentators believe that since Hindu nationalism has invaded Indian politics, there can be no assumption that the state is neutral any longer, with a resulting growth of cynicism about government. More than mere factionalism, this is arguably the greatest price of communalism, whereby the assumption that violence is normal creeps into one's political consciousness. The counter to the communalist forces is secularism, which was seen by Nehru as an essential component of the independent India. The term 'secularism' is used in India in a range of rather different ways. The obvious meaning is the separation of religion from state; this requires that the law is independent of religion and that religious motifs are not incorporated in the symbolic construction of the state.

However, this use of the term has been extended into a peculiarly Indian usage - that the state should be even- handed towards all religions. There is also the strange communalist appropriation of the idea of secularism, which claims that all (acceptable) belief can be incorporated within Hinduism which is uniquely tolerant of all. This last usage results in accusations of 'pseudo-secularism' being levelled at people who support either of the other more conventional uses. To criticize *Hindutva* is very definitely not to criticize Hinduism.

There are forms of Hindu belief which consider that the nation state is a modernist irrelevance; stress equality not only among people but also between people and nature; emphasize giving and selflessness; value non-violence and tolerance. There are many people who are not supporters of the Hindu Right or of communalism who regret the way in which Hinduism has been perverted into *Hindutva.* One sometimes sees the slogan 'Keep your politics out of my religion!' in protest against this. Such people often express an anti-secularist view, claiming that the way forward for India is to reject western ways and to espouse traditional Indian values, including a suffusion of spirituality in all aspects of life. Leading figures with this view are Ashis Nandy and T.N. Madan (1997a and b) who have been influential in establishing an anti-modernist trend in Indian intellectual life.

Their arguments are very appealing, particularly to people with orientalist leanings, as they offer the hope that there could be a way to shut out the unpleasantnesses of global competition and reorientate oneself into a whole different way of life. However, they present a romantic notion of traditional India which is difficult to apply to real conditions. Achin Vanaik (1997) and Partha Chatterjee (1994) are disinclined to believe that one can achieve true equality and heal the divisions within society within the bounds of tradition; both argue for a non-consumerist and totally secular modernity as India's contribution to contemporary global politics.

A HINDU BOMB

When India exploded nuclear devices at Pokhran in the Rajasthan desert in May 1998 there was jubilation in the streets of the major cities. The new BJP Government had been promising the tests in the light of the country's refusal to sign the Comprehensive Test Ban Treaty, seen as a western plot to enfeeble India. Crowds danced in celebration of this manifestation of national strength, even though the delight was soon to be tempered by Pakistan demonstrating that it too had the Bomb. Containers of sand from the site were distributed around the country as relics of the achievement. The tests were interpreted by all but a minority as being a matter for pride and patriotism, a demonstration of India's scientific and technical achievement. They were also a message not just to Pakistan, but also to the western nuclear powers that India would not be pushed around.

The secular Left is conducting an uphill campaign to educate people about the nuclear threat. Whilst the Left draws attention to the ironies of a desire for nuclear force in a country which fails to deliver clean drinking water to all its citizens, the Hindu Right appropriates the glory and the powerful imagery of weaponry named after gods. In the 1999 Kargil War, the most enthusiastic supporters of *Hindutva*, such as Bal Thackeray, periodically threatened to 'go nuclear'. The war was about national sovereignty - it was not a matter of Hindu versus Muslim; however, in contemporary situations in which state and religion are being brought into greater intimacy, the risks of conflation of national interest with faith become frightening.

8

Regional Movements

Although Independent India was constituted as a federal republic, it has always been highly centralized - the Union Government having power over defence, foreign affairs, planning, currency, major aspects of taxation and legislation. The majority of funding for the States comes from the Centre and the senior administrators are members of the All India Services, though they are attached to State cadres. Each State has a Governor, who acts as the representative of the Government of India; this person is appointed by the President and does not necessarily have a prior connection with the State. The President of India can, under Article 356 of the Constitution, suspend the individual State governments if these are deemed to have lost control of law and order, if there is a breakdown of the State economy, or during war.

The Centre can also declare a general State of Emergency where all State legislatures are dissolved, as did Indira Gandhi between 1975 and 1977. The strong Centre is largely the product of the Independence Movement, whereby India was imagined as a single nation in opposition to the colonial power. This sense of nationhood was intended to cut across community and region to create a strong and unified modern state and to prevent the emergence of sub-state nationalisms. One can see this vision of the unified state as being in the idealized image of the Congress Party - modern, pan-Indian but upper-caste dominated.

However, we can also see the new India reflecting the centralized structure of the colonial power, the States replicating the British administrative provinces, with the addition of the princely States. Nehru's modernizing project was opposed to the autonomous development of the States as ethnic and linguistic regions but it was in Indira Gandhi that the Centre strengthened to become all-dominating. Virtually all decisions at State level needed to be ratified by the Centre and State politics was conducted with an eye to Delhi.

Brass (1984) introduces the idea of a 'dynamic interpenetration' as being essential between Centre and State in a federal structure but considers the greatest weakness in Indian politics to be its ever-increasing centralizing tendencies (1994). This is a view shared by many Indian political theorists of the Left, perhaps most cogently expressed by Partha Chatterjee in his celebration of the potential demise of centralized power following the 1996 elections. Brass contends that the overcentralization of Indian politics, associated with Hindu majoritarianism, is the direct cause of minority regional and ethnic discontent, leading to secessionist and autonomist movements. He does not believe that inherent regional identity provides the motive force for autonomy or secession.

As he shows, the response of the Centre to demands for autonomy has always been the use of repressive measures, sometimes the use of considerable military or para-military force, since there is a fear that the Centre will not hold and that India will fragment into its component parts. For Brass, and many others, the only solution is to devolve power to the States and then right down to the level of local government, rather than to attempt further concentration.

Forms of decentralization at the lowest level, such as *panchayati raj* and the favouring of NGOs have been incorporated into the structural adjustment programme as a major aspect of the project of rolling back the bureaucratized state. The States vary considerably in terms of their economic fortunes and their influence nationally. This is not just a matter of location and physical geography but of histories of previous trade relations and investments, development strategies, and internal political relations. Today we see State governments increasingly promoting themselves directly on the global stage, seeking foreign investment, advertising their tourist attractions, offering concessions and bidding for international aid. There are regular State supplements in overseas newspapers and journals and State-based foreign deputations are becoming routine.

ARTICLE 356

However, there is little devolution of real power to the States, as was brought home very clearly in January 1999, when President's Rule was (briefly) imposed upon Bihar. Certainly the status of law and order in Bihar was at crisis point, but, as its Chief Minister was quick to point out, there were other States, such as Gujarat, Maharashtra and Uttar Pradesh, which also witnessed communal violence but were protected from President's Rule by having BJP/ Shiv Sena governments. In the case of Bihar, the Samata Party - a member of the Union Coalition Government but the minority party in the State - was determined to bring down the RJD administration.

Other States had already been investigated over their law and order status. Tamil Nadu's former Chief Minister, Jayalalitha, had been campaigning for President's Rule as a way of ousting the State's DMK Government and in June 1999 the leader of the AIADMK Parliamentary Party (part of the coalition government) walked out of the Lok Sabha on her instructions. In West Bengal, Mamata Bannerjee of the Trinamul Congress, yet another coalition member, stirred up a demand for President's Rule in opposition to the ruling CPI(M) government.

Since Independence, Article 356 has been invoked more than a hundred times, but in 1998 it became the subject of considerable controversy because it seemed to be being used very opportunistically. The scope for abuse of Article 356 is obvious. A precarious government at the Centre can intervene in State matters, so long as it can gain the agreement of the President. Refusing to meet the Central Home Ministry team of enquiry into alleged *panchayati raj* election violence, the West Bengal Home Minister declared:

It appears that the Trinamul Congress is pressurising the Centre to serve its own narrow political interests. The Centre, too, cannot do a thing as it is dependent on the support of parties like the Trinamul. If it is really worried about the law and order situation, it should send a team to Uttar Pradesh.

On the same page of The Hindu, the All-India Congress Committee accused the BJP Government of 'trying to erode federalism. This is nothing but an attempt of the Sangh Parivar to spread its wings all over the country.' The BJP was accused of having 'elastic standards' relating to its concern for law and order in the States, given that it was not imposing President's Rule in Rajasthan (with its appalling rate of violence against women and dalits), Uttar Pradesh (with its dacoity, kidnapping and rape record), or even Jammu and Kashmir with its troubled political situation (Swami et al. 1998). The leading indepth journal of current affairs, Frontline, brought out a special issue (Muralidharan 1998c) on the implications of the cynical attitude of the BJP-led coalition to the suspension of democratically-elected governments at the State level, arguing that the main problem was the Centre rather than the States.

Besides the simple expediency of retaining power, the BJP must adhere to the ideology of the RSS, with its ultimate project of a single Hindu *rashtra* with a strong central authority. Ironically, at present it can further this aim only by compromising with the minority parties in the regions. The intense debate in the late 1990s about the nature of federalism and the continuation of democracy in India formed around the realization that Article 356 is a loophole whereby a dictatorship can be imposed, regardless of the political will in the regions. As Kuppuswami maintains:

> The frequent misuse of Article 356 [is] possible ... because of the Governors aiding and abetting the Centre in imposing President's Rule when the state was ruled by a party in opposition to the ruling party at the Centre. The Union Cabinet appoints as Governors retired bureaucrats who were accustomed to serving the interests of the Union or politicians belonging to the ruling party who are not able to find a suitable place in the political arena ... The framers of the Constitution intended that a Governor be a person above party politics.

Although the RSS works through the umbrella organization of the *Sangh Parivar* which contains many traditionalist elements, its impetus is very definitely in terms of modernist imperatives. It gains its majority support from those lower-middle-class people who are squeezed by modernizing forces but who were also constructed by them. For this section of society, a strong centralized, even militarized, and state seems an essential bastion against the potential power of the mass, located at regional level.

NEW STATES

It is impossible to draw the State boundaries in India in such a way that each is ethnically and linguistically homogeneous, even though there have been boundary reorganizations as a consequence of agitation on linguistic grounds. In 1956 Madras Province was divided between Tamil Nadu and Andhra Pradesh; in 1960 Bombay Province became Maharashtra and Gujarat; in 1966 Punjab split into Punjab, Harayana and Himachal Pradesh. However, it is impossible for each minority to have its own State since each new State formation, as well as making former minorities into majorities, also does the exact opposite.

It becomes essential that the States, just as much as the Union should generate policies in which their own minorities are accorded equal rights. States, however, do not just segment internally along linguistic lines - like the nation, they contain religious, and caste and tribal divisions, which rarely have more than a loose fit to territory. The language and ethnicity issue is important not just for reasons of identity but because of economic and political opportunities. It is inevitable that as economic and political formations change, there will be new demands phrased in terms of old divisions. Recently, the stated policy of the BJP encourages the formation wherever possible, of smaller States has been far more significant than any grass-roots agitation for autonomy. Like the abuse of Article 356, this policy is intended to strengthen the Centre by fragmenting the States and removing the power base of some important players.

JHARKHAND/VANANCHAL AND CHHATTISGARH

One of the oldest demands for a new State is that of the Jharkhand Movement, whose history stretches back into pre-Independence days. It consists of an alliance of tribes in southern Bihar, western Orissa and eastern Madhya Pradesh which had long campaigned for a separate state called Jharkhand, where tribal people (adivassis) would be in the majority. It was intended that this new State should be carved out of all three existing States.

The southern part of Bihar is very rich in minerals; India depends upon this region for coal and iron in particular, but it is also becoming very important for the mining of uranium. It contains the steel city of Jamshedpur which is virtually controlled by the major industrialist firm of Tata. It is this wealth which so long stood in the way of separate statehood for the tribal people with their predominantly forest-based economic system. Like most sub-state nationalisms worldwide, the Jharkhand Movement was led by frustrated educated minorities who saw opportunities in a new political structure; it also drew upon the aspirations of the poorly unionized industrial workforce, drawn from the tribal rural areas.

In the political transformations of the 1980s and 1990s we can see the status of the tribal people of the Jharkhand region changing in the light of changes in the politics of the component States. At the national level, Bihar took on the role of the scapegoat State, the one which could always be called upon the show how bad things would get in terms of corruption, favouritism, disorder, caste violence and economic backwardness, and much of this was attributed to the way in which Bihar had become dominated by OBC politics.

Its Chief Minister, Laloo Pradad Yadav, was perceived by both Congress and BJP governments at the Centre as an overly powerful player in the national as well as State arena. The yadav power base is northern Bihar - the densely-populated, agriculturally-based, Hindu/Hindi heartland - but 70 per cent of the tax revenue of Bihar is generated through the mining and processing of the South. It is perhaps inevitable that this economic and political configuration, rather than the long struggle of tribal peoples for self-determination, should lead to successive Union governments becoming increasingly friendly to the idea of a separate Jharkhand State.

In 1994 the Jharkhand Autonomous Areas Council was established in the southern districts of Bihar as a consequence of economic pressure and popular unrest; it was predominantly composed of members of the *Jharkhand Mukti Morcha* (JMM). This organization had travelled a long way to the political Right since its days of violent agitation and association with Naxalite groups in the 1970s.

The initial impetus for Jharkhand grew out of demands for the rights of tribal people, particularly regarding access to forests and compensation for land acquired for mining and industry, but gradually, with increased investment, the non-tribal population of the region grew to constitute a majority; this was largely as a consequence of migration from northern Bihar.

The movement then came to represent far wider economic interests than those with a subsistence base and to have as its main focus a divorce from the impoverished and OBC-dominated North, which was seen as draining away the South's wealth. In 1993 there was a 'money for-votes' scandal when it was alleged that seven JMM members of the *Lok Sabha* were bribed with more than eight crores of rupees to prop up the tottering Congress Government, and the JMM was revealed as being as opportunist an organization as any.

There was growing BJP support in southern Bihar and the party at the Centre increasingly turned its attention to the region, promising that, if elected to government, it would grant a separate State. This new State, however, would consist only of the southern districts of Bihar and would be known as Vananchal (land of the forest) to distinguish it from the Jharkhand which had aspirations towards districts in Orissa and Madhya Pradesh. In 1998 the necessary bill was tabled.

On the Madhya Pradesh side of the border is the proposed new State of Chhattisgarh,. The original demands for a greater Jharkhand as a tribal people's State included two of the 13 districts which would make up the new Chhattisgarh, but the BJP set its sights on creating a new State in its own right, in which tribal aspirations would be incidental. The similarities with Vananchal are considerable. It is a mineral-rich region in a poor State and provides 45 per cent of the State's revenue. It has a substantial but fragmented tribal population which provides cheap labour for mining and industry and it has a new immigrant population of caste Hindus with commercial interests, who have swollen the non-tribal population to such an extent that it now constitutes a majority.

UTTARAKHAND/UTTARANCHAL

The hill districts of Uttar Pradesh are different in many ways from the more populous plains which constitute the greater part of the State. Most obvious is the difference in terrain which means that there is little rural opportunity other than a precarious living from forests and from terraced small-holdings. The hills have long sent substantial numbers of young men into the armed forces and they rely on government employment, some tourist activity and remittances from wage-earners on the plains. There are other less obvious differences, such as the predominance of the Pahari language and an unusual caste configuration, whereby Brahmins and Rajputs make up about 80-85 per cent of the population, as against about 11 per cent for the whole State.

Uttar Pradesh is India's largest State in terms of population (152 million) but the hill districts account for only 4 per cent of this. The lifestyles and economic interests of the hills are radically different from those of the plains and there have long been suggestions that the hill region could form a separate State; however, as Mawdsley shows, until recently there was little serious enthusiasm for this. These differences surfaced as an active demand for separate status in 1994 when the Chief Minister, Mulayam Singh Yadav (leader of the OBC-dominated Samajwadi Party), announced that he would apply reservations according to the Mandal recommendations in all districts in the State. More specifically he instructed the higher education institutions in the hills to reserve 50 per cent of places for SC/ST/OBC.

There was a sudden realization that the government service and the colleges would be swamped with lower- caste outsiders and that valuable job and opportunities would be lost (Ramakrishnan 1994a). The Uttarakhand Movement was initially launched by students who saw their job opportunities receding, but it soon grew, particularly after violent confrontations with the police in September 1994 in which 20 protestors were killed. As the campaign escalated, State and central government institutions were picketed, a district collector was murdered, *bandhs* (closure of shops etc.) were organized, and trains were stopped. When a bus carrying protestors to Delhi was fired at by the police in Muzaffarnagar, 15 of its passengers were killed and women allegedly raped (I have to say 'allegedly', since it has not yet been proven), and the tide of public opinion in India swung in favour of the movement (Ramakrishnan 1994b and c).

In 1995, a coalition of the BSP and the BJP replaced the Samajwadi Party as the State government. Mayawati, the first *dalit* woman to hold the rank, was Chief Minister and was opposed to demands for Uttarakhand; she was also demonstratively anti-upper caste and made life a misery for sympathetic civil servants by transferring them at will. However, the BJP part of the alliance was in full support of the separate State and it demonstrated this clearly on the anniversary of the rioting by helping to organize a rally in commemoration of the martyrs.

The Uttarakhand Movement is predominantly upper caste, middle class and BJP-voting; its demands are those of the new India, with very few echoes of the forest activists of the past. It has experienced violent opposition from both the State government and the Centre but with the BJP's accession to power at both levels, Uttarakhand (to be known as Uttaranchal) was assured its separate statehood. Reservations will be in proportion to its own unique caste composition.

Despite support from the Centre, the problem still rumbles on. The minority Sikh population of the Terai region on the borders of the proposed new State is resisting inclusion, enlisting the support of the Punjabi party, the *Akali Dal* - a partner of the BJP. The Sikhs in question were refugees from Partition and had been given grants of forest land which were not subject to the State's land ceiling laws. They had become affluent large farmers and owners of sugar and rice mills and had much in common with the rest of Green Revolution western Uttar Pradesh. They feared that Uttaranchal would impose land ceilings on them, and also that their products would have to pay duties when they crossed what would become a State border into Uttar Pradesh. They had nothing to gain from revised reservation laws and felt that there was much to lose from joining a smaller, poorer unit.

VIDARBHA AND TELENGANA

Vidarbha, on the north-eastern side of Maharashtra, is similar in many ways to Chhattisgarh or Vananchal in that it has a significant tribal population and is mineral rich. It is also a major cotton and orange producing region, but has received limited amounts of development funding from Maharashtra and is regarded as a 'backward' region. Where it differs from the claims for statehood already mentioned is that, this time, the opposition to its formation comes from a State government which is an ally of the BJP. Whilst the BJP at the Centre was willing to stand up to Congress-ruled Madhya Pradesh and RJD-ruled Bihar, its policy in relation to the opposition to claims from Vidarbha has been to back down. Similarly the bid for Telengana in northern Andhra Pradesh has been a virtual non-starter because of the ruling Telugu Desam Party's valuable opposition to the Congress Party in the State.

UNION TERRITORIES

At the same time as it tabled bills for the creation of the new States of Uttaranchal, Vananchal and Chhattisgarh, the central government announced the creation of the new State of Delhi and shortly afterwards, Pondicherry - both hitherto Union Territories. The Tamil Nadu opposition party, the AIADMK, immediately organized a victory procession to celebrate the new status of Pondicherry. As *The Hindu* of 15 March 1998 commented of Pondicherry, 'There is hardly any scope for the proposed State sustaining itself. In fact the clamour for statehood has very much to do with the thirst of the political class for more executive authority.' It was widely believed that Pondicherry received statehood only as a condition for AIADMK support for the Delhi Statehood Bill, which had long been a major ambition of the BJP.

The State of Delhi will exclude the separate area of the administrative capital but will consist of the major residential areas. It will be the most affluent and politically influential State in the Union and, most importantly, will be able to administer the allocation of some of the most valuable urban land in the country. Part of that power will extend to being able to displace illegal residents from good development land. Even as a State, Delhi will however still have all its old problems regarding the release of water by Haryana.

THE NORTH EAST

The States of the North East (Assam, Manipur, Meghalia, Nagaland, Tripura, Arunachal Pradesh and Mizoram) have always sat uneasily in independent India. With majority tribal populations they differ in virtually all respects from the rest of the country and have more affinities with neighbouring countries such as Burma and Bhutan. Mountainous States, connected to the rest of India by the narrow 'panhandle', it is easy to forget that they are part of the Union. They are off-limits to casual visitors from India because of the long-running armed struggle of separatist movements of two kinds: first, the radical demand for the secession of Assam from India, and second, the local demands for internal fragmentation to create Bodoland, based on tribal ethnicity, out of the present Assam.

Brass gives an excellent account of the issues involved until the early 1990s. These revolve around problems of multiple minority status and immigration. Assam's indigenous population is Assamese- speaking and Hindu, but this was overlain by Bengali administrators, estate owners and traders, both Hindu and Muslim. The Bangladesh War caused a huge immigration of Bangladeshis (Muslims) and Assam claimed that it was becoming flooded with foreigners. Assam's indigenous Hindus wanted its borders more effectively policed and to be able to deport outsiders; they also successfully campaigned for Assamese as the only official State language, gaining an advantage over the Bengalis.

The United Liberation Front of Assam emerged as a militant separatist organization, agitating for independence from India; its main base was educated, unemployed middle-class youth, frustrated by the lack of prospects in the State. As time progressed, its anti-immigrant stance waned and it became increasingly left wing. It maintains bases in neighbouring Bhutan, a country with an uneasy relationship with India. Meanwhile, tribal minorities in Assam resented the influence of the Assamese Hindu community and claimed that they were excluded from many State benefits on the grounds of both language and networks; they began their own violent campaign, under the Bodo Liberation Tigers, for separate statehood for Bodoland. Currently there are central government accusations that the Muslim schools in the area are harbouring Pakistani ISI-funded trainee terrorists.

There is little question of splitting or granting independence to Assam. The government's tactic has been to strengthen the Bodo Autonomous Council and to fund its development projects directly, rather than through the Assam Government. It has also sought to cut off the funding of the Liberation Tigers by getting tough with the big tea companies, demanding that they cease paying the militants protection money. Given that planters have suffered shootings, kidnappings and intimidation of their labour force, it is hardly surprising that they are willing to pay up; there are also plenty of indications that they are more interested in a stable regime than in giving any enthusiastic support to the Government of Assam.

The other northern States continue to be plagued by terrorism as militant elements fight for the same independence as Bhutan, and yet there are also women's peace movements, as in Manipur, where there are counter-campaigns simply against violence. Gorkaland seeks the status of an autonomous State, independent from West Bengal, whose CPI(M) government is sympathetic to its demands but intractably opposed to dividing the State, following the expressed party policy of support for strong States. We can probably expect Gorkaland to be in the next round of proposed States, unless its sensitive border position makes the Centre fearful of complete secession.

THE PUNJAB

The Punjab lies on India's most sensitive border. The line dividing it from Pakistan is nothing more than the slash of a cartographer's pen - more than half of the Punjab lies on the other side and many people have their ancestral homes there. The Punjab bore the brunt of the violence of Partition and has never quite shaken off its legacy. Muslim Pakistan may be the enemy, but part of the country itself is 'home'. It continues to be a State with its heart severed in two, never forgetting that everything can be taken away, nothing can be relied upon. In the three wars with Pakistan the Punjab has found itself in the front line.

Even in the Kargil 'War', continuing as I write, Punjabis are moving their families, livestock and valuables away from the border, just in case it escalates. It is no wonder that the State is never quite settled or that it sees itself as distinctive. For the present, the Punjab is relatively stable, its tensions channelled into internecine disputes between religious factions rather than political groups, but the stability cannot be taken for granted.

The Punjab has been betrayed many times over; it has a long history of invasions which trained its people to be aggressive and protective at the same time. Its population consists of both Sikhs and Hindus and there is a distinctive Punjabi culture irrespective of religion. The RSS would have us believe that Sikhism is nothing more than the militant wing of Hinduism; historically that is true - perhaps it is even beginning to become true again - but it is a long time since ordinary Sikhs and Hindus thought of themselves as one group and the dreadful events of the 1980s served only to increase the distance between them.

The State is probably the best example of Brass's claim that separatist tendencies are a consequence of over-centralization. In the 1980s, in an attempt to diminish the regionalist base of the Akali Dal and its demand for a confederation within India, Indira Gandhi's government actively encouraged rival Sikh fundamentalist groups, championing Bhindranwale, a Sikh sant (independent holy man). These groups quickly slipped out of governmental control and started to make demands for a separate State of Khalistan outside the Union.

The movement drew, as usual, upon young men with some education but limited prospects; it was heavily backed by the Sikh diaspora with fantasies of Khalistan. In 1984, after a prolonged campaign of rural terrorism, Indian troops launched Operation Blue Star and stormed the Golden Temple at Amritsar, which Bhindranwale and his supporters had established as a defensive position. Bhindranwale was killed, as were many of his supporters, and the temple was badly damaged.

A year later, Indira Gandhi was assassinated by Sikh members of her bodyguard. Delhi erupted in vengeful attacks on innocent Sikhs, particularly those living in the poorest quarters. The memories of Operation Blue Star and the Delhi riots are still too raw for Sikh Punjabis to trust the rest of India. The Punjab had been the showcase for the Green Revolution, but by the 1980s the miracle was fading. There was a general feeling that India had been prepared to see the advance of the Punjab as an agricultural producer but was not willing to allow it to progress beyond this.

Affluent Punjabis felt frustrated by the lack of backing for local investment in industry and for the modernization of the economy. Others saw the gap widening between rich and poor. The educated children of wealthy farmers frequently developed aspirations beyond agriculture and felt discriminated against when they could not find the sorts of employment they had anticipated. There has been massive emigration from the Punjab to the USA, Canada, Britain and the Far East and the non-resident Sikhs have not only invested back in buildings and small businesses in the Punjab, they have also maintained strong personal and emotional ties.

Terrorism was more or less extinguished in 1992, but the Chief Minister of the Punjab was killed by a car bomb in 1995 and there are still sporadic outbreaks. There is no effective demand for a separate country called Khalistan, but the desire has not been extinguished in the minds of frustrated young people or the romantic patriotism of those who will probably never return to live in India but continue to support fundamentalist tendencies 'at home'.

India alleges that Pakistan's Inter-Service Intelligence is actively promoting pro-Khalistan terrorist activities by funding such groups as the Bhabar Khalsa International, the Khalistan Zindabad Force and the Khalistan Commando Force. Whether it is Pakistan or the non-resident Sikhs, or both, who provide the finance, bombs on buses and at railway stations are still not a thing of the past - but the groups responsible are small and fragmented. At present the Punjab is ruled by an Akali Dal/ BJP coalition and the Akali faction is promoting itself now as a Punjabi party, rather than exclusively a Sikh party. It would however be rash to say that the Punjab is no longer a possible secessionist state.

KASHMIR

Young men are dying on the frozen wastes of the frontier between India and Pakistan in the Kargil 'War', the war we are not supposed to call a war, because it has never been declared and because the 'intruders' into India from Pakistan are not (are not supposed to be?) Pakistani soldiers but independent *mujahideen.* Kashmir is perhaps the main reason why the Indian government has a built-in centralizing urge. It stands as a permanent, unsolved, and insoluble remnant of the Partition of India. However, although the roots of the Kashmir problem lie in the past, like all political disputes it has to be interpreted in terms of the present; young men and women are not fighting their grandfathers' battles.

At Independence, Kashmir, then a princely State was allowed to opt whether to become part of India or Pakistan. The Maharaja was a Hindu, as were many of the ιlite minority - the pandits - of the Kashmir Valley, but the majority of the population was Muslim. The Maharaja chose India and signed the Instrument of Accession of Jammu and Kashmir State. It was given (temporary) special status under Article 370 of the Constitution, which limited the powers of the Indian government over Kashmir.

Its status has been contested ever since and it has been the cause of three declared wars with Pakistan and ongoing border skirmishes. Kashmir's northern boundary is not an accepted international border - it is a 'line of control' established in 1972 by the Shimla Agreement at the end of the 1971 Indo-Pakistan War. It is conventional in India to refer to the territory to the north of the line as 'Pakistan-occupied Kashmir', not conceding it to Pakistan. Ahmad (1999) sums the situation up concisely:

> The Kashmir problem ... has proved to be so very difficult to resolve politically, in accordance with the actual wishes and interests of the population, precisely because the territorial dispute between the two nation-states is based in irreconcilable geopolitical objectives.

But Kashmir is far more than just disputed territory; many Indians claim that, Kashmir before the violence with its Muslim majority, it is evidence of the validity of India's claim to be a secular State - one which is not composed along religious lines.

There is not sufficient space to outline the details of the background to the current insurgency, which dates back to 1986, but the political scientist Sumit Ganguly (1997) gives a masterly interpretation of this complex situation and Tavleen Singh's (1995) *Kashmir: A Ttragedy of Errors* is a meticulous and engaging personal account by one of India's most provocative journalists. Although the problems of Kashmir may seem unique, some of the underlying issues are general to those Indian regions which seek autonomy, at whatever level.

Most obvious is the matter of ethnic identity, but we know this to be something which emerges and recedes in the light of circumstance. Then there is the question of peripherality - Kashmir is remote from the rest of India and difficult to access. Most important in the late twentieth century, however, has been the consciousness of lack of economic opportunity, inability to share in the fruits of the new economy, and this consciousness is always felt most acutely by middle-class young men with some qualifications but few chances. It is easy for their ambitions to be channelled into ideological struggles.

Apart from tourism (now shattered), Kashmir had little modern economic activity and felt neglected in terms of development initiatives. Many saw themselves as colonized by India rather than a part of the nation. There is ample evidence that development funding has been syphoned off by 'the political middlemen who helped New Delhi keep a grip over its population, whose democratic aspirations were exceptionally high, thanks precisely to the promise that was once made but never kept'.

One can sum up the political positions in Kashmir as consisting of those who believe that Kashmir should be a part of Pakistan; those who believe that it should be a part of India (as at present); and those who believe that it should be a separate country in its own right. These are not reconcilable views.

The situation is, of course, perfect for the activity of Pakistan Inter-Service Intelligence which provides training, weaponry and bases for Kashmiri freedom fighters/rebels (according to one's perspective). It even recruits committed young men in foreign universities and infiltrates them, in the guise of NRI students on holiday, to carry the Kashmir campaign of terror into the cities of India. Virtually all of the Kashmiri pandits have left the valley and many will probably never return, whatever the outcome, given that they have set up successfully in business in the booming Indian cities.

Although referring to Kashmir throughout as if it were one place, the name of the State is Jammu and Kashmir and it contains Laddakh and Leh. In April 1999 the Regional Autonomy council recommended setting up three provinces in Kashmir and three more in Jammu, all generated along ethnic/religious lines. It is obvious that the policy is to fragment a difficult region so that defensive action can be concentrated where it is most needed (Kargil), and other areas can begin to rebuild. Jammu has a more mixed population than Kashmir, with substantial numbers of Buddhists as well as Hindus and Muslims. Pakistan exercises no claim over Jammu and local business interests are pressing for a severance of Jammu from Kashmir altogether.

Should Kashmir become an independent nation in its own right it is fairly clear that, given the circumstances of its history and location, it can never become economically independent or be left to its own devices politically? Its very geography means that it will not only be reliant upon international aid but that it will always be fraught with tensions generated outside its borders. But Kashmir is an issue for the rest of India as much as it is an issue for itself. It is because of disputed Kashmir that *Hindutva* forces can construct Muslims as the enemy within, undermining a united India. Those forces could never contemplate letting go of Kashmir for, if they did so, they would forfeit their most emotive cause. Not only was the Kargil War waged in 1999 but so also was an election campaign.

The BJP-led coalition was brought down in mid 1999 by the withdrawal of support from a minority regional party, but the caretaker government remained to conduct the war. It is clear that the war was used as political capital by all factions: the Left condemned the BJP for allowing the situation to escalate so far and for inefficiency in running the war; the BJP indulged in a rhetoric of heroism and patriotism which was hard to resist.

India Today devoted entire issues to paying tribute to the fallen and to sacrifices made by ordinary people for the war effort, quoting children who donated their pocket money as saying that they wished they could go to fight on the frontier. The battle of the Centre to control the States is encapsulated in the Kargil War but that battle is for more than just administrative control - it is for the deeper project of the Hindu rashtra. Praful Bidwai maintains that the costs of Kargil are greater than the loss of life and the military expenditure: 'They involve militarism and chauvinism, and "loyalty" tests for the minorities; growing intolerance in sections of the media towards those who question the conduct of Operation Vijay; and abridgement of democratic freedom through censorship and manipulation'.

9

Political Theatre in Contemporary India

In her rich and moving memoir of India from partition in 1947 to the present, Qamar Azad Hashmi, mother of slain theatre-activist Safdar Hashmi, lamented the tendency of revolutionary and politically active artists, particularly those on the left, to allow them to be co-opted into the central areas of power against which they once resisted. During the freedom struggle, she notes:

> Those who were poets and writers directed all of their anger against foreign [British] rule in their verses and songs; others orchestrated their resistance in the newspapers and articles; scientific and literary societies were founded to bring the common people and the artists together in one place; the suffering of the people was articulated through the theatre and forcefully made known to the people; those who participated in the struggle and those who were their leaders-before partition they used this entire array of means. [But] several members of the left-wing groups who had participated in the freedom struggle and who had spent time in British jails-after India became free, they accepted copper plaques and became the right hand of the ruling establishment, and thus in accepting payment for their sacrifices they became of one and the same color as the government.

The leaders of the freedom struggle, it seems, began to settle quickly and comfortably into chairs still warm from the recently departed British officials. Those who had only moments before considered themselves freedom fighters and revolutionaries began to ossify into a new establishment that to those outside the corridors of power began to look disturbingly similar to the old order against which they had struggled. Safdar Hashmi, left-wing activist and leader of the street theatre group Jana Natya Manch, knew well the power of theatre to make a political statement and also the lengths to which a government would go to quell the threat of dissension.

Many times his street dramas had been broken up by government thugs and his actors beaten and chased off. It was in one such tussle, on January 1, 1989, that Safdar Hashmi, defending the actors in his troop, was fatally wounded at the hands of a "mob attack" allegedly orchestrated by the ruling Congress Party. Although Safdar Hashmi's home theatre, so to speak, was the city of Delhi and its environs, the street theatre tradition of which he was a vociferous advocate is by no means confined to the capital city but extends into other regions and other cities of South Asia as well.

By and large, political theatre in South Asia tends to draw its inspiration from ideological sources that are opposed to the "center"-primarily, but not necessarily, from the political left. In most of South Asia, as elsewhere, the political left is identified with Marxist-Leninist parties of one sort or other, and the rhetoric of their manifestos, like the dialogue of their plays, is replete with calls for continuing "the revolution." Theoretically "the revolution" is the event in which the outsider party-the leftist party-takes power on behalf of the common people and political and social justice is finally served.

While Qamar Azad Flashmi's polemic is directed at those of the political left who have left their revolutionary perches f or the comfy confines of the central political establishment (the supposed antithesis of "the people"), in other parts of South Asia the embarrassment of revolutionary riches has posed a different sort of challenge for the theatre activist: what happens to political theatre when the revolution becomes the state? The general trends of political theatre in India are examined here with particular emphasis on a recent critical and controversial drama that satirizes the ruling Communist Party in one "revolutionary" state in southwestern India-the state of Kerala. Civic Chandran's Ninnal A is Kammunistaaki (Whom Did You Make a Communist?; 1995) indicates the direction toward which political or revolutionary theatre has been pushed both in India and elsewhere in South Asia.

Political practice and rhetoric have become so comical and absurd that left-wing, socialist, and "realist" dramas, if they are true to their task of representing the revolution as it is, must unwittingly and perhaps unwillingly tend toward a theatre of revolutionary farce (or farcical revolution)-or, indeed, a theatre in which farce and realism are indistinguishable. The ossification of the revolutionary state in Kerala is parallel ed throughout India by the pervasive sense of decaying nationalism out of which has emerged-to make things worse-a retreat to fundamentalist and culturally chauvinist governments (such as the Bharatiya Janata Party and the Shiv Sena).

The primary weapon that such governments have used to counteract this decay is to appeal nostalgically to a supposedly indigenous" but largely nonexistent, or at least misrepresented, "Golden Age" of the Hindu past. Political theatre in India, as in Kerala, has consequently become boxed in on two fronts. On one side it is boxed in by circumstance: there is the discomfiting similarity between the British and the Indian National Congress and between the centrist (Congress) and "revolutionary" or "fundamentalist" governments. On the other side it is boxed in by rhetoric: how can one evoke a people's theatre when everyone claims to speak for the people? As a result, political theatre has tended increasingly toward cynical satire and an involuted form of irony that is held together by absurd rhetoric made meaningful only by its absurd political context.

At the national level, then, political theatre finds itself in competition with an equally theatrical and dramatic state, one increasingly influenced by fundamentalist, or at least militantly nationalistic, forces. At the state level-and here Kerala will serve as the prime example-instead of revolutionary slogans, impassioned rhetoric, and socialist realism, political theatre has collapsed in on itself through the ponderous weight of its own ideological shortcomings in the face of a very different and less inspiring social "reality." The result in each case is an incestuous lexicon of self-reverence and self-reference that renders the idea of political theatre almost meaningless but at the same time suggests that abandoning the theatre would be to succumb to complacency and complicity. What, then, is a revolutionary playwright to do?

KERALA AND BEYOND

It is in some ways a misnomer to refer to leftist theatre as political theatre because in some sense all theatre is political-just in different ways. Even in so-called traditional forms of theatre in India, cloaked as they often are in the wholesome terms of preserving the values of the past, it is not too difficult to discern a political agenda of cosmic proportions that makes one wonder just how wholesome such traditional values really are.

Although modern theatre in Kerala and elsewhere in India is often contrasted to traditional theatre, the political continuity between them seriously weakens this historical and conceptual divide. Indeed, as we shall see, part of the absurdity confronting political theatre in Kerala stems from the urge to draw similarly artificial distinctions-between political ideologies or cultural practices, for instance-in places where such distinctions have no basis (whether in the theatre or in "reality").

We can see this in concrete form if we examine the parallel emergence of new ideas in theatre and new ideas in politics starting roughly from the 1870s: "political theatre" as it exists today in Kerala is in large part an offspring of both. In terms of theatre we begin in 1872, not in Kerala but in Bengal, with the opening of the National Theatre in Calcutta and the staging of Dinabandhu Mitra's polemical Bengali-language play Nil Darpan (The Blue Mirror).

Mitra's play, which highlights the exploitation of agricultural laborers in eastern India by British indigo planters, was initially both a commercial success-it was the first play in India to sell tickets to the public in a nondiscriminatory manner (by caste or class)-and a political disaster. Critical reactions were mixed: some praised its novelty and forcefulness; others thought it sacrificed literary merit for political sensation and resented its overtly political "European" style. Moreover, in terms of artistic creativity, the staging of the play had a profound (and, some might say, deleterious) effect in influencing the direction of political theatre.

According to Farley Richmond, the oppressive atmosphere created in the aftermath of the Dramatic Performances Act of 1876-a piece of censorial legislation issued in part as a response to Mitra's play and designed to mute the critical power of theatrical performance-pushed theatre in a new political direction. In the aftermath of the act, he notes, political and social protest was forced underground and Indian producers had to pass it off under the thinly veiled guise of historical and mythological subject matter. Frustrated by the harsh restrictions, many playwrights turned their attention to exposing the corruption within Hindu society and addressed a host of social injustices.

Common themes included the immolation of widows on the funeral pyres of their husbands, child marriages, the dowry system, the restrictive role of women at home and in society and politics, and love marriages, to name but a few of the more popular issues of the day that were addressed on the stage. Richmond's characterization, while generally accurate, is also incomplete. For the new directions toward which political theatre veered were not altogether random or even underground, nor were they necessarily a direct product of the act. A new center of political gravity was already forming at this time that would permanently change both the politics and the theatrical aesthetics of South Asia; this new center of gravity would ultimately be given the general name of "development."

As political theatre was gradually reoriented toward issues of development and social reform in the latter decades of the nineteenth century, so too were many political rulers following the newly laid paths to these issues, primarily for the same reason: the focus on social reform allowed the political ruler, just as it allowed the political dramatist, to be both radical and orthodox at the same time. This can be seen clearly in the fate of Dinabandhu Mitra. Although his play was originally banned, only a short while later the British awarded Mitra with an official title (Rai Bahadur) and began to patronize his play as a fine example of "native" theatre and exactly the type of politically driven public message that the British needed in order to advocate social reform.

In other words, a play that was originally intended to subvert the smugness of British rule ended up being applauded by the very group it was designed to critique. Here we have the first level of absurdity to be dealt with in modern political t heatre in Kerala and all over India: radical street performers of the present-as well as those who, as Qamar Azad Hashmi so acerbically noted, accepted copper plaques from the establishment-can both trace their political and theatrical lineage to the same source, a source that is simultaneously radical and orthodox.

The ideas of development and social reform were exceptionally important in Kerala, and historically Kerala has become known as something of a model of successful development but the development model of Kerala was not built merely by the British in Malabar and the princely rulers of Travancore and Cochin. It was also built by a radical opposition of nationalist and communist politicians that emerged in the early decades of the twentieth century and claimed to resist the entrenched powers of orthodoxy-even though they were engaged in the very same issues.

At least from the 1920s, for instance, political parties, caste communities, and royal patrons began to mobilize around crucial and contested issues of social reform such as temple entry for untouchables, public health, education, caste prejudice, and the status of women, to name just a few. The political battles revealed several fault lines in the political terrain of Kerala-established royal rulers versus "new" politicians; nationalists (Cong ress) versus communists; low caste versus high caste-and while political violence was certainly part of the "drama" of the period, the rhetorical side of the debate brought new modes of expression and linguistic arguments about the status of Malayalam to the political forefront.

This was an era of the mass and rapid circulation of words, and outlets such as street theatre and political pamphlets flourished in this atmosphere. Persons, words, and ideas quickly became muddled in what was in fact a very rich political stew, and by the 1940s every major political group in southwestern India-the British, the maharajas, the untouchables, the Congress, and the communists, among others-were all working on what was in essence the same political program of reform. The only thing that was radical was the rhetoric used by each to claim this program as its own.

By the time we get to the decades straddling independence, the 1940s and 1950s, the methods of popularizing and claiming ideas had become much more sophisticated than cheaply printed street plays and pamphlets-and the political stakes in doing so much higher. The "development state" that would become

Kerala was beginning to take shape, although who built it and who owned it remained unsettled. Much of the debate took place through the social drama of the period and also through carefully orchestrated "political theatre."

While the Congress Party was trying to wrest the claim of self-rule and nationalism out of the hands of British and traditional (princely) rulers, the Communist Party was busy staging secular and radical processions in which deities were replaced with hammer and sickle flags. Symbols were being continuously made and remade, and histories written and rewritten, by all parties.

Ideologically it was a volatile environment, and at times this volatility manifested itself in armed clashes and tuss les between competing groups. Wartime food shortages only exacerbated the general sense of tension and unrest. Words of revolution hung in the air. Other words were in the air as well-the words of politically active playwrights vying for politically loyal audiences. Out of this political and dramatic mayhem, one voice was to resonate clearly and suddenly, a voice that would literally change the course of Kerala's political and theatrical history: the voice of Thoppil Bhasi.

THE MAKING OF THOPPIL BHASI

To understand the concerns addressed in Civic Chandran's play, it is first necessary to examine briefly the Life and work of Thoppil Bhasi-in particular the play from which Chandran draws for his farce and which made Bhasi so extraordinarily famous in Kerala's modern political and theatrical history: Ninnal Enne Kammunistaaki (You Made Me a Communist). Bhasi wrote this play while in hiding-the new Congress government effectively banned the Communist Party when it came to power in 1947-and the spirit of the play is drawn from the "drama" of the attempted Communist uprising at Surnad (in present-day Kerala) in 1949 in which five policemen were killed, an event that is also central to his last play, Olivile Ormmakal (Memories in Hiding).

The former play was written in 1952; to give it popular appeal, songs were added by O. N. V. Kurup, in whose house Bhasi had taken shelter. After its initial performance, the Congress government responded first by breaking up performances and chasing actors o ut of town and then by banning performances altogether-a depressing dress rehearsal for the later action against Safdar Hashmi. But the play's popular appeal proved too great for the censors, and it became one of those works of art that appeared in the right place at exactly the right moment, capturing and creating the spirit of an era at the same time. Indeed, it is not too much of a stretch to suggest that the popularity of the communists, which allowed them to capture state power in the elections of 1957, stemmed largely from the popularity of Bhasi's play and its songs.

The plot of the play is part political propaganda, part melodrama, though the former is strangely muted in a play that is primarily a political statement. Kesavan Nayar, a capitalist landlord who is as hungry for more land as he is for sexual trysts with the young women of the village, wants to take the land of a certain Paramu Pillai, father of Communist Party member and worker Gopalan. Gopalan is in love with Sumam, the daughter of Kesavan Nayar, and Kesavan Nayar lusts after Mala, a beautiful young girl of the Pulaya (low-caste) community, whom he intends to seduce and dishonor.

Although Mala is in love with Gopalan, that love remains unrequited. Kesavan Nayar produces falsified papers to gain title to Paramu Pillai's lands. With no other possible recourse-Kesavan Nayar is connected to the Congress Party and is in fact trying to marry off Sumam to a Congress Party supporter-Paramu Pillai turns to the communists for help. Through agitations, demonstrations and processions, the communists ultimately galvanize enough popular support to gain concessions from big landlords such as Kesavan Nayar to protect the small landowners and tenants. Gopalan and Sumam promise to marry one another, and Mala fades to a pathetic demise and eventual death (which becomes significant in Civic Chandran's play).

The play ends with Paramu Pillai proclaiming to the young communists who fought on his behalf "You have made me a communist!" and demanding to carry the red flag of the revolution as the communists march off into the revolutionary-red sunset. Despite the play's popularity, not everyone in Kerala was a Communist. Indeed, opposition to the play and its simplistic story was voiced in other plays that became increasingly farcical. In 1953, Kesava Dev wrote a play titled *Nanippo Kammunistavum!* a satirical response to Bhasi's play. In Kesava Dev's play, characters threaten to join the Communist Party for the slightest insult or incident-in one case for dropping a teacup.

The play is not without a serious message, however. Along with the rest of Kesava Dev's farces and plays, it constitutes a warning against the type of politicking described earlier: the claim and counterclaim to the spoils of political victory, for example, or the rush to outdo the other parties in making increasingly outrageous claims as to the ownership of various agendas for action. When Dev parodies one of the landlords who becomes a communist in order to evict his tenants in *Nanippo Kammunistavum*, he is foreshadowing some of the criticisms that a ppear in Civic Chandran's play. From the perspective of "the people," revolutionary and reactionary groups began to look and sound remarkably the same.

Thoppil Bhasi began to see the emptiness of political rhetoric, and in later years he began to write articles and plays that criticized Communist Party rulers and functionaries for betraying the revolution. He even stated publicly that he regretted the violence of the Surnad uprising. His other plays continue to reveal a deep concern for social issues, and one of his best plays, *Asvameetam* (The Horse Sacrifice), published in 1962, deals with leprosy, then little discussed, and the issue of untouchability and "outcasting." It is of some interest to note that The Horse Sacrifice would not have had such an impact were it not for the long history of interest in issues of public health, hygiene, and untouchable contact in Kerala. Outcasting someone for contracting leprosy, Bhasi intimates, is little different from denying untouchables entry into a temple.

The disenchantment that began to emerge in Bhasi's writings up until his death in 1992 had its absurd side as well: because of his prominent role in the hist ory of communism in Kerala, anything he wrote, no matter how critical of the communists, was usually showered with prizes by those he sought to critique. For better or worse, the revolution for which Bhasi fought had become the state; Bhasi tried in vain to have his critique taken seriously. As the revolutionary rhetoric became increasingly empty over the years, the tradition of political farce that began early in the century reemerged as a central critical voice in the political theatre of Kerala. In short, to avoid co-optation by the revolutionary state, political theatre had to bring out the revolutionary clowns, so to speak-only this time, the clowns meant serious business.

CIVIC CHANDRAN AND THE REINCARNATION OF THOPPIL BHASI

Right from the start of Civic Chandran's play, it is clear that the icons and symbols of the revolution are in for a thrashing and Chandran is going to approach his subject with a nothing-is-sacred demeanor. The prologue begins with the sound of Communist Party songs (of the type that were written for Thoppil Bhasi's original play) which glorify the sacrifice of the great martyrs of the revolution. These songs, drawn from the music of older plays and movies, can evoke either a feeling of nostalgia or an implication of living in the past. As the curtain rises, Mala enters carrying the red flag of the revolution. She is in a graveyard, surrounded by "martyrs," and the juxtaposition of the glory songs and the somber gravestones could not be more startling. Slowly the other characters from Thoppil Bhasi's You Made Me a Communist enter.

The first to speak is Paramu Pillai-who, it will be recalled, speaks proudly at the end of Bhasi's play that he has been made into a communist, just as the characters march off w ith the flag held high. In the prologue of Civic Chandran's play, Paramu Pillai, shy and humbled, is surrounded by the graves of those who paid such a terribly high price to make him a communist: "All of you have made me into a communist, haven't you?" he ponders, adding weakly and diffidently, "That is what I am." When Kesavan Nayar, his supposed foe, comforts him by saying that times change, Paramu Pillai responds by saying he would like to lead a procession with the flag, an ironic statement considering the morose setting.

Finally Mala speaks, and Chandran's new take on Bhasi and the whole idea of the revolution becomes clear. Standing alone on the stage after the other characters have left, Mala transforms the symbol of the flag, changing its red from the proud color of revolution to the mournful hue of blood. "That flag is my flag, the flag of my community," she says, "but... but this time we lost. She is unable to finish and breaks into tears. As Mala cries, however, a shadowy figure appears smoking the cheap kind of cigarette called bidi. When the figure speaks, it becomes clear that this is none other than Thoppil Bhasi himself, back from the dead. "Mala," he says, "I have come to see you again." The figure of Bhasi then announces the play of Civic Chandran, describing it not as a drama (natakam), but as an antidrama (pratinatakam), and the curtain falls.

Although the prologue is relatively short, it is worthwhile to pause and examine some of the symbolic and thematic issues that have been introduced since they are not only very rich but suggest why Chandran's play was so controversial when it appeared. First, we have the image of the graveyard-itself a disturbing setting and a scene that (as Chandran points out later in the play) no one in the revolution wants to think about, except when placing wreaths for photo opportunities. The graveyard is also a common theme in the political literature of Kerala, a loaded image that portends the retribution of spirits who died unjust or unnatural deaths.

Here Chandran is implying that the revolution is dead or that the martyrs are "restless" because a failed revolution has rendered their deaths unjust. Second, there is the image of the red flag-probably the most prominent image of Bhasi's original play-which Chandran wastes no time deflating as an empty symbol of failed revolution. Much of Chandran's play is devoted to rewriting the symbol of the flag and the "heroic" processions in which it is carried; after he deflates and then ridicules it, he ultimately redeems it and appropriates it for "the people" by taking it out of the hands of the Communist Party leadership.

Third, there is the character of Mala, who, as we will see, is brought back from the dead and shown to be the "true hero" of Bhasi's play. Chandran's message here is that what is important about the revolution is not what it made-for example, a communist out of Paramu Pillai-but rather what it forgot: in this case, Mala and her (low-caste) community. Finally, lest anyone be ruffled by this disparaging of the "holy text" of Bhasi's original play, Chandran takes the outrageous step of bringing Bhasi back from the grave to lend legitimacy to Chandran's satirical interpretation. Just as Mala has reclaimed the red flag, Chandran has reclaimed the spirit of Bhasi to take the revolution away from the revolutionaries.

The first act opens with the character of the watchman, the symbolic guardian of the revolution and caretaker of the graveyard of the martyrs, asleep on the job, his face covered with a copy of Thoppil Bhasi's play You Made Me a

Communist. The image is as amusing as it is profound. In the background, the news is blaring over the radio that Gopalan has been elected chief minister and would like to come to place a wreath for the martyrs at the cemetery. The watchman wakes up and walks, without thinking, as if he is in a parade, signaling the empty and somnambulist tone of such official ceremonies as wreath laying.

At that moment, a different sort of procession enters: a funeral procession, led by Bharati, the adopted daughter of Mala, and an old man whose identity is not yet revealed. The watchman is upset-there cannot possibly be any burials in the graveyard to mar the chief minister's visit-and rushes to intervene: "Jesus, who is this? Whose corpse?" Bharati walks to the graveyard wall and writes Mala's nam e next to the date 1994: "This is Mala," she says. And picking up the copy of the play that was on the watchman's face, she clarifies that it is "Thoppil Bhasi's Mala." The old man then states: "It is now the moment to decide not only who is the hero of [Thoppil Rhasi's] play, but also of the movement. Mala, wake up!... History is forgotten."

Bharati then begs Mala to rise up and tell the people what has been hidden, how the flag of the revolution was taken away from Mala and given to Gopalan and Kesavan Nayar. Bharati then explains further what has happened to the revolution and the communists in terms that manage to conjure up the most painful issue of twentieth-century Kerala: not only was the flag taken from Mala and her community, but "Mala and Karamban [her father] are once again kept at a distance of sixty-four feet." The latter refers to the former practice of keeping untouchables literally at a distance from all higher castes. Through Bharati's statement, Chandran is claiming that the communists, far from saving the untouchables as they have often claimed, have instead become a high caste of their own, putting the untouchables back in their p lace and turning their backs on the revolution.

Mala eventually rises from the dead-she walks "as if asleep" so perhaps she was only sleeping a Snow White-like sleep-and erases her name from the wall. The watchman is nearly at his wits' end but then takes comfort, nervously, from the fact that "this is just make-believe, this is just a play." Chandran is beginning to pile deeper and deeper layers of meaning atop one another through references internal and external to the play and by repeated farcical statements that can be read in different ways. The serious rhetoric of the politicians in the play sounds ludicrous, and the ludicrous characters, like the watchman, appear as disturbingly serious (political) orators.

By having the watchman proclaim that "this is just a play," Civic Chandran is introducing an impossible conundrum that characterizes the politics of modern Kerala. If it is just a drama, then no one should be upset since the claims are not "real." But this also means that Thoppil Bhasi's original play was just a drama, too, and hence its claims, and perhaps the revolution of which it is part, cannot be "real." What is real and what is not becomes difficult to discern-in Act 3, for instance, many of the characters talk of how they were "invented" in various other works of fiction and movies. Hence fictional characters of one author begin quoting lines from other authors to show that they recognize the works in which the others were "invented." Everything is framed and highlighted as fiction.

But since Chandran is arguing that the claims of the communists (and other politicians as well) are equally fictitious, all of it, when brought together on the stage, is painfully real. Act 2 is taken up with a long conversation among Sumam, Mala, and another character, Matyu, in which the love triangle (Gopalan, Sumam, and Mala) is revisited. In the course of the conversation, it becomes clear that Gopalan could never have married Mala, since Gopalan, though a comrade (Communist Party member), is educated and virtuous and hence far above the station of the dark-skinned, uneducated, untouchable Mala.

Again Chandran is claiming that the communists have settled comfortably into the hierarchical society they supposedly fought to dismantle; the martyrs of that struggle are buried in the graveyard, where the conversation about love takes place. There are also intimations that Gopalan had a daughter by Mala. But since Gopalan married Sumam, it is hinted that the youthful revolutionary from Bhasi's play, despite his rhetoric of equality between caste and gender, could not overcome the attitude that there are some kinds of girls one gets pregnant (Mala) and other kinds of girls one marries (Sumam). Indeed, at the beginning of Act 3 Bharati says of Mala that "[she] is dark-complexioned, no? Moreover she is a low-caste pulakalli. A labourer.

Even though she is a comrade, she desired an educated Nayyar boy ... he, tut, tut." Civic Chandran has used the charact er of Mala to show exactly who has been forgotten, indeed despised, by the revolution: women and untouchables. Bharati is reproached by the Old Man and laments that the person who is now despised by everyone, Mala, is in fact the best of the lot. Any revolution that ignores these two groups or forgets the meaning of the term "comrade" or the value of the laborers, implies Chandran, is simply not worth its weight in red revolutionary flags.

As the play continues, Civic Chandran expands his farcical metaphors and images and weaves them together, not only within the text, but with characters, events, and scenes from other texts as well. The Old Man at one point confesses to the watchman that he is a rehashed character from previous revolutionary dramas and movies, claiming that his first "role" came in Rantitanazhi (Two Measures of Rice). Revolutionary literature and drama, Chandran seems to say, simply tells the same old story over and over again, changing a name or two here and there, but essentially telling the same old yarns. Chandran also mixes his literary figures with "real-life" historical figures such as C. P. Ramaswamy Aiyar or Ayyankali, and, as we have already seen, with Thoppil Bhasi himself, suggesting that it is difficult or perhaps irrelevant to separate real life from fiction in the current state of politics.

The lines are blurred not merely between real life and fiction but also between past and present. The Communist Party is repeatedly characterized as a remnant of the old order-not simply in the repeated discussions of caste, which slowly reveal the hypocrisy in the use of the word "comrade" (sakhave), but also in blunt statements such as Bharati's observation in Act 4 that during communist rule the red flag was merely a substitute for the maharaja's conch (a symbol of royalty and old Kerala). The blurring of past and present also reveals a pervasive sense of historical injustice.

The martyrs are restless, says the Old Man standing in the cemetery: "Tonight, right here, don't you see... Now the martyrs of the revolution, unknown to history, arise and awake, asking, Has the revolution come or not? Have our dreams come true? They thirst for their [proper] funerals." Until the revolution is properly done, their deaths were unjust-and hence they cannot, so to speak, rest in peace. By repeatedly pointing out that his drama is "merely a play," Chandran prevents the audience from losing itself in the "romance" of drama and revolution. At one point he implies that the people have forgotten the difference between fighting a revolution and watching a play about fighting a revolution. In Act 4, for instance. the Old Man says to Bharati:

Forty-five years ago [Bhasi's play] was written and presented more than five thousand times. You know, child, we loved that play more than the Party itself. For the old communists like us, performing the drama was the supreme deed. In every village where the play was performed, the red flag would be raised. Yet Chandran is not willing to put all the blame for forgetting the revolution on the shoulders of government officials. He also laments the tendency of contemporary laborers to forget the hardship of the original struggle now that they are used to government handouts and benefits. At one point he reminds the audience that the original goal of the workers' movement was not higher wages but recognition of their dignity.

Despite the trenchant and often bitterly sarcastic language of Chandran, the form of the play suggests a willingness to understand the ease with which revolutions are forgotten: by shifting the action of his play back and forth between real-time scenes in Chandran's play and the recreation of scenes from Bhasi's original play-and by bringing together references and characters from other revolutionary dramas past and present alongside historical figures and events-Chandran suggests that confusion may be an inevitable if unintentional by-product of revolutionary fervor, particularly as it decay s into revolutionary orthodoxy. Even so, Chandran seems clear on one point: the act of forgetting and the production of amnesiac history are the most powerful enemies of the revolution-hence the crime of forgetting Mala and those like her.

It comes as no surprise, therefore, that the action of the play and, to the extent that it is discernible, the moral of the story center on the awakening of the people to their revolutionary memories. The action of the drama builds to its climax in the last act with the grotesquely staged ceremony in which the chief minister wants to lay a wreath at the graveyard of the martyrs. The ceremony is to be conducted within a larger event composed of political processions that reveal, through Chandran's words, the hollowness of the revolution. In the processional dance by the lower castes, for instance, the watchman observes that most of them have forgotten their traditional dances (dances that tend to announce their place in the social order). Hence only those in the procession who have "remembered" their dances and can act "traditionally" will be visible to the audience.

The true revolution (to forget one's dance is to shed one's identity from the oppressive past) is thus ensconced in a hollow shell of indigenous, prerevolutionary culture. In the last act of Chandran's play, the old flag from Bhasi's play, tattered and worn, is found by the characters, sewn up, and renovated. This image is juxtaposed with the two red flags on the front of the chief minister's official car, which are bright and shiny and representative of the ruling elite.

The ghost of Thoppil Bhasi returns to announce the arrival of the new, "real" revolution, which has the communists quaking in their sandals. Still, Chandran's play is an "antidrama" and hence would not allow for a neat ending. We can read the ending of Civic Chandran's drama in at least two ways: either his political theatre is a polemic document, calling for a new revolution, or it is a play which says that any new revolution, if it emerges, will exist only in a play. The revolution is dead-long live the revolution.

THE FARCICAL MOSAIC

As we have seen, Civic Chandran describes his play as antidrama (pratinatakam), or antitheatre, and it is worth pausing for a moment to reflect on what this means. According to Jacques Scherer (1975), "antitheatre" was a form of drama that emerged in eighteenth-century Western Europe (particularly France) as "theatre" in the generic sense became associated with acceptable and establishment values-even in its farcical or satirical forms. What antitheatre represented, therefore, was a more extreme, more subversive, and more grotesque form of farcical drama that questioned the very idea of theatre as a concept even as it utilized it to articulate its venomous lexicon of ridicule and antiestablishment farce.

Although the action and nature of Civic Chandran's antidrama may seem a bit removed from eighteenth-century France, the situations are remarkably analogous: by calling his play an antidrama, Chandran is clearly suggesting that the formerly revolutionary art of the Communist Party in Kerala has ossified into an establishment of its own. Yet because the establishment still speaks through the language of resistance, radicalism, and revolution, the "normal" antiestablishment lexicon through which the people's theatre might speak has already been appropriated.

Hence just as subversive playwrights of eighteenth-century Western Europe had to "outfarce" the language of (establishment) farce, revolutionary playwrights in present-day Kerala must outradicalize radical theatre with the extra burden of being stripped of their natural vocabulary. The words of the antidrama are thus overloaded with meaning-and in another sense, one that is perfect for the language of farce, antiliterary. One can, of course, recognize in all of this a trace of Mikhail Bakhtin's belief, interpreted through Rabelais, in the liberating and subversive power of laughter.

What is interesting about Civic Chandran's play in this regard, however, is that it poses an altogether novel and disturbing question: Rabelasian laughter may be a form of resistance in that it portends the ever-present possibility of subversive revolution, but what if it turns out that the revolution itself is a joke? Leftist theatre, indeed leftist regimes in general, reveal a pathetically low threshold of tolerance when it comes to self-ridicule; revolutionary theatre as a state-sponsored endeavor, whether in its Chinese, Soviet, or Malayali models, has as a rule been decidedly unfunny. In the glory days (if such a description is possible) of the Soviet Empire or the Communist Bloc, literary works such as Mikhail Bulgakov's Master and Margarita or Milan Kundera's The Joke, which hinted at the possibility of self-directed ridicule, were deemed subversive and often banned entirely.

The revolutionary theatre of the Communist Party in India has similarly remained straight-faced and remarkably intolerant of self-ridicule: Thoppil Bhasi's plays may have been popular, but they were serious to the point of melodrama. Certainly there were those who ridiculed Bhasi's revolutionary melodrama, but that was before the revolution came to town. Civic Chandran wants something truly different: a revolution that is not afraid to laugh. Even without the revolutionary aspects of theatrical farce in Communist-ruled Kerala, Civic Chandran is writing in the context of a well-established postindependence and India-wide trend of theatrical performance.

This trend has relied on increasingly sophisticated and subversive approaches to keep farce in the realm of people's theatre when the political spectacles of the actual state itself seem designed to act as competition in a contest of farces. Girish Karnad's Kannada-language play Muhammad Tughalak (Tughlaq), published in 1964 just as the era of Nehru's rule was coming to an end, has taken on an increased sense of relevance and resonance as post-Nehru politics-particularly the totalitarian period of Indira Gandhi's emergence in 1975-1977-reveals itself as a continuous canard of grotesque proportions.

Karnad's play is not an antidrama but a complex farce (prahasana vinod) in which "serious" political rule becomes increasingly indistinguishable from political charade and brute force masquerades as ide alism in the hands of Muhammad Tughlaq, a fourteenth-century monarch of northern India. In the final, thirteenth act, the "clown" of the play, Aziz, who has undertaken a series of increasingly grandiose and bizarre schemes in which he masquerades as something other than what he is (an ordinary, low-status washerman), finally schemes his way into Tughlaq's palace disguised as the religious leader Ghiyas-ud-din. When Tughlaq finds him out, Aziz admits to killing Ghiyas-ud-din and coming in his place. In an interesting twist, however, he begins to recount his personal history of scheming to Tughlaq and concludes with self-confident arrogance that he should not be punished but rewarded:

It is true that I killed Ghiyas-ud-din and deceived you, master. But even with all of this, I am in truth your disciple. In the last five years I have considered my every act to be done in your hired service. You might ask who else is there in this kingdom that has devoted the past five years of his life in your service? Tughlaq is at first angry with Aziz's insolence, calling him a fool because of his sophistic reasoning. Yet Tughlaq soon sees the "reason" in Aziz's words-bursting out with buffoonish, almost insane laughter at his point of "enlightenment"-and, referring to himself as a fool in the next moment, awards Aziz with an official post for his "services."

The point here is to show that even outside the charged context of revolutionary, leftist theatre in Kerala, the subversive and political potential for laughter has been denied through its co-optation and inclusion in the words and deeds of the state-here represented by analogy through the character of Tughlaq. The nonsensical reasoning through which Aziz, as the clown, justifies his heinous actions turns out to be synonymous with the reasoning through which Tughlaq has pursued his own political intrigues: government action is itself a farce.

The clown does not merely imitate the king-part of the power of farce is in recognizing the clown and the king as separate characters-but in fact elides with the king: the clown becomes the king and the king becomes the clown. And in that moment the possibility of clowning, or even of laughter, disappears. Karnad's play implies that a despotic or totalitarian state is one that precludes the possibility of laughter. By extension, then, and in the same vein as Karnad's critique (or warning), we can interpret the unamused reactions of communist officials to Civic Chandran's play-some considered it nearly "sacrilegious"-in Kerala as corroboration of one of Chandran's key points: that the communist state has become the very tyranny against which the revolution was originally waged.

Yet the laughter-thwarting political machinations that have hindered or complicated the development of people's theatre in Kerala specifically and in India generally have not always come from outside sources (such as government action or inaction). Many of the problems have been self-inflicted. If we look at the development of revolutionary theatre in Bengal, for instance, as it is interpreted through the eyes of Rustom Bharucha, we can see how the maturation of a true "people's theatre" has been stunted by a rather large bundle of cultural and ideological baggage. Bharucha interprets the evolution of a people's theatre in Bengal as the movement away from foreign, especially European, dramatic models and toward more indigenous models that are presumably closer to "the people."

Thus while the nineteenth-century Bengali playwright Michael Madhusadhan Dutt is praised for using Western ideas to "throw off the fetters forged for us by a servile admiration of everything Sanskrit" (Madhusadhan's words), Bharucha tak es pains to point out that Madhusadhan was, "in all probability, embarrassed by the aping of Western manners and customs by English-educated Indians of his day". Similarly, Bharucha quotes another pivotal figure in the rise of political theatre in Bengal from the 1920s, Sisir Bahaduri, who lamented: "We have made the mistake of imitating the English models, of forsaking our own truth for the falsity of an alien import. We have to rectify the mistake and go back to the ways of our yatra".

Yet if what is "alien" is inherently false, then we arrive, both through Bharucha and through the playwrights he quotes, at an egregious contradiction: when the "people's theatre" emerges in Bengal in recognizable form in the 1930s, it does so in association with groups such as the Progressive Writer's Association, which was inspired by literary and cultural movements in Europe, and the Indian People's Theatre Association, which served as a conduit for the importation of (European) Marxist models of theatrical performance. (Indeed, the "Internationale" was often sung at performances.)

Hence the arrival of the people's theatre in rural Bengal was not so much a triumph of the Indian (or, better, the Bengali) voice acting out against the oppressors of the people as it was a forum in which one Western alien voice (Marxism/communism) was translated into local dialect to serve as the people's opposition to another alien voice (colonialism/capitalism). In fact, the layers of irony and contradiction are even more rich and complex. P. Kesava Dev's short story "Otayilninnu" (Out of the Gutter), for instance, one of the most important pieces of radical literature in Malayalam, drew heavily in both content and ideology from Victor Hugo's Les Miserables implying that the vocabulary of social justice need not rely exclusively on the lexicon of the orthodox (Marxist! communist) left.

There are even problems with the claim that certain "folk" drama styles, toward which radical or people's theatre in India has tended, are somehow more authentic or more indigenous than other types of theatre. The yatra (jatra) of Bengal-and its Malayali counterpart the jatha-both claim to be folk theatre styles which have their origins among the people; heir significance for political theatre in India stems from the fact that they were supposedly an indigenous folk model that, among other things, questioned the Western conventions of the proscenium arch or the passive, paying audience.

Yet the "procession" that lies at the heart of the concept of yatra has gone through a number of transformations since its putative origins as an orthodox ("top down") missionary activity among the followers of Ghaitanya's tantric vision of Vaishnavite devotionalism. In the mid-nineteenth century in Bengal, the yatra became secularized in content and heavily westernized in form-the proscenium arch, for instance, was incorporated during this period-and, as the story goes, only returned to its "original" form as a theatre intended for the rural masses (and eventually the urban) when it was reclaimed in the twentieth century by radical leftist playwrights in Bengal, most importantly by Utpal Dutt.

The story of its reclamation for the people and by the people, however, has a few kinks in it that tend to get smoothed over in the heroic version of the tale. Before the communist and leftist playwrights reinvented the yatra as a secular form for missionaries of radical propaganda, colonial development workers and social reformers had already done much of the groundwork in this direction by utilizing traditional forms of mass communication (folk drama) as well as novel forms (movies, magic lanterns) to indigenously express the messages of agricultural development, public health and hygiene, village improvement, and civic social relations.

Again the accomplishment of Civic Chandran in this respect should not be underestimated. For he is working in an environment which faces new conceptual challenges that early revolutionary playwrights did not have to face-at least not to the degree witnessed in the 1990s. In addition to facing the orthodox wrath of the communist state government in Kerala, Civic Chandran is also searching for a true people's theatre, one with "indigenous" roots, at a time when the national government and many state governments in India are increasingly under the influence of the politics of filling old symbols with new political meanings, a process arguably perfected by the Bharatiya Janaṭa Party (BJP).

The BJP government, along with other "cultural" organizations with a Hindu fundamentalist agenda, such as the Rashtriya Svayamsevak Sangh (RSS), are currently in the process of trying to reclaim and classify as indigenous anything that they want to have positively associated with an exclusively Hindu India. What this means for playwrights and troupes who are experimenting with folk or ostensibly indigenous modes of theatre is that the people's theatre suddenly aligns discomfortingly well with the political program of a quasi-fascist state.

Looking for indigenous roots for people's theatre simultaneously draws such theatre into the hands of the people and the state, and in fact might unwittingly bring the state deeper into the lives of those who are in fact seeking to distance themselves from it or resist its pervasive power. The absurdity of such a situation introduces a new series of challenges for politically active or civic-minded playwrights in contemporary India and helps to explain the type of extreme farce of which Civic Chandran's play is but one prominent example.

So if borrowing from the "alien" source is inherently false-yet searching for the indigenous source brings the unwelcome approval of the state (with the threat of incorporation)-what then, to return to our original question, is a revolutionary playwright to do? Some have argued that this state of indeterminacy-of being neither above nor below, neither indigenous nor foreign-constitutes the essence of the postcolonial condition. Indeed, some have gone so far as to suggest that this state of indeterminacy, insofar as it denies the categorization and classification supposedly reminiscent of colonial hegemony, is in fact both a state of suffering and a state of resistance.

But indeterminacy and the inability to be categorized easily are surely not the monopoly of non-Western or postcolonial peoples. Hence this argument is misguided to the extent that it privileges the uniqueness of alienation and indeterminacy for the postcolonial world. The difficulty of sorting through the history and current s tatus of yatra, for instance, remains a difficulty only insofar as the mixture of styles and influences is perceived as a problem. The Indian (and South Asian) past and present are inhabited by the spirits of many different cultural influences that can only be rendered "Indian" or "alien" by imposing the colonial boundaries of the Indian nation anachronistically.

It seems to me that it is the artifice of searching for pure cultural traditions or dramatic styles that produces the absurdities currently facing radical playwrights in contemporary India and South Asia: the supposed tension between the indigenous and the alien is false and illusory. When Nandi Bhatia tries to explain away the "embarrassment" of the fact that the radical Indian People's Theatre Association often staged European plays and used European influence by stating that they did so "to escape censorship" and "to camouflage their messages and propagate their anti-imperial ideas in covert ways," we can see the same disturbing process of tying to excise the "alien" and reclaim it as indigenous that we see in, for example, the BJP's attempt to pass off Western nuclear technology as an "indigenous weapons system".

If a true people's theatre is to emerge in contemporary India, one that can resist the machinations of the state and assist in procuring social justice for the p eople who constitute its primary audience, then it must embrace the mixing of styles and influences and unmask the insidious politics of inventing the indigenous by dissolving the putative contradiction between alien and pure sources in the construction of civic culture. The oppressed and downtrodden of India (and elsewhere) come from many different cultures and classes-they are, to use a much vaunted but poorly understood term, multicultural-and hence only a multicultural theatre in India, one that reaches across cultural boundaries both within India and without, can lay claim to being in any true sense a theatre of the people.

BEYOND FARCE

In much of the literature on the "people's theatre" or any theatre that deems itself radical or political, there is a tendency to assume that such theatre, especially insofar as it eschews formal scenarios of theatre and formal methods of presentation, is somehow closer to the masses of common people and somehow more in tune with their day-to-day challenges and sufferings. This may be the case, but not necessarily. Forms of theatre that allow for intimacy between audience and actor and are presented in public forums designed to attract a mass audience are not the exclusive domain of theatres that present the "truth" as opposed to "artificial" theatres. In India, political theatre has tended just as easily toward a theatre of liberation or a theatre of propaganda-and as the state itself has come to rely increasingly on public spectacles of mass politics, the line between the two will be increasingly difficult to negotiate.

Not all theatre in India must tend toward farce to escape the gravity of nationalism. G irish Karnad's most recent play, for instance, Agni Mattu Male (The Fire and the Rain), has managed to draw deeply from a little-known tale from the Mahabharata without sliding into a nationalistic call for the revival of indigenous theatre by utilizing universal themes that extend beyond the confines of Hinduism or the Indian nation. This would suggest the possibility of another direction in which political theatre in contemporary India might proceed: not toward a drama that revives and evokes a heroic past, but toward one that interrogates that past as well as the urge to relive it.

A vibrant political theatre in contemporary India need not assume the task of choosing which approach works best-this was one of the main shortcomings of the rigidly Marxist Indian People's Theatre Association. What it can assume is the responsibility for creating a public space that allows for the possibility of multiple and diverse approaches through which civic culture may reach into and beyond the power of the state.

Civic Chandran's multilayered satire of contemporary Kerala politics and history is certainly one of the richest and most sophisticated texts to date offering an artistic critique of Communist Party rule. Gone are the days when a political drama took the form of a melo dramatic, simplistic play such as Thoppil Bhasi's You Made Me a Communist. The division of the world into good and bad, into revolutionary versus reactionary, is no longer a viable approach to social justice through the means of political theatre. It is neither the king nor the rebel who in the end takes the revolutionary day.

Rather, implies Civic Chandran, it is the public-spirited commoner who is part critic, part clown, and who is not afraid to laugh, publicly or privately. Negotiating the fine line between orthodoxy and rebellion is no longer so simple as accepting or refusing a copper plaque, as Qamar Azad Hashmi put it. Rather, it is the incorrigibly ambivalent rhetoric of the clown or jester that will fight through the hazy rhetoric of orthodoxy emanating from the corridors of power, regardless of who inhabits their labyrinthine passages.

The absurd or convoluted nature of contemporary politics in Kerala (and India in general) may have emptied revolutionary passion or rhetoric of meaning. Yet Civic Chandran is not willing to let us recede into cynical narcissism. His point-if I read his antiplay correctly-is that farce and satire sustain us both through good times and through bad, for without this intermittent laughter there would only be tears. Political theatre has often relied upon farce and satire to make a veiled but effective critique of political trends. In contemporary India, however, political theatre is facing a new challenge in trying to find ways to "out-force" a political arena that already has become inherently farcical. There are two special challenges addressed here.

The first comes from the state of Kerala in southwestern India, where a self-styled progressive state government in the hands of the Communist Party has come under attack by critical playwrights for ossifying into orthodoxy and complacency. The second challenge centers on the difficulties faced by playwrights who have turned toward so-called indigenous or folk models of theatre to voice their critiques. Since the national government in Delhi has tried to utilize the symbols of an invented indigenous past to establish its legitimacy, critical theatre often finds itself applauded and even co-opted by the very political forces against which it has directed its dissent. This chapter examines the difficulties of establishing a "pure" space for political theatre in contemporary India and offers as a conclusion a possible path toward resolution.

BIBLIOGRAPHY

Adas, Michael. *Machines as the Measure of Men: Science, Technology, and Ideologies of Western Dominance*. Ithaca: Cornell University Press, 1989.

Barraclough, Geoffrey, and Geoffrey Parker, eds. *The Times Atlas of World History*. 4th ed. Maplewood, New Jersey: Hammond, 1993.

Brass, Paul R. *The New Cambridge History of India, IV.1: The Politics of India since Independence*. 2d ed. Cambridge: Cambridge University Press, 1994.

Chanchreek, K.L., and Saroj Prasad, eds. *Crisis in India*. Delhi: H.K. Publishers, 1993.

Davies, C. Collin. *An Historical Atlas of the Indian Peninsula*. London: Oxford University Press, 1959.

Ellinwood, DeWitt C., and S.P. Pradhan. *India and World War I*. New Delhi: Manohar, 1978.

Gascoigne, Bamber. *The Great Moghuls*. London: Cape, 1971.

Habib, Irfan. *An Atlas of the Mughal Empire*. Delhi: Oxford University Press, 1982.

Heinsath, Charles. *Indian Nationalism and Hindu Social Reform*. Princeton: Princeton University Press, 1964.

Inder Singh, Anita. "Decolonization in India: The Statement of February 20, 1947," *International History Review* [Toronto], 6, No. 2, May 1984, 191-209.

Keay, John. *Democracy and Discontent: India's Growing Crisis of Governability*. Cambridge: Cambridge University Press, 1992.

McLane, John R. *Indian Nationalism and the Early Congress*. Princeton: Princeton University Press, 1977.

Park, Richard L., and Bruce Bueno de Mesquita. *India's Political System*. Englewood Cliffs, New Jersey: Prentice-Hall, 1979.

Robb, Peter G. *The Evolution of British Policy Towards Indian Politics, 1880-1920*. Westwood, Massachusetts: Riverdale, 1992.

Sharma, Kususm. *Ambedkar and Indian Constitution*. New Delhi: Ashish, 1992.

Sharma, Ram Sharman. *Aspects of Political Ideas and Institutions in Ancient India*. 2d ed. Delhi: Motilal Banarsidass, 1968.

Singh, Mahendra Prasad, ed. *Lok Sabha Elections 1989: Indian Politics in 1990's*. New Delhi: Kalinga, 1992.

Sitaramayya, B. Pattabhi. *History of the Indian National Congress*. 2 vols. Bombay: Padma, 1947.

Smith, Donald E. *India as a Secular State*. Princeton: Princeton University Press, 1963.

Tully, Mark. *India: Forty Years of Independence*. New York: Braziller, 1988.

Washbrook, David A. *The Emergence of Provincial Politics: The Madras Presidency, 1870-1920*. Cambridge: Cambridge University Press, 1976.

Wolpert, Stanley. *India*. Berkeley: University of California Press, 1991.

Woodruff, Philip (pseud.). *The Men Who Ruled India, 2: The Founders*. London: Cape, 1963.

INDEX